THE COMMON
UNCOMMON

Stories of the Past
Hopkinton, Massachusetts

By

James F. Ward

To
Claire

James F. Ward

Copyright © 2014

James F. Ward

First Edition

Image credits begin on page 272.

Every effort has been made to present accurate information. Corrections are welcome. Every effort has also been made to document and/or contact the copyright holders of material in this book. However, where an omission has occurred, the publishers will gladly include acknowledgement in any future edition.

Library of Congress Control Number: 2014937611
ISBN: 9781941573013

Published by Damianos Publishing
59 Fountain Street, 4th Floor East, #10
Framingham, MA 01702 USA
www.DamianosPublishing.com

Produced through Silver Street Media
by Bridgeport National Bindery
Agawam, MA USA
First printed 2014

Contents

CONTENTS
CONTINUED

CONTENTS
CONTINUED

Introduction

The "common," or village green, is at the center of many New England towns. Early on, it often provided pasture for livestock or room to train the local militia. The common gradually transitioned into a public park. It became a place to gather for public events or perhaps listen to a concert from the bandstand on a warm, summer evening.

One such common is located in the town of Hopkinton, Massachusetts. Today, as in many surrounding towns, long lines of cars wait to pass by the Town Common during rush hour. Once a year, tens of thousands wait for their chance to cross the starting line of the B.A.A.'s Boston Marathon. Few know the unique stories of how this area developed and of some fascinating people who lived and worked here. Yes, there were the minister, an innkeeper, a blacksmith, a wheelwright, doctors, lawyers, merchants, and many local farmers. However, here also lived the celebrated Madam Price. A unique group of English gentry gathered here, one of whom later commanded militia in defense of Boston. Another commanded one of the most famous ships in history. Here worshiped a Baronet with estates in England, who later experienced the horrific Lisbon earthquake of 1755. In the first half of the 19th century, the Common was the pioneering center of one of the largest industries in Massachusetts and a center of the anti-slavery movement. The largest coal dealer in New England would reassemble his ancestral lands here. The houses and other features, which line the streets around the Common, are the remnants which connect us with these stories.

Here is an opportunity to explore an area which saw rapid industrial development and then virtually stopped. The leaders of industry built substantial homes during particularly fine periods of architecture and craftsmanship. Most of these houses remain and their history can be traced. Had the factories remained, the scene would be quite different. This work attempts to connect what you see today, as you stand on the Common and walk the nearby streets, with visual images from the past and the stories behind them.

EARLY DEVELOPMENT

Boston was the center of the most densely populated colony in New England. The original Massachusetts Bay Colony was restyled as the Province of Massachusetts Bay in 1692. New towns were developed as the population grew and pushed west or north from Boston. Grants of land were usually made to individuals who were willing to meet the requirements of clearing land and building a house, barn, etc. However, the Town of Hopkinton started out quite differently.

Eight-thousand acres of land was purchased by Harvard College from the previous residents. These were Native American residents who had made up a small settlement named Magunco,[1] one which had been artificially created by the Court. It was really the western part of John Elliot's congregation at Natick.[2] Of course, this was prior to the ravages of the French and Indian wars. There had also been earlier land grants in the eastern part of what became Hopkinton and then Ashland. Harvard made its purchase as an investment—making use of a legacy from Edward Hopkins. The land was then leased to new tenants willing to relocate there. The Legislature added more land to make up the new *"Hopkins Town"* or Hopkinton, which then encompassed twenty-five thousand acres. Hopkinton was incorporated on the 13th of December, 1715. In 1735, part of the town was set off to form Upton.

As a result, early property records exist in two places! Two towns, namely Hopkinton and Upton, located in *two different counties* (Middlesex and Worcester) share a set of volumes containing transactions stemming from these original leases.[3] Another set of property records is located at the Middlesex South Registry of Deeds in Cambridge. These records are the foundation for appreciating how the Common area properties developed. Fortunately, especially for the historian, several early maps exist. These help to put the puzzle together. A study of these records, and of the exhaustive work of previous researchers, has made it possible to trace the origins of the subject properties. There is room for additional research. Unfortunately, several fires destroyed records pertaining to the buildings which occupied these lots over the years. Thankfully, some wonderful photographic collections have been preserved.

---

[1] Spelling varies.

[2] Elliot Street in Hopkinton (now Ashland) once connected through to Elliot Street in Natick, connecting the two Puritan Indian settlements.

[3] The Hopkinton Registry of Deeds was created by the General Court in 1741 and recorded deeds for the town until the record books were transferred to the Middlesex County Registry, in accord with 1811 legislation. However, the actual deeds cover the period from 1743 to 1833. The residents of Hopkinton protested the removal of the records, and in February 1813, the Massachusetts Legislature revised the laws to allow for the appointment of a Hopkinton Register and called for the return of the land records to Hopkinton. The restored volume set resides at the Hopkinton Town Hall today. A microfilm copy is at the Hopkinton Public Library where there are also some additional indexes.

PLEASE NOTE:

Family charts and specific dates are included (1) to help the reader understand the family relationships in time and place; And (2) to aid future research. Feel free to skip over these and concentrate on the people, architecture, and/or industrial development.

Maps are also included for reference. An attempt has been made to present information in chronologic and geographic order. However, due to the complex ownership transfers between members of the same families, it was necessary to deviate from this plan a few times.

The properties which originally surrounded the Common were very large. Original bounds were not well defined. It would take much more research than I am willing to do in order to trace every property which now exists on those original lots. Instead, I have traced the houses which face the Common and nearby sections of Hayden Rowe and Main Street. At the end of the book is a summary of ownership discovered during research, with transaction dates for each property, if known. In tracing the industries which the families developed, I went wherever the story took me. As a result, I have included information and pictures beyond the Common and indeed, beyond Hopkinton. Let's begin by looking down from above.

Plan & Topographical Views

Plan view[4] of the Hopkinton Town Common and surrounding landscape:

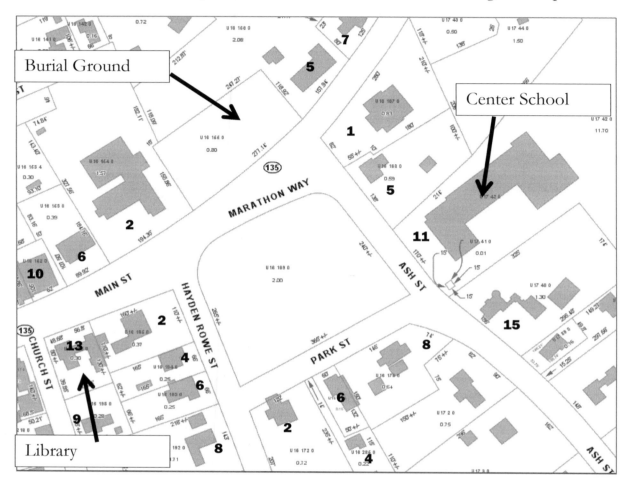

Hayden Rowe Street was originally called the "Road to Milford." Ash Street was called "Fitch Road" or the "Road to Holliston." Park Street was first called Common Street. East Main Street begins at Ash Street. The Stone Tavern (the "L" shaped building right of the Burial Ground) is the first house and its address is "5 East Main." However, Main Street has even numbers on the north side, starting with the Korean Presbyterian Church at number 2. The Hopkinton Public Library, on the south side, is number 13.

---

[4] Town of Hopkinton Assessors Map.

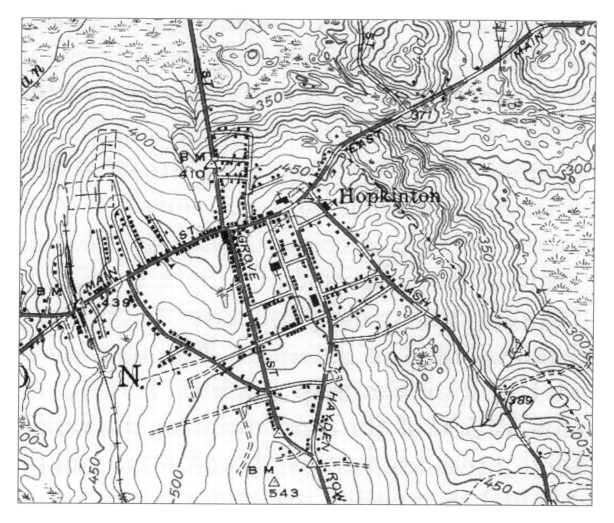

On this U.S.G.S. topographical map of 1946, the Common is located just left of the name "Hopkinton." Though the crest of the ridge on the "Bay Path" was chosen for the center of town, the top of the hill is actually near the current high school and the intersection of Hayden Rowe and Grove. The Common is at an elevation of 480-feet. The top of the hill is at 543-feet. The Little Cedar Swamp is on the right edge in this view and the Great Cedar Swamp is at the top. Like the plan view, this map is provided for reference as you read the following chapters.

Now let's go back to 1715 and picture the scene. Heading west, settlers may have been somewhat dismayed to see the amount of granite ledge and all the boulders along the trail. Though they found good farmland in sections (such as that developed along Hayden Rowe), much of Hopkinton was covered in rocks.

Main Street & the Burial Ground

The earliest feature of the surrounding landscape is not the Common, but rather, Main Street. It is likely that the oldest, east-west trail through this region was located somewhat to the north of the present street, where it skirted the hill, rather than coming straight up what was a very steep grade with exposed rock at the top. The trail became known as "The Bay Path," as it developed into a primary travel, transport and communications route from Boston, Massachusetts **Bay** to Hartford, Connecticut.[5] A 4-rod (66') wide road was laid out in the spring of 1724/25. With minor adjustments, this became Main Street.

The next existing feature is the old burial ground opposite the Common. For the center of the new town, the settlers chose the edge of the hill. The first meetinghouse was constructed in November of 1725. On early maps, the hill is thus identified as "Meetinghouse Hill." The burial ground was set aside to the north of the Bay Path on land owned by the Barrett family.

On the 24th of December, 1807, John Barrett, Schoolmaster, and Nancy Freeland, Widow, conveyed "a certain tract or parcel of land lying and being in said Town and is now enclosed and improved for Burial Ground in the center of said Town, bounded on the westerly side by the meeting house and contains 40 rods more or less." The Town Selectmen purchased this "Burial Ground" for the sum of $40.00.

Old Burial Ground

---

[5] Thus, it is also sometimes called the "Old Connecticut Path."

The Barrett Family and the First Meetings

As close as can be determined, the first meetinghouse was located a little south of the burial ground, partly on the Common and partly in what is the much wider Main Street of today. It was a plain, wooden, unpainted structure, 48' by 35', with a double row of windows and a large sounding board over the pulpit. After its sale in 1829, it was moved and used as a barn on the Valentine estate and then as part of a boot factory (see page 168). The moving and reuse of buildings was not uncommon in those days. Timber frames, with their hand-made, mortise and tenon joints, were valuable. Sometimes, teams of oxen were used to move complete buildings.

When Hopkinton was incorporated, towns were still organized under the Puritan arrangement. Town meetings and religious services were held in the same building. Two large buildings were more than was deemed necessary. Even when the new Congregational (or First Parish Church as it was also called) was built in 1830, opposite the end of Hayden Rowe, the stone basement was leased to the town for use as a town hall.

Just to the west of the new church was the old home of Samuel Barrett II, the first minister (Harvard, class of 1721 and of 1724). His father, Samuel I, was a well-to-do merchant in Boston, who owned 100 acres on the Mendon line.[6] He built a wharf in Boston which bore his name. He married Sarah Manning and they had fifteen children, of whom Samuel II was the eldest.

Minister Barrett's grandson, John Barrett (1759-1821), was a teacher and, in 1819, author of an English grammar. He was also one of the early teachers of Horace Mann.[7]

The following is a genealogy of the Barrett family. The chart indicates the connections the Barrett family had to well-known citizens of Boston.

---

[6] The area which became Hopkinton was once bounded by Mendon, Sutton, Westboro, Sudbury and Sherborn. The Barrett property on the Mendon line was sold by Samuel Barrett II, by deed of 17 Nov. 1745, signed by Samuel on the 2nd of March, 1746, in the presence of Charles Morris and Samuel Barrett Jr. (III).

[7] Horace Mann – Education reformer and founder of the Framingham "normal school" to train teachers. He was a brother-in-law of Nathaniel Hawthorne. His statue is in front of the Massachusetts State House.

SAMUEL BARRETT I b. 8 Feb. 1669/70, Cambridge – d. bef. 1741, Boston
    m. 8/12 March 1693/94, Sarah MANNING b. 19 Mar. 1669 – d. 29 Jul. 1741
    Fifteen children, including:

    1. SAMUEL BARRETT II b. 9 Dec. 1700, Boston – d. 11 Dec. 1772, Hopkinton
        m. 28 Nov. 1723 Ann MORRIS b. 23 Sep. 1702, Boston – 19 Oct. 1771,
            Hopkinton, one son:

    SAMUEL BARRETT III b. 10 Sep. 1726, Hop. – d. 10 Mar. 1800, Hop.
        m. after 9 Feb. 1758 Mrs. Mary Caswell,
        Widow of Dr. Samuel Caswell (1724-bef. 1758)
        She, b. c. 1725, Norton or Taunton – d. 7 Oct. 1812, Hopkinton
        Two children:

        1. JOHN BARRETT b. 2 Jan. 1759, Hopkinton – d. 4 Apr. 1821, Hop.
            m. Bridget _____ b. c. 1733?? – d. 17 Apr. 1816, age 83

        2. NANCY (ANNA) BARRETT b. 23 Feb. 1761, Hopkinton - _____
            m. 5 Apr. 1781, Hopkinton,
            Thomas FREELAND bef. 13 Jun. 1756 – 16 Aug. 1805 Hopkinton

    2. GEORGE BARRETT b. 11 Jun. 1706, Boston – d 17 August, 1745, Hopkinton
        m. Mary _____
    (They had at least five sons: Manning, George, James, Thornton, & John)

    3. JOHN BARRETT b. 12 Jun. 1708, Boston – d. 9 Sep. 1786, Boston
        m. 3 Jun. 1732, Sarah Gerrish b. 23 Jul. 1713, Bos. – d. 9 Feb. 1798

        1. SAMUEL BARRETT b. 17 Jan. 1738, Boston – d. ?
            m. Mary CLARKE

        SARAH BARRETT b. 13 Mar. 1763, Bos. – d. 17 Feb. 1809
            m. 27 Nov. 1781, Samuel Cabot b. 9 Nov. 1759, Salem

John Barrett of 1708 was a wealthy Boston merchant like his father. He commissioned John Singleton Copley to paint portraits of himself and his wife. Their daughter-in-law Mary's sister, Susanna Clarke, married Copley.

The homestead lot of Samuel Barrett was divided by Main Street, with most of the property on the south side, leaving just a narrow strip on the north side. Minister Barrett's house was located on this strip of land.

No known drawings of the Barrett house survive. However, when Nancy (Barrett) Freeland was appointed administratrix of her husband's estate, she had to sell property to pay debts. Thomas Freeland was only 49 when he died. Nancy and Thomas Freeland had been living in the Barrett house on Main Street. She sold their half of the house at an auction held on the 28th of April, 1806. Samuel Valentine Jr. and his brother Joseph Valentine were the high bidders at $548.59.[8] The deed contains a description of the divided house. The sale included the west room with cellar under, the chamber and garrets above and "the closets belonging to the same," and the kitchen with bed and cheese rooms adjoining, a privilege in the Entry and to the stairs leading up to the chambers and garrets, a privilege to the well or wells." Nancy reserved "a privilege in the Kitchen for my Mother the widow Mary Barrett to do her baking, washing, and other necessary work." The house was torn down in, or just before, 1831. Mary Barrett, widow of Samuel III, lived until the 7th of October, 1812, when she was 87. See the chapter on the Central Coffee House for more details on the sale of this property in 1831.

Records indicate that the first town meeting was held in the house of John How(e) (1664-1740) on the 25th of March, 1724. This is why it is sometimes called the first meetinghouse, thus causing some confusion. We may remember this as the home of Betty Strong, who served as Director of the Hopkinton Public Library from 1955 to 1972. It is the white house set back on the north side of East Main Street,[9] just down the hill to the east of the Common. At least, most sources identify this as the house of John How.

According to Josiah Temple's 'History of Framingham,' John How had a house located 75 rods *east* of the town center. That is approximately the location of the house identified above and pictured next. However, the will of John How, dated 1740, mentions his house located on his leased lot *west* of the town center. The location of this lot is well established. The land primarily went to his son-in-law, Jacob Gibbs. On this land, Davenport & Gibbs later built a boot factory (see pages 98 and 101).

---

[8] The deed also describes a parcel across Main Street which contained a barn. Ownership of the barn was also divided in half, with the Barrett's retaining ownership of the east half. More than 3 acres were sold with the half of the barn.

[9] The house is set back because Main Street used to be closer, in fact the old roadway is still in place, flanked by stone walls.

c. 1718 House of John How

The dormer and bay window are later modifications to an otherwise authentic Cape Cod-style house. It was an affordable and popular style throughout New England. Most of the first houses in Hopkinton would have looked similar. His larger lot was just west of John Taylor's (see page 11).

Why consider John How when none of his properties seem to front on the Common? Well, John How was called an Innholder, when, in 1728, he was indicted for selling alcohol to the Indians.[10] John Taylor was also called an Innholder. Just to the east of the old burial ground is the Stone Tavern. If you look at the map on the next page, you will see that it is located on a parcel owned by the Barrett/Manning family.[11] John How and John Taylor had leases just west of Barrett's land. In fact, Samuel Barrett sold the 49-acre lot to John Taylor. It was part of 100 acres that had been leased to Ralph Hemenway. No record exists for a transfer from Hemenway to Barrett and no deeds exist for the original Hemenway and How lots (at least none that I can find).

A deed dated 5 May, 1742 from the Harvard Trustees to "John Barrett of Boston, Shop Keeper, Assignee of John Manning of Cambridge," describes a lot containing 34 acres which had been "laid out to his Honorable father, Samuel Barrett, late of Boston, deceased. The map for this deed shows the lot just north of the burial ground. This lot is thus labeled "John Manning" on the following map.[12]

---

[10] See the Massachusetts Archives, Boston for more information. Also, the records of the Wayside Inn, Sudbury.

[11] The exact property lines can no longer be determined. The landmarks have long disappeared, such as "an oak tree" or "stake & stones."

[12] Several of John's children were baptized at the Congregational Church in Hopkinton.

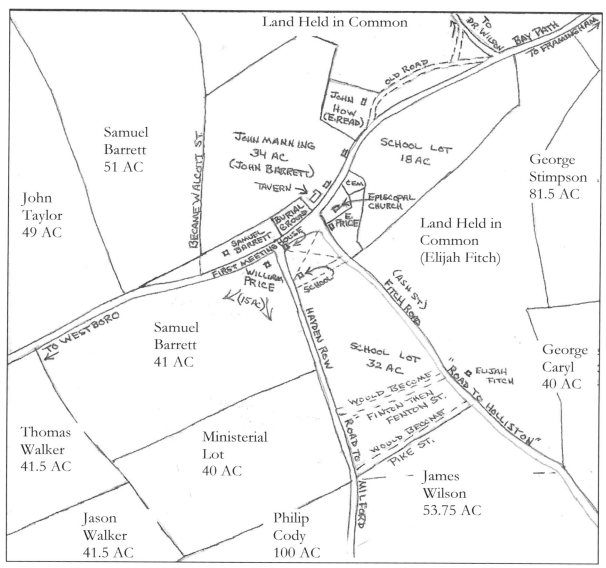

This is a portion of a map modified from one drawn by Beryl Osborn about 1940 and based upon his analysis of the original land leases.[13] The meetinghouse is depicted here by a square and located near the corner of the "road to Milford" (later Hayden Row, then Hayden Rowe). The Price Mansion House was built on the opposite corner, on fifteen acres of the original 41-acre lot of Samuel Barrett. The other Barrett/Manning lots are shown.

The 32- and 18-acre School Lots are defined. The Common is designated "Training Field" in the deeds which were created as the 32-acre portion of the school

---

[13] All the pieces of the puzzle never precisely fit together. The map provides a good guide to the approximate location of the lots granted to the first lease holders.

lot was divided and sold. An additional 45 acres were located at "Whit Hall" adjacent to land of John Kelley. All these parcels together added up to 100 acres.

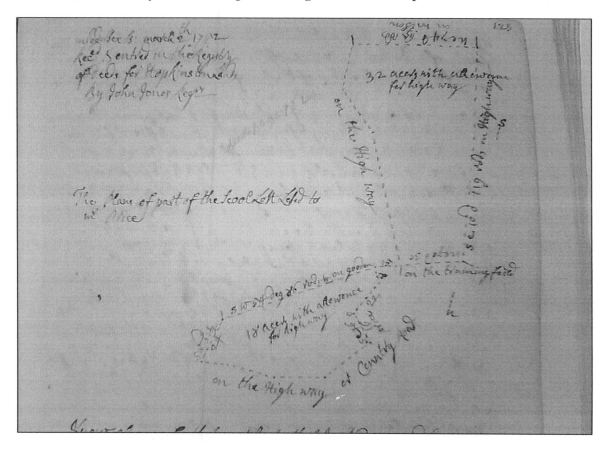

This is an image of the survey which accompanies the original deed conveying part of the school lots to Roger Price, dated the 2nd of March, 1752.[14] The lease would run from the 25th of March, 1720 for a period of 99 years. Roger was to pay 4 ounces of silver annually. See page 22 for more details on this transaction. It is included here for the benefit of showing the location of the school lots.

The survey shows the "Highway or County Road" on the bottom, so we are looking south, with the Common to the right, or as it is shown here "on the training field." Just above the word "County" is a jog around land labeled "Price." This is land previously purchased by Roger Price. The cemetery with the tombs is located on part of this property. The other abutters of the 18-acre parcel are George Kingston and James Gooden. Above the training field is the 32-acre parcel, bounded by Ash on the left and Hayden Rowe on the right. It was bounded southerly by land of the "Widow Wilson," since James Wilson had died by the time this deed was written.

---

[14] Hopkinton & Upton deed books, Volume I, part II, page 217 (originally page 123).

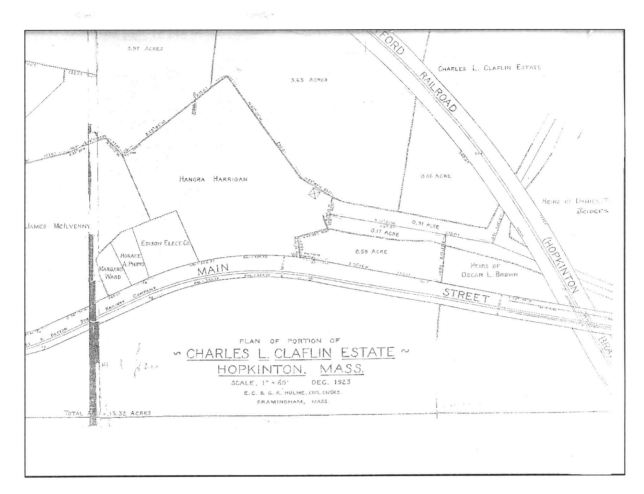

On this map from 1923, part of the old route of (East) Main Street is shown parallel with the current route. The old intersection with Wilson Street is also visible. Cutting across these former streets and under Main Street is the Hopkinton Railroad (more on that later). In 1923, Hanora Harrigan was the owner of the former How property. Not shown is the part of Main Street which formerly cut through this Harrigan property with a sharper curve to connect with the part of the old layout which is shown. The parcels to the north (top) were owned by the Charles L. Claflin Estate and were joined to the parcel containing the Stone Tavern.

The Stone Tavern

The oldest, existing building at the Common is the one pictured below.

Pub. by Frank Phipps.   Tavern where Geo. Washington & Daniel Webster dined on their way to Boston, Hopkinton, Mass.

This is an early photograph of the tavern. A date of 1745 is usually given for this building. The stone was quarried just up the hill to the south (see page 61). It is impressive that it was constructed in stone and thus it has long been known as the "Stone Tavern." Many meetings and social events were held in the large ballroom with a cove ceiling on the second floor. Barns can be seen behind the tavern.

Various articles have claimed that the tavern was originally built of wood in 1706. John How was a carpenter, as well as an "innholder." He may have constructed a wooden house on this site, which is not far from the house attributed to him and pictured earlier. As a comparison, the more famous Wayside Inn in Sudbury has functioned as a tavern since 1716. It began in 1707 (in wood) as a two room homestead by David How, John's younger brother. Did John start building in Hopkinton the year before?

A likely candidate for the first innkeeper would be John How. Its location next to the church made it convenient for parishioners to gather for lunch during the long day at Sunday services. Each town was required to have a "public house." The tavern long continued to be a popular meeting place for social events.

What we do know for certain is that in the latter part of the 18th century, Isaac Claflin was the innkeeper. In a deed dated the 2nd of April, 1804, Isaac sold the tavern and seventy acres "more or less" to Samuel Valentine Jr. for the sum of $2,666.00.[15] The property ran from Walcott Street to Wilson Street, behind the Barrett house (then owned by Thomas and Nancy [Barrett] Freeland), behind the church and burial ground, along Main Street at the tavern and behind the property of Ephraim Read (the John How house).[16] Samuel and Elizabeth Valentine had a large family. This led to a complex division of the property among the heirs. Ownership of the Stone Tavern remained in their family and heirs throughout the 19th century.[17]

The next discovered deed records the sale of the tavern by William H. & Martha M. Gleason of Framingham to their daughter Carrie E. Taylor. She was married to James F. Taylor. The Taylor family had long owned the house just to the east of the tavern, at 7 East Main St. Luther Taylor and his son, James F., did business as L. Taylor & Son, working as carpenters and builders. In 1915, Carrie Taylor sold the Stone Tavern to Alice D. Tebeau of Hopkinton (Mrs. John H. Tebeau) and Mary F. Hines of Boylston (Mrs. John H. Hines). The Stone Tavern remains the oldest inhabited dwelling facing the Common.

About the time the Stone Tavern was under construction, changes were about to take place on the south side of Main Street. As indicated on the previous map, the Barrett family controlled all the choice property around what was developing as the center of Hopkinton.

It is somewhat ironic that the south side of Main Street was soon purchased by the Episcopal minister from Boston, Roger Price. His house was built across the street from that of Samuel Barrett. He also built a church on the south side of the street. It was located on the site of the One Ash Street building (see the previous aerial view). He gave a one-and-one-half acre lot of adjacent land for a churchyard. This later became a private cemetery of Valentine, Claflin, and other families. Several stone tombs are still located there. Due to the central role of the Price family with regard to the land surrounding and including the Common, we should consider this family in detail.

---

[15] H&U deed books, Vol. 15, page 346.

[16] This implies that the two 18th century homes between the tavern and Ephraim Read's (John How's) house were part of Valentine's property.

[17] We will consider the Valentine and Claflin families in connection with other properties.

View of the cemetery created by Roger Price in the 1740's
The back of the Episcopal Church was just up the hill to the right

Before the doughboy statue and its triangle of land, Main Street extended in width from the cemetery to the Common. Thus, it was even wider than it is today. It was so wide because of the Episcopal Church. When approached from the west, as one reached the top of the hill on Main Street, the Episcopal Church was centered in your view, with the Congregational Church to your left. The gable end of the Congregational Church faced the end of Hayden Row. It was centered in your view when approached from Milford to the south.

Roger Price & Elizabeth Bull

Roger Price was born on the 6th of December, 1697, in Whitfield, Northamptonshire, England. He was educated at Oxford, where he received his A.B. from Balliol College in 1717. On his way to become a chaplain at Widdaw, Guinea, West Africa, he was captured by pirates. He came down with a fever in Guinea, once he finally arrived there. This led to a transfer to Jamaica, where he served as chaplain to the Duke of Portland and minister of the local parish. Roger stayed three years until his health deteriorated once again. The Duke then sent him back to England with letters of recommendation to several of his relatives and to the Bishop of London, Edmund Gibson. The Bishop first offered him a small living at Leigh in Essex. Then he was offered the position of representing the Bishop as Commissary of the Anglican (Episcopal) Church in the Massachusetts Bay Colony.

Roger became the Rector of King's Chapel in Boston, the original of which predated the 1748 stone edifice now on the corner of Tremont and School. He married Elizabeth Bull on the 11th of April, 1735. She was known as one of the beauties of Boston. For her wedding to Roger Price, she wore an elaborately embroidered gown which has long been in the possession of the Bostonian Society. From 1735, the Price family lived in a mansion erected by Hezekiah Usher in 1684, which was in the middle of an extensive tract of land on Tremont Street, known then as Common Street, between Temple Place and West Street, facing Boston Common.[18] This was just a short walk from King's Chapel. It is difficult today to picture the bucolic scene of gardens and orchards where tall buildings now stand (see page 20 for a period map).

ROGER PRICE (1697-1762) & ELIZABETH BULL (1712-1780)

1. Elizabeth Price (1737, Boston-1826, Cambridge)
2. William Price (1739, Boston-1802, Hopkinton)
3. Henry Yelverton Price (1740, Boston-1780, London, England)
4. John Price (1741-1741, Boston)
5. Mary Price (1742-1742, Boston)
6. Mary Ann Price (1744, Boston-1763, Hammersmith, England)
7. James Price (1747-1747, Boston)
8. John Price (1748-1751, Boston)
9. Thomas Price (1749, Boston-1770, Hyde Park, London, England)
10. Andrew Price (1752-1752, Boston)
11. Andrew Price (1753, Leigh, England-1851, Downhampton, England)

---

[18] Robert Means Lawrence, M.D., The Site of St. Paul's Cathedral, Boston, and Its Neighborhood, (Boston: Richard G. Badger, 1916).

A modeling of Elizabeth Bull's wedding gown[19]

Elizabeth Bull inherited her father's estate. He had been an innkeeper and businessman. Bull's Tavern was located at the foot of Summer Street and included a store and wharf. The Tavern had been the property of Nicholas Baxter until 1668 when it was sold to John and Mary Bull.

---

[19] <u>Days and Ways in Old Boston</u>, (Boston: R. H. Stearns and Company, 1914).

John Bull (1646/47-1723) married Mary Woodward, step-daughter of Nicholas Baxter, on the 21st of April, 1692 when he was 45. They had eight children. The youngest son, Jonathan, inherited and successfully expanded their business interests. He married Elizabeth Mann on the 1st of January, 1706/07. Elizabeth Bull was their only surviving child.

Various reports of the Boston Selectmen mention the tavern and wharf. For example:

"At a meeting of the Select Men, April 30, 1739....the safest Way for Conveying Powder to the Powder House is to do it by water,....while the River remains frozen, that it be brought from on board Ship in Cover'd Boats to Bull Wharf at the South end of the town, and from thence Convey'd to the Powder house in Cover'd Carts as aforesaid…"

The powder house was on Boston Common. Also:

"At a Meeting of the Select Men, March 23, 1736….Samuel Adams, Esq. being Present, desiring the Select Men to run the line, in Order to Ascertain the breadth of Summer street, at the lower end thereof, near the sign of the Bull." Also, "On Fryday last the 27th of June Current (1740), The Select men met at Bulls Wharf, the lower end of Summer Street, upon the Desire of mrs. Dyre and run the line between the Town and Said Dyre, and Staked out the High Way, taking the Measure from the Well on the North Side of the said High Way, which is agreeable to the Record thereof made in the Year, 1683…"

And finally:

"August 1, 1744, Rev. Roger Price may bring his fence in Sea St. on to a line with Capt. Darby in Summer St."

The Tavern was described as a wooden house of two stories and thirty-one windows. It was demolished in 1833, to make way for Atlantic Avenue. The wharf area is now under Dewey Square, near South Station.[20]

---

[20] Samuel Adams Drake, Old Boston Taverns and Tavern Clubs, (Boston: W. A. Butterfield, 1917);
A Report of the Record Commissioners of the City of Boston, Containing the Records of Boston Selectmen, 1736 to 1742, (Boston: Rockwell & Churchill, 1886); and,
Annie H. Thwing, The Crooked and Narrow Streets of Boston 1600-1822, (Boston: Marshall Jones Co., 1920).

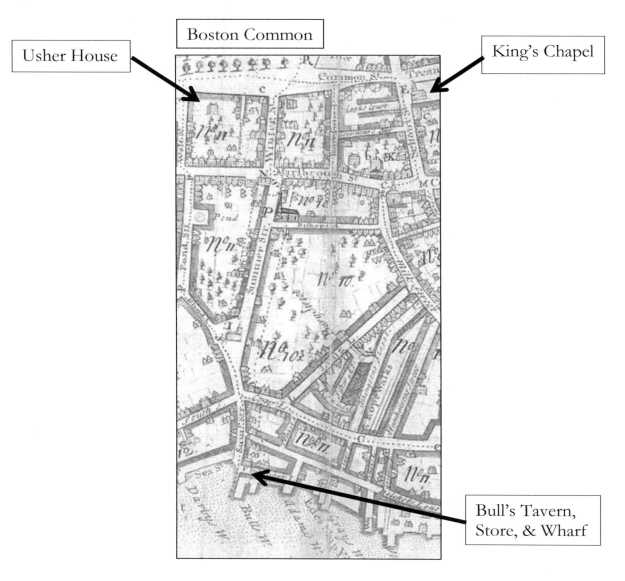

Usher House

Boston Common

King's Chapel

Bull's Tavern, Store, & Wharf

A portion of a 1769 map of Boston[21]

---

[21] William Price (a Boston printer), <u>A New Plan of ye Great Town of Boston in New England in America</u>, 1769.

Roger Price was often at odds with his fellow clergymen in Boston. This led to an attempt to provide himself with a church living in the quiet countryside of Hopkinton. Some of his wealthy parishioners, such as members of the Valentine, Gooch, and Wilson families had already located there. Roger was enamored with the beauty and tranquility of the location. By promoting these attributes, he was successful in getting more families to acquire property in Hopkinton, including Sir Charles Henry Frankland, who acquired a large estate. This resulted in a rather unique, genteel society some twenty-five miles west of Boston. With a core of parishioners, Roger tried repeatedly to convince the Bishop of London to establish a mission church in Hopkinton. He was unsuccessful. The Bishop wrote that he didn't have the funds to support a minister in Hopkinton. In 1739, Roger was able to secure funding from a benefactor to purchase a "glebe," consisting of one hundred and seventy acres of land <u>with house and barn</u>, to support his dream.[22] The benefactor was Christopher Jacob Lawton of Leicester, Massachusetts.[23]

Roger Price purchased other tracts of land starting in 1744.[24] One purchase consisted of an unfinished house and "a large tract of land with a fine grove" from Charles Morris, Gentleman. He paid Mr. Morris two hundred pounds in province bills on the fifteenth day of August, 1746. Roger and his wife completed the house and made it their home during the summer months. In all his letters, the Price house is referred to as the "Mansion House." It is designated on the town seal as the "Price Mansion House" as a result. This is the house which was opposite the house of Samuel, the Congregational minister. When Roger proceeded to build a church as well, Samuel argued that Hopkinton already had a church.

On the first of March, 1735, the lots which had been designated to support the schools were leased to Charles Morris, brother-in-law of Samuel Barrett.[25] So at that time, the family controlled the choice property on the top of the hill on both sides of the street.

---

[22] The glebe land is now a part of the Hopkinton State Park. When driving north on Route 85 (Cedar Street) from Hopkinton center, the former glebe land is on both sides of the road from the Park Headquarters, past Rafferty Road, to the reservoir. This was once open farm land.

[23] Henry Wilder Foote, <u>Annals of King's Chapel from the Puritan Age of New England to the Present Day</u>, Vol. 1, (Boston: Little, Brown & Co., 1881). Also from: Kewaunee and Door, <u>Commemorative Biographical Record of the Counties of Brown, Wisconsin</u>, (Chicago: J. H. Beers & Co., 1895): Christopher Jacob Lawton was born in 1701 in Rhode Island. He became a respected lawyer and member of the General Court after moving to Leicester, Massachusetts in 1735, birthplace of his wife Abigail Kellogg. See also: Rev. Amos Hill Coolidge: <u>A Brief History of Leicester, Massachusetts</u>, 1890.

[24] According to Clement Meserve of Hopkinton, writing in 1891, these lots totaled 709 acres, plus 142 acres of common land (for firewood and building materials). Each tenant got a percentage of the common land based upon the size of their leased land - in this case, 142 acres.

[25] See the chart on page 8 and the chapter on Charles Morris, starting on page 39.

But now picture the situation in 1744. Along comes Roger Price and effectively begins to take over the south side of the street. On the 2nd of March, 1752, the Town Selectmen transferred "two certain tracts or parcels of land containing fifty acres, being part of the School Lot" to Roger Price for the sum of 19 Pounds, 1 Shilling, and 10 Pence.[26] Roger also had the funds to pay the back rents which Mr. Morris had let accumulate. The plan which accompanies this deed was depicted earlier on page 12.

It is no wonder that Samuel, whose religious teachings were founded on the nonconformist views of the Puritans, was uncomfortable with the reemergence of the Episcopal (or Anglican) church. Also, the minister's income came from the townspeople, who were already hard-pressed to support him. Samuel started out with just £30 per year for the first three years, along with providing for the cutting and carting of his firewood. This was to be raised to £70 afterwards. The Trustees also voted to give £30 towards "building his house upon his own land" and £60 (later raised to £100) in day labor and materials towards his settlement and the building of his house. In effect, Main Street would now divide the gentry, who supported the Episcopal form of worship, from the yeoman farmers, who supported the Congregational form.

The Episcopal congregation remained small and, in 1753, the Price family returned to England. By then, Roger no longer had a wealthy supporter, such as the Duke of Portland. He no longer had the influence within the church to find a lucrative living in a large parish. He ended up with just his small living from the parish at Leigh, where he died, impoverished, in 1762. In 1764, at the age of 52,[27] Mrs. Price applied to the "Governors of the Charity for the relief of poor widows and children of clergymen," much to the consternation of her friends and wealthy relatives in Boston. Just the year before, the family had been hit by smallpox. Daughter Mary Ann had died. Mrs. Price still had two teenage boys at home. Clearly, she needed financial support. Elizabeth Bull Price died in Beckley, England on the 5th of August, 1780.

In the years between 1750 and 1780, the Price Mansion in Hopkinton had many tenants. These included Sir Henry Frankland in 1751, while he was building his grand house, and John Troutbeck,[28] who officiated at the Episcopal Church as curate.

---

[26] H&U Deed Books, Volume I, Part II, pp. 216 and 217.

[27] In her petition, she states her age as 47, so she was shaving five years off her real age.

[28] After leaving Hopkinton, John Troutbeck became the assistant to Henry Caner at King's Chapel in Boston. He was one of the signers of an address to General Gage. He was subject to the banishment act as a Loyalist and died in England.

Sir Charles Henry Frankland,
4th Baronet of Thirkleby

Of the gentry who lived and worshiped on Meetinghouse Hill, none were more influential than Sir Charles Henry Frankland, Baronet of Thirkleby. He has been the subject of much research. Even Oliver Wendell Holmes wrote about him. We will consider some highlights here. For an in-depth study of his life, I refer you to the excellent work of Elias Nason, M. A., entitled "Sir Charles Henry Frankland, Baronet: or Boston in the Colonial Times," 1865, and now online. Mr. Nason had access to original documents and living relatives when he compiled his book. He also purchased what had been Sir Henry's mansion in Hopkinton. The story of Henry's dalliance with, and eventual marriage to, a "bar girl" from Marblehead, named Agnes Surriage, became a popular and embellished romance tale of Victorian times.

To his friends, Henry (he didn't use his first name Charles) was known as Harry Frankland. 'Henry' in the North Yorkshire dialect is pronounced 'Harry', closer to the French pronunciation of Henri. For example, the 2nd Duke of Buckingham, Henry Stafford, wrote his name as 'Harre Bokynham.' Names were spelled as they sounded. Spelling sometimes even varied in the same document.

Henry was born in Bengal, India on the 10th of May, 1716. His father was Henry Frankland, Esq., president of the East India Company's factory at Bengal and fourth son of Sir Thomas Frankland, 2nd Baronet of Thirkleby. The hereditary title of Baronet had been conferred on Sir Thomas' father, Sir William Frankland M. P., by Charles II in 1660.[29] The Frankland's represented Thirsk, North Yorkshire, in Parliament for some 200 years. Sir Thomas married Elizabeth Russell, granddaughter of Oliver Cromwell. Sir Thomas, 3rd Baronet, and a Lord of the Admiralty, was the eldest son. He only had two daughters. One married the Earl of Litchfield. This was remarkable because the Earl was a descendant of Charles I, who was beheaded before Oliver Cromwell took over the government. Without male issue, the title passed to Sir Thomas' nephew, Charles Henry Frankland, who was now living in Boston.[30]

---

[29] The use of 'Sir' designates one who has been knighted. Knighthood was for life, but could not be passed on. However, the title of Baronet (Bart.) is hereditary and was conferred on the eldest male child. Hence, a Baronet is a hereditary Knight and he uses 'Sir' before his name. To distinguish one baronet from another, the title contains the location, as in 'Baronet of Thirkleby'.

[30] The 3rd Baronet died in 1746. His brothers had all died too, so the title went to the next male in line.

Henry had arrived in Massachusetts Bay by September of 1739. He was keeping up the family business tradition as a merchant trader. The family had been trading in Barbados for a long time and Henry was supplying dried cod from Marblehead in exchange for such items as fruit, sugar, wine, and rum from Barbados.

Thomas Pelham-Holles, Duke of Newcastle, was influential in getting Henry the post of Collector of His Majesty's Customs at the Port of Boston. About the same time, Sir William Shirley received the position of Governor of the Province of Massachusetts Bay, partly due to the writing efforts of his wife.[31] Henry got the choice office. Both Sir William Shirley and Henry Frankland took up their respective offices in 1741. It wasn't until 1747 that Henry became Sir Frankland.

---

[31] William Shirley was the son of William and Elizabeth (Godman) Shirley, and was born on the 2nd of December, 1694, at Preston Manor in East Sussex, England. The large c. 1747 residence of Governor Shirley, located in what is now Roxbury, has been preserved and is open for tours.

Thirkleby Hall, near Thirsk, Yorkshire, was the family estate. Henry did not get to live there since his uncle's (much younger) wife had inherited a life estate. The house pictured above was built to plans of James Wyatt for the 6th Baronet, nephew of the Hopkinton resident. It replaced a Jacobean house. The new house was constructed of fine ashlar stone and included a quadrangular stable and matching triumphal arch gate lodge. When the last male heir died in World War I, the distraught family sold the estate and the house was demolished. The façade was purchased by an American in 1927. The stable and lodge remain and the estate is occupied by a number of holiday rental trailers. It is located in an agricultural area to the north of the city of York.

Another estate was in Nottinghamshire. Henry Frankland, Esq., the father of our subject, maintained estates in England while working in India. In 1720, Henry, then of St. Andrews, Holborn, purchased Mattersea Manor from the family of Sir William Hickman. In 1725, he bought further Mattersea lands in Nottinghamshire. But, he died in India in 1728. So this estate also passed to Sir Henry of Boston and Hopkinton. In the East Sussex Record Office in England, there is an archive of Griffith, Smith, Dodd and Riley of Brighton, Solicitors. Contained in the papers is correspondence and notarial letters from Sir Henry's attorney in Boston, regarding his Mattersea estate.[32] The estate produced a sizable income, but so did Henry's position in Boston, where he chose to live. The Mattersea estate stayed in the family until purchased for £40,000 by Jonathan Acklom, Esq. By 1832, it had passed to his son-in-law, Lord Althorp.[33] Mattersea Hall still exists. It is part of a religious college and has undergone many changes since the 18th century.

---

[32] National Archives, East Sussex Record Office, United Kingdom.
[33] William White, History, Gazetteer, and Directory of Nottinghamshire, (Sheffield, England, 1832).

ESTATES IN THE PROVINCE OF MASSACHUSETTS BAY

When in Boston, Sir Henry was a member and principal supporter of King's Chapel, and therefore, an associate of Roger Price and the wealthy members of his congregation. He was persuaded that Hopkinton would be a favorable place for a country estate. According to Elias Nason, he also wished to get away "from the annoyance of the busy tongues of Boston" due to his immorality. Sir Henry had fathered an illegitimate son in 1740/41, who he named Henry Cromwell. Now he was living openly with Agnes Surriage. Though immorality was often "winked at" among the upper classes in England, this was Massachusetts Bay. The Puritan influence continued, so Biblical standards of morality were still valued by many in Boston. Roger Price, however, was an Anglican clergyman and used to depending on the patronage of the nobility and this took precedence in his mind. He remained a close friend to Sir Henry.

Sir Henry purchased the Gooch lease in 1749, the Preston lease in 1750, and several others to form a 482-acre estate in Hopkinton. Construction of the manor house began in 1751 and was completed the following summer. According to Nason, the façade was about one hundred feet long. It had three floors and a dining room which could seat fifty people. The central hall was flanked by fluted columns and hung with tapestries.

There was once a one-hundred foot long barn to the west of the house. The houses for the servants rivaled those of the neighboring farmers. From the following photograph, it is possible to get an idea of the setting. It shows the third and much smaller house built on the site. It exists today, though surrounded by housing developments. Frankland Road is named in memory of Sir Frankland.

And the three Elms high-arching still, are seen at the Sir Harry Frankland Farm and home of Agnes Surrage. Pub by Frank Phipps Hopkinton Mass

The terraces leading up from Frankland Road were constructed by his slaves. This portion of Frankland Road is now part of the town of Ashland. The property extended west from the house to Cross Street in Hopkinton.[34] It encompassed much of Magunco Hill and stretched south beyond present-day Olive Street in Ashland.

On the estate were planted a great variety of fruit trees, as well as elms and other ornamental trees. The hill behind was covered with chestnut trees. The walks of his garden were lined with box lilac and hawthorn. Sir Henry enjoyed hunting and fishing with his neighbors. Boxes of the latest books were sent over from England. He also had a large wine cellar, and he had a special glass made which was of double thickness so he could remain sober, while his drinking companions did not!

In 1754, Sir Henry and Agnes went to England in connection with a dispute about ownership of Thirkleby Hall. His family did not approve of his unwed state either. Agnes was not received. So they embarked on the customary European tour. They were in Lisbon during the worst possible time. Mid-morning on "All Souls Day," the 1st of November, 1755, a great earthquake destroyed much of Lisbon. The churches were crowded when it struck. A tsunami and fires resulted. Henry was trapped under his carriage for more than an hour. Agnes discovered him and he was extricated from the rubble. Like most Europeans, Henry was profoundly struck by his experiences. He determined he should marry Agnes without delay. After a Catholic

---

[34] Cross Street was actually moved west at Sir Henry's request. He wanted it on the western edge of his property.

ceremony in Lisbon, they left for New England. Aboard ship they had an Anglican ceremony to be sure the marriage was official.

In October, 1756, Sir Henry purchased the famed, twenty-six room, Clarke House on Garden Court in Boston from Thomas Greenough, for twelve hundred pounds sterling. It had been built to rival in splendor its neighbor, the Hutchinson House owned by Royal Governor Thomas Hutchinson. Lady Agnes was now received in society.

Clarke-Frankland House

The house was built about 1711 on the corner of Garden Court and Prince Street in the North End of Boston for the Honorable William Clarke, Esq., a wealthy merchant and member of the Governor's Council. The following is a description from the book "Loyalists of Massachusetts and the Other Side of the Revolution" by James H. Stark, published in 1910:

"The principal feature which distinguished this house was the rich, elaborate and peculiar decoration of the north parlor, on the right of the entrance hall, which was a rich example of the prevalent style, found in the mansions of wealthy citizens of the colonial period, in and around Boston. The peculiar decoration consisted of a series of raised panels filling these compartments, reaching from the surbase to the frieze, eleven in all, each embellished with a romantic landscape painted in oil colors, the four panels opposite the windows being further enriched by the emblazoned escutcheons of the Clarks, the Saltonstalls, and other allied families. Beneath the surbase, the panels, as also those of the door, were covered with arabesques. The twelfth painting was a view of the house upon a horizontal panel over the mantel, from which this engraving was made,[35] and beneath this panel inscribed in an oval, was the monogram of the builder, W. C. At the base of the gilded and fluted vault of the buffet was a painted dove. The floor was inlaid with divers woods in multiform patterns. In the center, surrounded by a border, emblazoned in proper colors, was the escutcheon of the Clarks, with its three white swans. The mere enumeration of the details fails to give an idea of the impression made by this painted and gilded parlor, not an inch of whose surface but had been elaborated by painter, gilder, carver or artist, to which the blazoner had added heraldic emblems; so that, as you looked around these walls, the romantic ruins and castles seemed placed there to suggest, if not to portray, the old homes of a long line of ancestors, and the escutcheons above to confirm the suggestion, thereby enhancing the splendor of the present by the feudal dignity of an august past."

The land for the house was purchased from the widow Ann Hobby on the 10th of December, 1711 for £725. She was likely Ann (Wensley) Hobby, wife of John Hobby who died on the 7th of September, 1711. His brother was Sir Charles Hobby of Boston. Charles had a daughter Elizabeth who married James Gooch in 1715. James and Elizabeth lived in Hopkinton until they sold their property to Sir Henry Frankland. The Gooch's daughter Elizabeth married Thomas Valentine in Hopkinton in 1735.

During the winter of 1756/57, Sir Henry Frankland experienced health problems. He suffered from gout, brought on by a rich diet. In July of 1757, he sought and obtained the position of Counsel-General to the Court at Lisbon, Portugal. On the 23rd of February, 1758, the couple set sail on the ship Mermaid, a man-of-war, Alexander Innes, Captain.[36] In the summer of 1760, they attended the wedding of Don

---

[35] The engraving is the one pictured on the previous page.

[36] Diary of Sir Henry Frankland, Bart. From the spring of 1755 to the end of his life, Sir Henry kept a journal or diary. It survives in the archives of the Massachusetts Historical Society and consists of some two hundred pages.

Pedro and Donna Maria[37] and spent the rest of the summer at Caldas de Rainha, a fashionable, hot sulphur spa.

Sir Henry and Lady Frankland returned to Boston for a brief visit in 1763. While away, their property in Boston and Hopkinton was left in the charge of Ralph Inman. The Hopkinton farm was advertised for lease in the Boston Evening Post of 7 January, 1765, "suitable for a gentleman or farmer…now tenanted by Joseph Villiers." This was Jacques Joseph Villiers de Rouen. The house in Boston was advertised in July of 1765.

Sir Henry died at Bath on the 11th of January, 1768. Henry's brother Thomas, the next Baronet, purchased the Mattersea estate for £20,000. Lady Agnes returned, along with Henry Cromwell, to their home in Hopkinton. She stayed there until May of 1775. Henry had apparently left for England before then. As the wife of a former British official, she wisely sought the safe haven of British-controlled Boston. But, it meant a dangerous, twenty-six mile trip through militia-controlled territory. Lady Agnes requested and was granted safe passage by the Committee of Safety. The permit was signed by Dr. Benjamin Church. Interestingly, Dr. Church was later tried and convicted of "illegal correspondence with the enemy." He had secretly been sending messages to General Thomas Gage with the hopes of aiding a peaceful solution to the situation.

On the way to Boston, Lady Agnes was arrested by a party of armed men and detained. The Provincial Congress subsequently appointed a six-man, armed guard as escort to Boston. The Committee of Safety and Provincial Congress were organizations of the Colonists and they became the de-facto government as the former authority broke down.

Lady Frankland moved into her fashionable home in Boston. There she entertained General John Burgoyne, who had just arrived from England with two other generals in response to the rebellion. He had been a friend of Henry and Agnes in Portugal.[38] The British forces evacuated Boston in March of 1776 and the Loyalists fled to Nova Scotia or England. Lady Frankland sailed to England where she had a home with her Frankland relatives. In 1782, Lady Agnes married a prosperous banker in Chichester, Sussex, named John Drew. Unfortunately, she died the next year, the

---

[37] Queen Maria I and Pedro III of Portugal.

[38] General John Burgoyne (1722-1792) was an English Brigadier-General in Portugal in 1762. His success there played a major part in thwarting a Spanish invasion of Portugal. He was in Boston only a short time. In 1777, George III gave him command of a campaign to divide New England from the rest of the Colonies. His overconfidence and lack of support from armies of two other generals led to his defeat and a turning point in the war. The two other generals (Howe and Clinton) had been with him in Boston.

result of a bad cold. She was 57 (23 April, 1783). Her Hopkinton estate was willed to her relatives. Who were they?

Lady Agnes Surriage Frankland was the fourth child of Edward and Mary (Pierce) Surriage. Edward was a fisherman in Marblehead. Mary Pierce was the impoverished granddaughter of John Brown, who had a huge land grant in Maine.

Two siblings of Lady Agnes moved to Hopkinton. One was Mrs. Mary (McClester) (Surriage) Swain (b. c. 1722). The Boston estate on Garden Court was willed to Mary Swain. It passed to her son Daniel McClester, who willed it to his uncle, Isaac Surriage in 1807.

Isaac (b. c. 1734 - September, 1813) was a mariner who became a farmer upon settling in Hopkinton. He married Ruhamah Pedrick and had a house on Pig Lane (Howe Street). Their daughter Jane (1773-1839) married Peletiah Bixby Jr. (intentions recorded 7 April, 1795). They raised a large family in Hopkinton. Isaac continued to rent out the estate in Boston until he sold it to Josiah Ellis, Esq. in 1811 for $8,000.[39] According to historian Stark, when Bell Alley was widened in 1832, the famed Clarke-Frankland mansion, along with the neighboring Foster-Hutchinson mansion,[40] was "ruthlessly swept away."[41]

During the War of Independence, the Hopkinton property was occupied by Mary Swain and her daughter, Sally Dupee, widow of John Dupee. Because it was occupied by the family and "Three negro slaves of which one is old and blind,"[42] it was not confiscated. However, Henry Cromwell, Esq. inherited the property from Lady Frankland. Through his Boston attorney, he sold it all in 1793 to Dr. Timothy Shepherd of Sherborn for £950.[43]

The Hopkinton estate remained the property of Dr. Shepherd and then his wife until her death in 1857. In that year, the house and one hundred acres were purchased by Elias Nason. The house accidentally burned on the 23rd of January, 1858. Many artifacts of the Frankland family from a hundred years before had remained in place

---

[39] Based upon average wage conversion, this would be about $6-8 million in 2013.

[40] The Hutchinson house is thought to have been the first Palladian mansion in Boston and had been owned by Royal Governor Thomas Hutchinson. It was built for John Foster, Esq. between 1689 and 1692, partly of imported stone.

[41] James Henry Stark, Loyalists of Massachusetts and the Other Side of the Revolution, (Salem, MA: The Salem Press Co., 1910) and Nathan Perkins Sanborn, The Fountain Inn, Agnes Surriage and Sir Harry Frankland, (Marblehead, MA: Marblehead Historical Society, 1904).

[42] Massachusetts Archives, Vol. 154, pp. 52, as quoted by Elias Nason.

[43] Based upon average wage and a current British pound to US dollar conversion, this would equal $1.8 million.

until then. The house was rebuilt, but then burned again. In 1904, there was nothing but charred ruins. The great gardens extended from the house, across Frankland Road and down to West Union. Thus, when passing on the Central Turnpike (West Union /Route 135 today), you would have had a long view of the house sitting high up the hill to the north.

The reconstructed c. 1860 Frankland Mansion as viewed from Frankland Road

Its c. 1905 replacement is partly seen in an early view reproduced below

In 2013, the row of great elms planted by Sir Henry is long gone, but successors have grown large. They give some perspective on the passage of time since this third house was built more than one hundred years ago. The original would be over two hundred and sixty.

But what happened to Sir Henry's son? Loyalists were often left out of history books. Local, historical accounts simply say he "disappeared." But did he?

Admiral Henry Cromwell

Henry was born in Massachusetts in February of the year 1741.[44] He joined his father in Hopkinton in 1752. He began a career in the Royal Navy at the age of fifteen, when he joined the ship "Success," then in Casco Bay (Falmouth, Maine). He attained the rank of Lieutenant on the 6th of July, 1761. His Uncle Thomas was having great success with his career in the Navy and this may have helped Henry's prospects.

Henry settled in Chichester, Sussex and married the widow Mary Ventham on the 2nd of January, 1779. They had a son and daughter.[45] On the 10th of May, 1779 he was made Commander and received the ship Cabot in June. The Cabot was a captured American Brigantine of fourteen guns. On the 14th of November, 1781, he was elevated to the rank of Captain. Either he was a very accomplished mariner or his family connections were remarkable, because just days later, on the 23rd, he was made Captain of H.M.S. Victory. H.M.S Royal George was also put under his command! H.M.S. Victory was the flagship of Rear-Admiral Kempenfelt at the time.[46] Captain Cromwell may have been serving as his chief of staff.

It was an important time to be Captain of the Victory. The ship was involved in just three significant battles. The first of these took place on the 12th of December, 1781, while under Cromwell's command. It became known as the Second Battle of Ushant. The weather played a part, or the outcome would probably have been quite different. The French force turned out to be far superior in strength. A storm prevented any action between the armed forces, but it allowed for the capture of a large French convoy.

H.M.S. Victory is more famous for its role as Lord Nelson's flagship at the Battle of Trafalgar in 1805. It is a 104-gun, First Rate Ship-of-the-Line, launched in 1765. It remains the oldest, commissioned warship in the world. For reasons of preservation, it remains in dry dock, rather than floating.[47]

---

[44] Calculated from entries in Henry Frankland's diary, see: F. Marshall Bauer, Marblehead's Pygmalion, Finding the Real Agnes Surriage, (Charleston, SC: The History Press, 2010).

[45] Ibid.

[46] Sir William Laird Clowes, The Royal Navy, A History from the Earliest Times to the Present, Vol. 3, (London: Sampson Low, Marston and Company, Limited, 1898).

[47] If you have seen the U.S.S. Constitution in Boston, a comparison may be helpful. The Constitution is a 44-gun, Frigate, launched in 1797. It is the oldest, commissioned, warship *afloat* in the world. It was built 30 years after H.M.S. Victory. H.M.S. Victory is 227' long, with a displacement of 3,500 tons, and a crew which totaled 850. U.S.S. Constitution is 204' long, with a displacement of 2,200 tons, and a crew which totaled 450.

H.M.S. Victory in Portsmouth Harbour, Portsmouth, Hampshire, England

As she appeared c. 1900, without her elaborate gilt decorations

H.M.S Royal George was also a very famous ship for other reasons. When launched in 1756, it was the largest ship in the world. It was a 100-gun, First Rate Ship-of-the-Line. On the 28th of August, 1782, H.M.S. Royal George was anchored off Spithead, preparing to join Vice-Admiral Richard Howe's fleet in another relief of Gibraltar. With an estimated 1,200 aboard, the ship was heeled over to make some repairs to the hull. The officer in charge did not realize that ports were open on the low side. Barrels of rum were being loaded through these gunports from a lighter at the time. Water rushed in and the ship rolled over onto the lighter and sank. Hundreds of men, women, and children died, including Rear-Admiral Kempenfelt. He was trapped in his cabin when the doors jammed. Captain Cromwell was not aboard. In August, 1782, he was aboard the Bienfaisant with fellow Captain John Howarth.[48]

Model of H.M.S. Royal George

Oil on panel by Joseph Marshall

Greenwich Hospital Collection, National Maritime Museum, Greenwich, London

---

[48] Op. cit., Clowes.

Henry became a Rear Admiral in 1801. After that he continued to move up in rank, but not in active service. In 1810, he was elevated to the rank of Vice-Admiral of the Red. During this time he continued to maintain his house in Chichester.

Henry's Uncle William lived not far away at Muntham Court, a very large (1,860-acre) estate in Findon. Findon is near the English Channel in Sussex. William became a somewhat eccentric inventor after his retirement as an East-India merchant. His house was full of marvelous inventions. He commissioned portraits of his ancestors leading back to Oliver Cromwell. Only the likeness of William himself (shown below) is publicly known to exist.

William Frankland 1720-1805 by Mather Brown[49]

When William Frankland died in 1805, he bequeathed his house and contents to Henry, with the proviso that Henry Cromwell would become Henry Frankland. He did. After Henry's death in January of 1814 at the age of about 72, his widow, Mary, continued to live at their home in Chichester and at her death in 1823, Muntham Court passed to Roger Frankland, Henry's cousin. There is a carved stone funerary monument to Henry Cromwell (Frankland) by John Flaxman in Chichester Cathedral.

---

[49] Mather Brown (1761-1831) was a portrait and historical painter. Born in Boston, he was a student of Gilbert Stuart and, later in London, of Benjamin West. He also painted Thomas Jefferson and Charles Bulfinch. He was a descendant of Increase Mather, the famous Boston minister. His uncle was Mather Byles, a Loyalist.

Muntham Court Estate, prior to 1835

Muntham Court remained in the Frankland family until it was put up for sale in 1835. In 1850, the estate was purchased by the Dowager Marchioness of Bath, Harriet Thynne. After her son John reached the age of twenty, Harriet Thynne moved out of Longleat, the famous Thynne family estate, and into Muntham Court. She had greatly enlarged the old brick house by 1877.

Here we see the house in its final form. In 1961, Muntham Court was deemed "surplus to local council requirements" and demolished.[50]

---

[50] Pictures and quote courtesy of: Lost Heritage – Demolished Country Houses of England - www.lostheritage.org.uk.

Charles Morris

As mentioned in a previous chapter, Charles Morris sold his property at the Common to Roger Price in 1746. This is the year Charles first went to Nova Scotia, where he ultimately became Privy Councillor and Chief Justice. His father was a prosperous sail-maker and Charles received a good education, including instruction in methods of land survey.[51] We will call him Charles III because his grandfather was also Charles (b. 1650 in Wales). Charles II was born in Bristol, England in 1675 and came to Boston in 1696. Three years later he married Esther Rainsthorpe, daughter of James of Boston. Esther was born about 1676 because she was 79 at her death in 1755. Her gravestone is in the famous Granary Burial Ground in Boston. Charles and Esther Morris/Morrise/Morriss had nine children, including Ann, born 23 September, 1702. She married Samuel Barrett II on the 28th of November, 1723 in Boston. Her brother, Charles III, was born in Boston on the 8th of June, 1711.[52]

Charles Morris III moved into the highest levels of society in Boston upon his marriage in 1732 to Mary Read, daughter of the famed lawyer and Attorney General of Massachusetts Bay, John Read, and Ruth (Talcott) Read. John Adams, in writing to a friend, said of John Read "that he had as great a genius, and became as eminent as any man."[53] John Read graduated from Harvard in 1697. Interestingly, he was a Warden of King's Chapel in 1735 and 1736. This helps to explain why his son-in-law would sell land to Roger Price in spite of Samuel Barrett's position on the matter. John was also a member of Governor Shirley's Council in 1742. For more on his many accomplishments, I recommend George Bowlend Reed's "Sketch of the Life of the Honorable John Read, of Boston, 1722-1749," 1903, reprinted, (Whitefish, MT: Kessinger Publishing, LLC, 2010).

After his marriage, Charles and Mary Morris lived in Hopkinton on a farm which had been established by his father at the Common. Charles taught school. Then in 1745 he volunteered for the expedition to capture the French stronghold at Louisbourg, Cape Breton. Governor William Shirley of Massachusetts Bay and

---

[51] Rev. Arthur Wentworth Hamilton Eaton, D.C.L., "Eminent Nova Scotians of New England Birth," The New England Historical and Genealogical Register, Volume LXLII, (Boston: 1913). See also, Phyllis R. Blakeley, "Morris, Charles (1711-1781)," Dictionary of Canadian Biography, Volume IV (1771-1800), (University of Toronto/Université Laval, University of Toronto Press, Toronto, 1979).

[52] A Report of the Record Commissioners of the City of Boston, Containing Boston Births from A.D. 1700 to A.D. 1800, (Boston: Rockwell & Churchill, City Printers, 1894). Also, the report from 1898 for marriages.

[53] Charles Francis Adams, Life and Works of John Adams, Vol. 9, (Boston: Little, Brown & Co., 1850-1856) p. 572.

Governor Benning Wentworth of New Hampshire rallied support among the other colonies and eventually gathered a significant force. Charles Morris served as a captain under William Pepperrell from Kittery. The fort was captured. In 1746, Governor Shirley gave Charles a commission as captain of a company of 100 men being sent to Annapolis Royal. There was great concern for the safety of Annapolis Royal, and even Boston, at the time, due to a large French fleet which was expected to arrive. However, the fleet was hit by storms and British attacks and never did arrive.

Captain Morris was present at the battle of Minas/Grand Pré. His troops were joined by those of Jedediah Preble and others. Colonel Arthur Noble arrived by sea in early January with an additional 100 men, for a total of about 500. Due to the severe winter conditions, they felt that any attack was impossible. But they were surprised when the French did attack. About 70 soldiers were killed and another 69 were wounded and taken as prisoners. Captain Morris rallied the others, who fought their way to a large stone building in the middle of town. Offered an honorable surrender, they were permitted to return to Annapolis Royal. The Duke of Bedford wrote to Governor Shirley regarding Captain Morris "who commanded one of the six New England companies, an officer who has distinguished himself…by his behavior at Minas against the enemy."

Due to his performance, Governor Shirley asked him to survey large areas of Nova Scotia and Charles went on to lay out the towns of Halifax and Lunenburg. He was appointed Surveyor-General in 1749, Justice of the Inferior Court of Common Pleas in 1753, created Privy Councillor in 1755, and Chief Justice in 1776. His son and grandson, both born in Hopkinton, succeeded him as Surveyor-General.

Though he accomplished much, he was also one of the persons responsible for the cruel Acadian expulsion which paved the way for a large immigration from New England. The following is a quote[54] from a work by Peter Landry of Dartmouth, Nova Scotia:

"Morris was appointed to the Council on 30 Dec., 1755; he was therefore not a member when it was decided in July of that year to expel the Acadians. In 1751, however, he had already made the significant suggestion that the Acadians be rooted out of the Chignecto region in his 'Representation of the relative state of French and English in Nova Scotia,' which he transmitted to Shirley, then leaving for England as one of the British commissioners empowered to settle the Anglo-French dispute over the boundaries of Acadia.

[54] www.blupete.com.

Morris believed that the presence of the Indians and French on the north shore of the Bay of Fundy and at Chignecto made effective British settlement of the province impossible, and he recommended that the Acadians be removed 'by some stratagem . . . the most effectual way is to destroy all these settlements by burning down all the houses, cutting the dykes, and destroys all the Grain now growing.' As the official most knowledgeable about the Acadians, Morris was consulted by the Council during its deliberations on their fate. His opinions had not changed, and the Reverend Andrew Brown found his report 'little honourable to his heart . . . cruel advice and barbarous Counsel.' "

Charles Morris III, 1711 – 1781

Charles Morris IV was apparently born in Hopkinton in 1731 or 1732. The record of his birth is missing. He married Elizabeth Bond Leggatt/Leggett on the 5th of September, 1756, in Lancaster, Massachusetts. His sister Mary Elizabeth Morris was born on the 27th of March, 1742, in Hopkinton. She married Thomas Balch Leggett on the 20th of April, 1760, in Halifax, Nova Scotia. Thomas and Elizabeth were brother and sister. They were the children of Captain Thomas and Madelane (Dupree) Leggett of Boston. Captain Leggett (b. 1705/06 in Yarmouth, England) was killed in the siege of the fort at Louisburg. He was a friend of Charles Morris III.

In addition to his many responsibilities, Charles was a large land speculator. As a member of the Saint John River Society[55] in the mid-1760s, he participated in its grants, and he also held land in Maugerville Township, around Passamaquoddy Bay (both in New Brunswick), and in and around the Annapolis valley. In 1774 he sold 10,000 acres on the Saint John River to James Simonds for £150. Despite the many expenses of his offices, Charles amassed a considerable estate, probably through his property transactions. When he died in 1802, he left assets worth more than £17,000.

Charles Morris V was born in Hopkinton on the 28th of November, 1759. Since his aunt was married in April, in Halifax, we can deduce that the family moved to Halifax early in 1760. It was the time period when some seven thousand moved to Nova Scotia from New England. They came to be known as the "Planters." The "Loyalists" went later, after the Revolutionary War. By 1760, land was already scarce in southern New England. The Planters were usually the younger sons in a family — ones who did not expect to inherit the family homestead. They went north seeking farm land. Other Planters were fishermen who had been fishing off the Grand Banks. During the summer they stayed in Nova Scotia to be close to the rich fishing areas. Now, they could establish permanent settlements. The District of Maine, then a part of Massachusetts, became safer from attack as well and settlement progressed north from Portland.

There was frequent travel between Nova Scotia (New Scotland) and New England. A little known fact was the intention at one point of establishing New Ireland between New England and Nova Scotia. It would have included much of Maine. The death of King Charles I put an end to many early plans for Maine.

Because thirteen colonies broke away from all the rest of the English colonies in America, the conflict which ensued has been called the first civil war. When the southern states tried to do the same later on, it caused what we know as the "Civil War." Both conflicts caused people—many of them professed Christians with the same heritage—even members of the same family—to slaughter one another.

---

[55] Beamsley Perkins Glasier from Newburyport, Mass. was their agent on the St. John River. In 1765, Beamsley worked with Charles Morris III on an exhaustive survey of the St. John. 125,000 acres were granted to Glasier. Due to the parsimony of his backers, Major Glasier eventually returned to his regiment. This was after building mills and roads in the area. His brothers remained on the St. John where they became famous lumbermen. Beamsley went on to survey copper deposits around Lake Superior. He was commandant of the fort at St. Augustine, Florida from 1778. He died on his way to England on the ship "Nancy" out of Halifax in 1784. Extensive travel was more common than we might think.

Madam Price

In Volume 20 of the New England Historical and Genealogical Register, dated 1866, she is called the "celebrated Madam Elizabeth." Long before women's suffrage, Elizabeth Price was a woman of independent means and an independent lifestyle. She owned much property in her own name and acted in her own behalf in legal matters. She lived in a time when all but the wealthiest women were excluded from these aspects of life.[56] Who was she and what made this possible?

Elizabeth was born in Boston on the 3rd of April, 1737 as the eldest child of Roger and Elizabeth Price. She was therefore about nine years old when they moved to the country setting in Hopkinton, and a teenager of fifteen or sixteen when they made their voyage to England in 1753. For the next three decades, Elizabeth lived in England. There, her youngest brother Andrew was born. But, during that time she also lost three of her five siblings. Elizabeth herself nearly died of smallpox. The effects on her appearance may have contributed to her decision not to marry. However, she is said to have had many suitors, both in England and America, so she may have just preferred to remain single.

In 1783, three years after their mother's death and after the end of hostilities, Elizabeth and her brother, Major William Price, returned to Hopkinton. William was just two years her junior. He had retired from the British army by then, after serving in Gibraltar, and was now forty-four.

When they returned to Hopkinton in 1783, it had been thirty years since Elizabeth and William had been home. They found the old house at the Common in a dilapidated state. Soon, repairs were underway.

---

[56] For example, Elizabeth Hardwick, Countess of Shrewsbury, married four times, outliving each in turn, the last being George Talbot, 6th Earl of Shrewsbury, who left her the wealthiest woman in England after Queen Elizabeth I. In conjunction with Robert Smythson, she designed her own magnificent manor house in Derbyshire, completed in 1599 when she was 72. Her wealth gave her independence and, on a much smaller scale, wealth did the same for Elizabeth Price.

Did the Price house look something like this, or was it more humble?

The only image we have of the Price Mansion House comes from an ink sketch made by Sally Dupee in 1805, during a visit with Madam Price. Sally was the daughter of John and Sally Dupee, and thus, a grand-niece of Lady Frankland. Her sketch depicts a smaller house than this one which is located on the corner of Chamberlain Street in Holliston. This is a "three-quarter" Georgian Colonial, whereas the sketch shows a "half" house. But it is located on a corner much like the site of the Price Mansion. The use of "half" and "three-quarter" to describe the size refers to the number of windows on the first floor front. A "full" house would have two windows on each side of the front door. It would also be known as a "five-bay" house, easily recognized by five windows on the second floor, each in a "bay" between the upright posts of post and beam construction. The style fits the period of construction and the social standing of the Price family. However, a survey of properties in Hopkinton, dated 5 October, 1798, describes the homestead of Major William Price as being of one-story, 38' x 16' and "bounded North and East on a road," the lot containing fifteen acres. Contemporary maps confirm that William lived in the house on the corner of Hayden Rowe and Main. It is possible that the house was enlarged and the sketch shows how it looked in subsequent years.

COUNTRY HOME OF REV. ROGER PRICE,

(NEAR THE FIRST PARISH CHURCH)

AT HOPKINTON.

From an 1805 sketch by Sally Dupee, signed "F. E. W." and dated "1876"

The Price Mansion (left) and the Meetinghouse (First Parish Church) (right)

William Price had two daughters by an unknown woman when he was in his fifties. Mary Ann was born on the 24th of January, 1792 and her sister Olivia a year later. William died in Hopkinton on the 7th of December, 1802. This is where the story of Elizabeth becomes truly remarkable.

On the thirteenth day of April of the following year, Elizabeth was appointed "…administratrix of the Estate of William Price, late of Hopkinton, aforesaid, Esquire, deceased." This was after "Elizabeth Price, singlewoman; Samuel Parker, Doctor of Divinity; and David Watts Bradley, wine merchant;" deposited with Oliver Prescott, Esquire, Judge of the Probate of Wills, the astonishing sum of thirty thousand dollars[57] to secure the probate of the estate!

---

[57] By one method of price comparison (using average earnings), $30,000 in 1803 would equal $26,800,000.00 in 2013.

The inventory of the estate is also quite revealing. The real estate in Hopkinton, consisting of many parcels, was valued at $12,395. This did not include Bull's Tavern, store and wharf in Boston, which were valued at $8,000. The homestead in Hopkinton, still containing fifteen acres, was valued at $1,500. William's personal estate was valued at $660.

The personal estate included a noteworthy item. It was "A lease of fifty acres of land known by the name of the School Lot for ninety-nine years. Sixteen years are yet to run at thirty dollars per year at one third part at $160.00." The value was one third because it was split with his sister Elizabeth, as well as his brother Andrew in England (16 x 30 = 480 /3 = 160). The land was still leased at thirty dollars per year, but this was considered an asset, not a liability. When the leases came to an end,[58] each tenant was given title to his or her respective lots. The leases pertaining to the school lots ended on the 25th of March, 1819. In effect, the leases ended up being a "rent to own" arrangement. In addition to the Price homestead on the corner of Hayden Rowe, Elizabeth owned another, newer house on the Common, as we shall discover later. In this case, the house still exists.

Another interesting aspect of the administration of the estate of William Price concerns the interest of his youngest brother Andrew. By now, he was the only other surviving child of Roger and Elizabeth Price. Andrew would live to the age of 98, dying in 1853. At the time of the probate in 1803, an affidavit was sent from England, authorizing Elizabeth to represent his interests in the estate. This affidavit was attested to by none other than the Lord Mayor of London, Charles Price, Esq.[59]

In the years after her brother's death, Elizabeth Price continued to manage hundreds of acres in Hopkinton. She continued her brother's practice of hospitality and charity.[60] She farmed part of the "glebe" land which was located off Howe Street, then called Pig Lane.[61] Her brother Andrew wrote to her from England in 1805, urging her to move to Boston. It was another fifteen years before she agreed to go live with her niece and husband in Cambridge. By then (1820), she was 83 years old. The 99-year leases on the school lots had reached their end the previous spring. She thus claimed ownership of all her property. As she was preparing to leave Hopkinton,

---

[58] The last of these leases came to an end in 1832.

[59] As far as I have been able to determine, Charles Price was not a close relative. A copy of the affidavit is contained in the set of Hopkinton & Upton deed books, Vol. 14, beginning on page 186.

[60] The New England Palladium (published 1803-1814) carried an obituary notice after William's death. The obituary relates details of his internment with military honors, accompanied by "a large concourse of the most respectable inhabitants of the neighboring towns…to whom his hospitality and extensive charity had endeared him."

[61] At the time there was no direct access to this land. An access road to Howe Street was constructed later. Eventually, Cedar Street was constructed through the property.

Elizabeth sold a house and more than nine acres to Willard Aldrich for $400.00. Willard Aldrich and Lucy Morse were married later that year.

Both Willard and Lucy had been raised in the household of Madam Price.[62] There is also a record of another girl who was sent to live with Madam Price. Ann Bent, born 19 June, 1768, was the eldest daughter of Rufus and Ann (Middleton) Bent. "She was early called to aid in the support of the family." There were seven children and "...while still quite a child [Ann] went to live with Madam Price at Hopkinton, for two pistareens a week.[63] Madam Price was very kind to her, and always remained her firm friend. After some years she returned to Milton, and taught school on Milton Hill."[64] The arrangement with Madam Price provided much needed income to the Bent family.

The Census of Hopkinton in 1820 shows Elizabeth with two females between the ages of twenty-six and forty-four, one female sixteen to twenty-five, one female under ten and one male under ten. This indicates that she was still providing charitable employment.

Madam Price lived at a time when class distinctions were the norm. One who had traveled or had more refined manners was held in high regard. In her book "Brampton Sketches," published in 1890, Mary Bucklin Claflin writes of Madam Price:

"...a stately, solemn-looking dame, who wore a turban with a large lilac-colored bow on the top and high-heeled boots and carried a spacious bag on her arm, and always maintained her English style of living. She kept two Negro servants, and was looked upon by the village people as somebody quite above common. She had kept up the grounds around the old-fashioned mansion, and had introduced many new plants and shrubs, so that her garden, with its box borders and lilac hedges, was the wonder of the village people, and was regarded as a marvel of landscape gardening. Her house was just opposite the meetinghouse, and the wall which surrounded it was lined with lilacs. She was the first person who introduced lilacs to the village."

---

[62] From The New England Historical and Genealogical Register, Vol. 20, 1866, pages 260-261, deaths: "Aldrich, Willard, Hopkinton, Mass., 24 Feb., aged 70 years. Himself and wife Lucy, daughter of Arnold Morse, were brought up in the family of the celebrated Madam Elizabeth, daughter of Commissary Roger Price, once rector of King's Chapel, Boston."

[63] Pistareen: A small silver coin originating in Spain and used as common currency in the Americas during the 18th century.

[64] Albert Kendall Teele, History of Milton, Mass. 1640-1877, (Boston: Rockwell & Churchill, 1887).

Madam Price is said to have planted an elm tree, which she had brought from England, near the school house on the Common. In the mid-1870's, Mary Ann Price reflected upon the time she spent in Hopkinton at her aunt's house. There she saw "the very best of society in the country."[65]

When Madam Price went to live permanently in Cambridge, in 1820, the rest of the school lots went to benefit the schools and all the rest of her lands went to Lawson Valentine. Lawson Valentine (1792-1828) had married the eldest daughter of William Price (Mary Ann, 1792-1881) and lived in Cambridge. Madam Price also deeded a mortgage on the Watch Farm, containing 139 acres, to Joseph Valentine for $700.00. This would have been the remaining interest she had in a mortgage given by Joseph Belknap of Westborough in 1813.

Madam Price had a large circle of friends in Boston.[66] This indicates that she had continued to spend time there over the years, while maintaining her residences in Hopkinton. After moving to Cambridge, she lived for another six years, dying at the age of 89 on the 23rd of July, 1826. We can conclude that it was her charity, as well as her independence and work ethic, which gained her the respect of her contemporaries and the designation: "the celebrated Madam Elizabeth."

~

The original Episcopal Church, constructed by Elizabeth's father Roger Price, was severely damaged in the "Great Gale" of September, 1815. This was the first major hurricane to hit New England in 180 years.[67] The building was deemed too far gone to repair. Samuel Valentine Jr. was contracted to rebuild and Elizabeth Price provided the funds. She then proceeded to deed the property to the Church in September, 1818. The second church burned on the 15th of July, 1865. After that, the membership dwindled and the land was taken over by the town. About the year 1875, a school was built on this lot, but it is a little closer to Ash Street than the church had been.

On the 17th of June, 1820, the Massachusetts Legislature created a seven-member group of trustees to manage the remaining school lots and the proceeds of any sales. The group was appropriately called "Trustees for the School Fund." Dr. Thomas Bucklin, Col. Joseph Valentine, and Moses Chamberlain were among those appointed.

---

[65] T. W. Valentine: The Valentines in America, (New York: Clark & Maynard, Publishers, 1874).
[66] Op. cit., Foote.
[67] The next was in 1938.

The First Schools

On August 13, 1734, the town voted to erect three schools, one in Woodville, one in Hopkinton (center), and one on Frankland Road. A school was erected on what became the Common (near the corner of what is now Park and Hayden Rowe Streets) in 1748 by "several worthy and pious men." This may or may not have been the unfinished building acquired by Roger Price from Charles Morris when he purchased his property on the south side of Main Street in 1746.

In any case, this school on the Common, or its successor, is where Henry Ward Beecher taught during his winter break from Amherst College in 1832.[68] He attended Amherst from 1830 to 1834, beginning at the age of seventeen. He became a famous abolitionist preacher and was the brother of the author, Harriet Beecher Stowe.[69] One of Henry's Hopkinton students, by the name of Johnson, is said to have dropped him out the window of the school into a snow bank! In "A Brief History of Hopkinton," 1915, by Mrs. Frances A. Stafford, she states that this story is factual, unlike other stories which "lack verification." One hundred years later, I think we can take her word for it. The school building itself was eventually moved to Hayden Rowe opposite Pike Street by Lee Claflin for use as part of his boot manufacturing operations. A straw hat shop was established upstairs. A. Coburn, Son & Co. was still using the building in 1889. It later became the residence of Curtis Smith. When he cleaned out the attic, he threw out many hat forms and much straw. He also found many strips of leather and, on the beams, bars of shoe wax.[70] This house was recently and extensively remodeled. Evidence of its use as a school was seen during demolition. A few of the original boards were salvaged. The current address is 50 Hayden Rowe.

---

[68] Wm. C. Beecher and Rev. Samuel Scoville, Biography of Henry Ward Beecher, (New York, 1888).

[69] They were children of Lyman and Roxana (Foote) Beecher of New Haven, Connecticut. Lyman Beecher was a Presbyterian minister, a co-founder of the American Temperance Society, and president of the Lane Theological Seminary in Ohio. Both Henry and Harriet would later be among the visitors to the Newton home of Governor William Claflin. Harriet was the famous author of "Uncle Tom's Cabin" and her brother became one of the most well-known clergymen and the first minister of the Plymouth Church in Brooklyn, New York. He was known for his entertaining oration. Not only was he entertaining, but Henry taught people what they wanted to hear, namely that Christianity should adapt to changing culture. Henry's trial for adultery with a friend and fellow abolitionist's wife became a sensational scandal in 1875, though he had publicly denounced Victoria Claflin Woodhull's advocacy of "free love." A jury could not come to an agreement, but members of his own family believed he was guilty. Victoria, by the way, was a distant relative of the Hopkinton Claflin family. She was the first female candidate for President. Her sister, Tennessee Claflin, was 'involved with' Cornelius Vanderbilt. She was a feminist who advocated legalized prostitution. The two sisters founded a Wall Street brokerage firm. They were also deeply involved in Spiritism, which was quite popular at the time.

[70] Harold S. Wood, "Our Little Old School Houses," for the Hopkinton Historical Society, 1960.

Intermediate School
Hopkinton Mass

This is the four-room school of 1875 which replaced the Episcopal Church. It is shown as it originally appeared, with an entrance for girls on one side and boys on the other. They had separate outhouses attached to the rear of the building. This late Greek-Revival-style building exists as the One Ash Street office building. The entrance front has been modified and there is a large addition on the back; constructed in such a way as to match the original architecture.

The Boston Athletic Association has an office in this building, overlooking the start of the famous marathon they host. Walter A. Brown (1905-1964) of Hopkinton was the President of the B. A. A. from 1941 to 1964. He founded the Boston Celtics.

Willard Aldrich at 5 Ash Street

Willard Aldrich was born about 1795 in Smithfield, Rhode Island. Lucy S. Morse was born on the 1st of January, 1798. Willard & Lucy were married in Hopkinton on the 4th of October, 1820. Willard was a blacksmith by trade.

As mentioned, he purchased a property from Elizabeth Price earlier that year. Which property was this? It contained "nine acres and forty rods." When Elizabeth deeded land to the Episcopal Church in 1818, it included the adjacent graveyard and land extending down Main Street beyond, which included part of the 18-acre school lot. It also included part of the land adjacent to Ash Street which had belonged to her father. The sale to Aldrich was another portion of these lots.

The deed from Price to Aldrich describes the parcel as beginning at the northwest corner of the premises, *near the dwelling house*. It extended east to the land of Smith, then south to other land retained by Elizabeth Price, then west to the road leading from the meeting house to Mr. Fitch (Ash Street) and back to the point of beginning. This "dwelling house" is still on the site. It is the elegant, Federal-style house (c. 1812) with later, (1840-42?) Greek-Revival details, facing the Common at 5 Ash Street. The property line still runs close to the house on the north side.

Madam Price Manor at 5 Ash Street

Willard Aldrich retained land on this side of the Common, but the next owner of the house at 5 Ash was Silas Moore. Silas was the contractor for the road to Cordaville (Cedar Street). He is called a stable keeper on some deeds. On the 3rd of October, 1836, Silas sold the property to William Godfrey of Milford.

William brought the first stagecoach to Milford in 1822 and had a row of shops and sheds on the west side of the Parish Common there. He was a representative to the General Court in 1832 and one of the prominent citizens of Milford. After his death, the administrators of his estate, John Erskine and David S. Godfrey, put the property up for auction. It included a house, barn, and shoemaker's shop. The highest bidder was Artimus W. Johnson, carpenter, of Hopkinton. His high bid was $745.00. However, the property was also subject to a mortgage to Samuel B. Walcott of $400.00, plus interest from 1 July, 1833. The sale to Johnson was finalized on the 21st of March, 1840. On the 30th of March, Artimus Johnson sold an undivided, half interest in the property to Sylvester Phipps for the sum of $372.50. Sylvester was also a carpenter. Less than two years later, they sold the property to Joshua Tucker of Framingham for the sum of $795.00 and passed on the mortgage. So, they made a profit of $50.00. This sale was finalized on the 18th of January, 1842 and signed by A. W. and Experience Johnson and Sylvester and Laura A. Phipps. Experience and Laura were sisters.

Artimus Ward Johnson married Experience Briggs on the 31st of December, 1837. Sylvester Phipps married her sister, Laura Ann Briggs, on the 9th of October, 1841, thus just a few months before they purchased the property. Artimus was 28 and Sylvester was 23 at the time of the sale. Again, they were both carpenters by trade and probably remodeled the house, principally with the Greek-Revival entrances. The average wage of a carpenter in 1840 was about $1.40 per day, so $50.00 (minus expenses) was a substantial amount.[71] Artimus and his wife moved to Holliston. In 1865, he was contracted to build St. Malachi's Church on Cedar Street. This was the first Catholic Church in Hopkinton.

Joshua Tucker owned 5 Ash Street for many years. Before we take a closer look, let's back up just a little and look at the neighborhood around the Common ten years after Willard Aldrich bought the property.

---

[71] Stanley Lebergott, Trends in the American Economy in the Nineteenth Century, (The Conference on Research in Income and Wealth, UMI, 1960), chapter title: Wage Trends, 1800-1900.

1830

1830 marked a significant milestone in the development of Hopkinton and the Common area. All the leases were coming to an end. The school lots were being sold off. Industry was about to take off. Fortunately, Matthew Metcalf recorded the property owners on his map in 1831. An expanded view of a section is shown below.

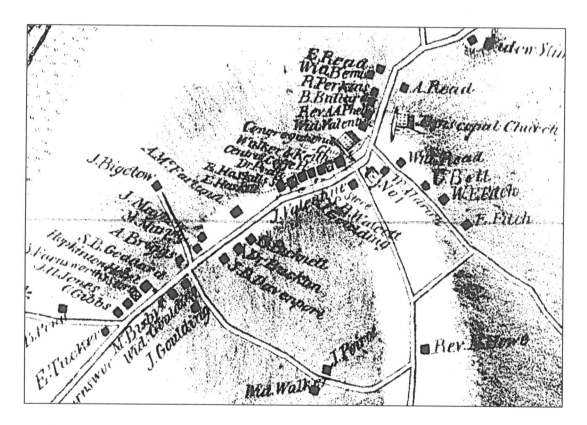

The Hartford Turnpike was extended through Hopkinton to Upton in 1830 along Main Street and the newly constructed West Main. The Boston & Worcester Railroad reached Hopkinton at Unionville in 1834. Unionville would become the center of Ashland in 1846.[72] In the 116 years since incorporation in 1715, gradual development had taken place. On the map we can see Main, East Main, West Main, Hayden Rowe, Ash, Pike, Pleasant, Wood, Mt. Auburn, and Wilson Streets. School No. 1 is on the Common.

---

[72] Hopkinton had four villages in addition to the town center. They were Unionville, Woodville, Hopkinton Springs and Hayden Row. Today, Woodville is a well-preserved village with its own interesting history. Hopkinton Springs was west of Lake Whitehall. Hayden Row is now just a cluster of houses at the intersection of Chestnut and Hayden Rowe.

The Episcopal Church of 1818 is shown, as is the brand new Congregational. Willard Aldrich had built a new house facing the south side of the Common. The house he bought in 1820 is now occupied by Betsey Read, widow of Rezin (1787-1827). Next to Widow Read is the family of Gilman Ball (sometimes "Bell") (1809-1843) who would marry the following year. His wife-to-be was Mary Ann Fitch, daughter of his neighbors, Elijah and Mary (Valentine) Fitch Jr. William Fuller Fitch, son of Elijah and Mary, was next door. William F. and his wife Eliza (Lyon) would later move to Lewiston, Maine. Next is the house of Elijah and Mary Fitch Jr. Elijah would eventually buy up much property in the neighborhood.

Widow Polly Valentine is at the Stone Tavern. Next to her is Rev. Amos A. Phelps, who was assisting the elderly Rev. Nathaniel Howe, whose house is located opposite the intersection of Hayden Rowe and Pleasant. Next to Phelps are B. Bullard, Reuben and Hannah (Clements) Perkins, Widow Bemis, and Ephraim (1757-1837) and Hannah (Cargill) (1755-1823) Read (parents of Rezin). The Read house is that formerly of John How. Across Main is the house of Read's son, Aaron (1796-1848) and his wife Betsey (Corbett).[73] They later moved into his parent's house across the street. Col. Joseph Valentine's mansion is shown. The word "store" below it applies to the one across Main Street. Next, to the west, are the houses of Levi (a housewright) & Clarissa (Barrett) Bicknall,[74] Dr. Thomas & Sally (Claflin) Bucklin, and Samuel D. & Mary (Freeland) Davenport.[75] Along Main Street, to the west of the Congregational Church, is the business of Walker & Keith and the "store." Next is the Central Coffee House, followed by houses of Samuel B. and Martha Walcott, John Goulding, Dr. Jefferson Pratt, and finally, Ezra Haskell's house and store—all in a row.

Further west on Main Street are several more houses built on what were the lots of John How and John Taylor on either side of Mt. Auburn Street, which then just led to the house of J. Bigelow. Near the corner of Pleasant is a house identified as that of Samuel Brigham Goddard (see page 92). His name "S. B. Goddard" is spelled out across the street from his house. On the bottom of the map is a house identified as that of Widow Walker. This house was built on the lot of Thomas Walker, an early lease-holder (see page 11). His uncle was John How.

---

[73] Aaron Reed would later marry Mary Swain Bixby, granddaughter of Isaac Surriage.
[74] Levi Bicknall of Boston married Clarissa Barrett (b. 9 Mar. 1789, daughter of John & Bridget). Marriage intention: 17 Apr. 1803. This would indicate that this portion of the Barrett lot was still in the family and not part of the 15 acres deeded to Roger Price and subsequently to Joseph Valentine.
[75] Samuel Davenport's first wife was the daughter of Dr. & Mrs. Bucklin next door. She died on the 13th of March, 1826. Samuel married Mary Sophia Freeland on the 17th of June, 1827, thus before the 1831 map was made.

Joshua Tucker at 5 Ash Street

Joshua Tucker was a tailor by trade. By the Census of 1860, he was working as a mechanic and from then on, he is listed as working in a boot shop. On a map of 1856, Joshua is shown as the owner of two buildings. The following is a detail from that map.

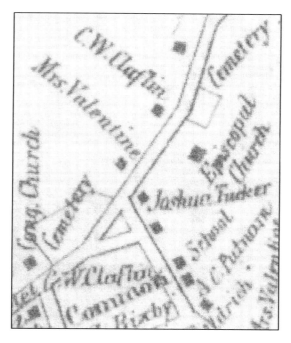

One building is right at the corner of Ash and Main and may have been used in his business. He did not own land all the way to the corner. It is important to note that the squares denoting buildings on this map are not always accurately placed. For example the building marked "C. W. Claflin" is really much closer to the stone tavern of "Mrs. Valentine." However, the Episcopal Church *was* closer to the cemetery than the school which replaced it. The building marked "school" is the Greek-Revival one with four columns, as shown on the next page. It was likely built in the 1840's on what had once been part of the Tucker property.

Joshua was born in Hardwick, Worcester County on the 12th of May, 1811. He married Ede (Edith A.) Claflin on the 7th of June, 1837. Ede was the ninth child of Amaziah and Ede (Watkins) Claflin, born on the 11th of September, 1813.

Ash Street from Main Street, Hopkinton, Mass.

This is a view of Ash Street and early schools which faced the Common. In the lower right corner can be seen the stone curb along the Common. Ash Street remained a narrow, gravel road. A small photo shop can be seen in the lower left corner. It is not on the school property, but "connected" by fence to the 5 Ash Street property. The photo is undated, but likely taken after 1900.

In 1901, Joshua and Ede's son, Frances Eugene Tucker of Lennox, mortgaged the property to Martha A. P. Everett of Dover for only $400.00. The mortgage was never discharged and no record of any payments was found. On the 27th of August, 1918, Martha sold the property to Sara Humphrey. In 1925, a court ruled in favor of Sarah E. Humphrey vs. Frances E. Tucker. In her deed, the bounds are listed as: west by Ash Street, south by Town of Hopkinton and Land of J. Mahon, east by land of J. Kelly and the Episcopal Church, and north by Town of Hopkinton.

Sara Humphrey sold the house at 5 Ash Street to Honora A. Harrigan in 1925. In May of 1927, more land was taken from this lot in preparation for building Center School. The new school was opened on the 9th of January, 1928. The old schools in front had remained in use during construction, but they were torn down when the new one was complete. The school was expanded with a new east wing in 1950. 5 Ash has now been owned for decades by the Kelly family.

The 1928 Center School at 11 Ash Street

Willard Aldrich at 8 Park Street

Meanwhile, Willard Aldrich went on to purchase more of the school lot and build a second house. Facing the Common on the east end of Park Street is his second Federal-style house. The present house was rebuilt after a destructive fire in 1925. Though damaged, it was not a total loss. Recent restoration revealed charred timbers. It is apparent that some design elements were updated in the 20's when the house was rebuilt. As to a date for initial construction — shortly after 1823.

Willard purchased this lot from Cornelius and Patience (Aldrich) Gibson on the 6th of October, 1823 for $364.00. Remember that the Trustees for the School Fund were appointed when Elizabeth Price moved to Cambridge in 1820. The 32-acre parcel was divided roughly in half lengthwise and offered for sale to raise money for the schools. John Gibson Jr. and Elijah Fitch bought up much of this land. Cornelius was John Gibson Jr.'s younger brother, so this is probably how he came to own the lot at 8 Park.

Cornelius Gibson was born in Hopkinton on the 11th of November, 1781, the son of John and Elizabeth (Barnes) Gibson. (Mary) Patience Aldrich was born on the 1st of September, 1782, in Gloucester, Rhode Island.[76] She married Cornelius Gibson on the 9th of November, 1804, in Uxbridge. Her father, Joseph, died in 1785, so Willard Aldrich (b. 1795) may have been her nephew, but certainly not her brother.[77]

Willard and Lucy Aldrich had one daughter. Susannah Valentine Aldrich was born on the 14th of November, 1828. She was a published author of both poetry and prose. The following is a quote from "A Woman of the Century: Fourteen Hundred-Seventy Biographical Sketches Accompanied by Portraits of Leading American Women in All Walks of Life" from 1893:

"From her earliest years she showed that fondness for putting her thoughts on paper which seems to be the unerring indication of the possession of literary talents. When other children were satisfied with dolls and playthings, the little Susan was always asking for paper and pencil to use in 'writing letters' as she then called her work. In her schooldays she always found it far easier to write compositions than it was for her to commit lessons to memory, and she was generally permitted to choose her own subjects for the regular 'composition day' in school. Her studies were interrupted by a severe illness which lasted for several years. She was long a victim to insomnia, and she always kept paper and pencil within reach in order to be able to jot down the fancies that thronged upon her in long hours of wakefulness."

Miss Aldrich contributed to a number of papers and magazines. Her father died in 1866 at 70 years of age. She continued to live at her Park Street address until

---

[76] Another Aldrich relative, born in Gloucester about 1754, was Job, grandfather of Senator Nelson Aldrich of Rhode Island. Nelson's daughter married John D. Rockefeller Jr. - the major society wedding of the Gilded Age.

[77] The Aldrich family of Gloucester, RI came from Smithfield, RI, birthplace of Willard. The Aldrich family apparently started with the immigrant George Aldrich of Mendon (the section which later became Uxbridge, where Cornelius and Patience were married).

1879, when she moved to Roxbury. But, she retained ownership of 6 (later 8) Park Street.

SUSANNA VALENTINE ALDRICH.

To understand what happened to the Park Street property next, we need to consider the sale of land which Willard Aldrich had retained on the east side of Ash Street. On the 28th of November, 1877, Susanna sold the property she had inherited from her parents on the east side of Ash to her aunt, Susan E. Morse, for $1,200.00. She retained the right to use the well on this property, both for herself and for John Gannon, who lived further down Ash Street. Before the advent of town water, a good well was important and thus, a valuable asset.

The parcels on this side of Ash Street are easier to understand by looking at a map. The following is a section from a map of 1875. Notice that W. A. Morse is shown with a house on the property before his wife Susan bought the property from Aldrich.

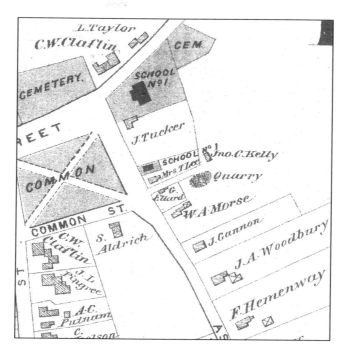

1875

By 1875, the nine-acre lot sold to Willard Aldrich in 1820 had clearly been reduced. Joshua Tucker still had a good sized yard to the south of the house, but it was already being squeezed by the schools (both labeled #1) on either side. Mrs. Timothy Lee is living in what would become another school. There is a small lane (called simply "old lane" on deeds) leading to the property of John C. Kelly and separating the Lee property from those of W. A. (Willard Aldrich) Morse and George Ellard. Notice too, the Quarry. A portion of this can still be seen behind 15 Ash Street. Stone from this quarry was used to build the Stone Tavern. Next is the property of John Gannon and then that of John A. Woodbury. John Woodbury was postmaster. The house of Fisher Hemenway is next. Fisher was a house painter and window glazier. He tried his hand at boot manufacturing too. His wife was Elizabeth Jones Fitch, another daughter of Deacon Elijah and Mary (Valentine) Fitch. Their son, George L. Hemenway became a prominent lawyer with offices in Boston. Susannah Aldrich's lot on Park Street was still large.

Willard Aldrich Morse at 15 Ash Street

Yes, Willard Aldrich *Morse*, not to be confused with Willard Aldrich! Willard came to live with his eldest sister Lucy S. Morse, who had by then married Willard Aldrich. Their mother Betsey Morse had died when Willard was just two, in 1816. Their father, Arnold Morse, lived in Pomfret, Connecticut, where he remarried and would have four more children. Little Willard was sent off to live with his sister, who had herself been sent to live in the household of Madam Price when she was young. Willard Morse must have been named for the boy who would later become his brother-in-law.

Arnold Morse was born in Natick, on the 15th of May, 1774, as the fifth child of Elisha and Jemima (Tomblin) Morse. Elisha was a soldier throughout the Revolutionary War. Arnold married Betsey Hunting and they had ten children. Of the ten, Lucy S. was born in 1798 and her brother Willard in 1814.

Willard must have come to live with his sister after 1820, so he was at least six years old. When he was about twenty, he went to Boston to work as a blacksmith, after learning the trade from his brother-in-law. He later had a shop in Millbury. He was considered an expert in horse-shoeing. He moved on to Springfield, then Grafton, then out to Rockford, Illinois, where he worked for the Manny Mowing Machine Company for about eight years.

From Illinois, Willard went to Fairfield, Iowa and then came back to Spencer. He moved from there to Millbury. He was associated for three years with his father-in-law, Captain Samuel Hall of Grafton. Willard married first, Sarah Simmons, who died in Millbury and second, Susan E. Hall. This is the Susan E. Morse who bought the property on Ash from Susanna Aldrich. After working for three years in Worcester, Willard moved back to Hopkinton were he and his wife built a house and he retired. For a short time, Willard Morse went to live on a farm in Norfolk and then moved to Brookline. He died there on the 12th of May, 1886, at the age of 71.

Morse house, c. 1875, at 15 Ash Street
Queen Anne-style

  The property at 15 Ash Street was still in the name of Susan E. Morse when she sold it to John A. Woodbury for $2,000 on the 15th of December, 1877. John already had a house two doors down on Ash. He also bought the small lot in the corner of this property, which had been owned by George Ellard of Salem. George had bought this lot from Artimus C. Putnam on the 18th of July, 1866, for $400.00. He lost it as part of the settlement of a lawsuit. On the 8th of October, 1875, George Stedman was the high bidder at $256.00. John Woodbury acquired the property from Stedman on the 18th of December, 1877, or just three days after getting the rest of the land from Morse. In his will, John left the property to Amy W. Perkins of Hopkinton. She sold both parcels to Charles L. Claflin, who will be considered later.

Willard Morse and his first wife, Sarah had one daughter who lived to adulthood. Her name was Lucy F. and she married Luther W. Bixby of Roxbury. Now it becomes clearer why Susannah Aldrich moved to Roxbury and Mrs. L. W. Bixby is seen on a map of about 1907 as living at 6 (now 8) Park Street. They were cousins. Susannah Aldrich moved from Roxbury to 2817 Washington Street, Boston, where she died on the 30th of November, 1905. She was 77.

Mrs. L. W. Bixby sold the Aldrich house on Park Street and its large lot to William D. Mosher on the 6th of October, 1920. As mentioned earlier, the house had a fire about 1925. William subdivided the property into ten lots in October of 1927. The house and lot 1 were sold to Francis V. Kennedy on the 1st of June, 1931. Kennedy had purchased Lot 2 on the 19th of October, 1927. Francis was a mail clerk.

Lots 3, 4, and 5 went to James H. Murphy, also on the 1st of June, 1931. Lots 6, 7, and 8 went to Julia M. Riley on the 3rd of October, 1932. Lots 9 and 10 were sold to Mosher Bros., Inc. in 1935.

ALDRICH and MORSE

Willard Aldrich & Lucy Morse - - - - - - - - - - - - - Willard A. Morse & Sarah Simmons
(1795-1866)　　　　(1798-?)　　　　　　　　(1814-1886)　　　& Susan E. Hall
　　　Susannah Aldrich　　　　　　　　　Lucy F. Morse & Luther W. Bixby
　　　　(1828-1905)　　　　　　　　　　(She sold 8 Park)

Patience Aldrich & Cornelius Gibson (8 Park aft. Madam Price, bef. Willard Aldrich)
(1782-1882) 100!　　(1781-?)
(Patience came from the same area as Willard and was likely a close relative.)

Maria Gibson & Alanson Stearns - - - - - Emeline Stearns & Samuel Crooks
(1805-1890)　　　　(1803-1860)　　　　1795-1864　　　　1792-1873

　　　　　|　　　　　　　　　　　　John, Samuel, & Abram Crooks

Priscilla Stearns & Charles Morse (Morse not closely related to Lucy or Willard)
(1838-aft 1906)　　(1832-1899)

　　Emma Morse & Edward Winslow Pierce (Owned 15 Ash and 2 and 4 Park)
　　(1869-1918)　　　　(1867-1925)

　　William Stearns Morse & Etta M. Roberts (Owned 15 Ash)
　　(1871-1960)　　　　　(1880-?)

The Valentine Family

Despite her middle name, Susannah Valentine Aldrich was not related to the Valentine family. Valentine was another of the genteel families who moved out from Boston and eventually came to own two properties bordering the Common.

The Hon. John Valentine was born at Bencliffe Hall, Eccles, Lancashire, England on the 28th of December, 1670. He became "His Majesty's Advocate General for the Provinces of Massachusetts Bay, New Hampshire and Rhode Island." He married Mary Lynde of Boston in 1702. Their eldest son Samuel inherited Bencliffe Hall in 1766, but it was sold about 1792. Their daughter Elizabeth married Joseph Gooch of Boston in 1724. Joseph's brother-in-law was John Franklin, brother of (the) Benjamin Franklin.

Thomas Valentine was the fourth son of John and Mary and he had one of the original leases in Hopkinton. It was 100 ¼ acres of land, located at what is now the intersection of West Union, Frankland, and Olive streets in Ashland. The second house on the site remains today.

By 1834, when Thomas' son, Samuel, died, the property contained "by estimation" 250 acres. Samuel's grandsons, Andrew Price Valentine and William Price Valentine, successively owned the property. William made extensive changes to modernize the house in 1870. He didn't tear down the house, as is sometimes reported. The misconception apparently stems from the dissatisfaction some members of the family had with the changes. The barn was moved from up on the hill to where it could be connected to the house. There was an old cider mill across the street.

Unfortunately, the Hopkinton Railroad (and West Union) divided the land and spoiled it for farming. By 1918 the house was owned by Miss Francis (Fanny) Wadsworth Valentine, granddaughter of John Tyng Valentine. John was a cousin of Andrew and William. Fanny was a teacher like her aunts. Her brother Robert was a musician. He was living in Ashland at the time of his death in 1952. Fanny continued to live in the house after that. The following is a picture of what the farm looked like about 1920, when it was still in a quiet country setting.

Once in the center of a quiet 250-acre farm

Now on busy Route 135 in Ashland
Valentines lived on this property for more than 225 years

THOMAS VALENTINE 1713-1783 & ELIZABETH GOOCH 1717-1752
11 Children, including Samuel

SAMUEL VALENTINE 1745-1834 & ELIZABETH JONES 1750-1828
12 Children, including:

2. SAMUEL JR. 1773-1823 & POLLY FISKE 1783-1861 (Stone Tavern)
9 Children, including:
Susan Gilbert 1810- m. Homer Tilton (as 2nd wife)
John Tyng 1818-1852 m. Mary W. Claflin
Ann Maria 1819-1894 m. Charles W. Claflin

4. JOSEPH 1776-1845 & FANNY HAVEN 1780-1841 (Valentine Mansion)
7 Children, including:
Harriet Jones 1800-1871 m. Dr. Jefferson Pratt
George Washington 1809-1840 m. Mary W. Claflin

5. MARY 1779-1835 & ELIJAH FITCH JR. 1778-1847 (Ash St. Properties)
12 Children, including:
William Fuller Fitch 1801-1857 m. Eliza Ann Lyon
John Augustus Fitch 1803-1883 m. Lucy Ann Howe
Mary Ann Fitch 1807-1862 m. Gilman Ball
Elizabeth Jones Fitch 1813- m. Fisher Hemenway

6. THOMAS 1780-1823 & HELENE READ 1782-1850
5 Children   (Helene, daughter of Ephraim & Hannah Read)

8. BETSEY 1784-1843 & ELIJAH FITCH JR. 1778-1847

11. FANNY 1790-1850 & HOMER TILTON 1792-1869
5 Children, including
Edward Lafayette 1824-1887
Lawson Valentine 1828-1897

12. LAWSON 1792-1828 & MARY ANN PRICE 1792-1881 (Homestead &
5 Children, including: Price Mansion)
Andrew Price 1818-1895, William Price 1820-, and
Edward Lawson 1823-

13. CHARLES 1797-1850 & ISANNA CHAMBERLAIN 1801-
(Isanna, daughter of Moses & Rhoda Chamberlain)
12 Children, including: (Price Mansion)
Lawson 1828-1891 and   Henry Chamberlain 1830-1912

Thomas Valentine was born on the 3rd of August, 1713, in Boston. After taking up his lease in Hopkinton, he married his neighbor, Elizabeth Gooch, on the 17th of July, 1735, when he was 21. Her father, James Gooch, had 214 acres adjoining to the west. The Gooch property was later sold to Sir Henry Frankland as the core of his large estate. James Gooch was married to Elizabeth Hobby, daughter of Sir Charles Hobby, a leading merchant in Boston, who was knighted by Queen Anne at Windsor Castle in 1705. He was the Lieutenant Governor of Annapolis Royal (named for Anne) in Nova Scotia in 1711. He and his father William had been wardens of King's Chapel in Boston (see page 29 for the connection to the Frankland house in Boston).

Thomas and Elizabeth Valentine had eleven children. Sons Samuel (1745-1834) and William (1750-1825) were farmers and innkeepers like their father. Each married a different Elizabeth Jones and each had large families. We will not consider the large family of William in any detail.

On the 5th of December, 1770, Samuel married Elizabeth, daughter of John and Mary (Mellen) Jones. It is their children who moved up to the center of town. They had thirteen children, some of whom are charted on the previous page. Elizabeth Jones was the great-granddaughter of another member of King's Chapel, Savil Simpson. He was the owner of a large tract of land which covered much of what is now Ashland to the south and west of the Sudbury River. Savil was also a cordwainer (shoemaker), a trade which would come to have a huge impact upon Hopkinton. Samuel Valentine Sr. established, with others, a wire mill below his grist mill on the Sudbury River. Several of the children will be considered in their own chapters, but three are briefly mentioned here:

#4 Mary (1779-1835), married Deacon Elijah Fitch (1778-1847), son of the second minister (of the Congregational Church), Elijah Fitch Sr.

#5 Thomas (1780-1823) married Helene Read on the 4th of September, 1803. She was the daughter of Ephraim and Hannah Read. As we saw, Ephraim's house is identified on the 1831 map. It was previously the house of John How (pages 10, 54).

#7 Betsey (1784-1843) married Deacon Fitch after Mary died in 1835. She was the second of his three wives.

Elizabeth (Jones) Valentine was a "fleshy"[78] woman and she died suddenly in 1828. Her children inherited cardio-vascular problems and didn't live as long as she.

---

[78] Op. cit., Valentine.

Samuel Valentine Jr. at the Stone Tavern

The family who owned the Stone Tavern the longest was that of Samuel Valentine Jr. As noted earlier, he purchased the property in 1804 from Isaac Claflin. Samuel was born on the 14th of February, 1773. His first wife was Frances (Fanny) Clark, daughter of Isaac and Elizabeth (Hill) Clark. They were married on the 25th of May, 1800 and had three children together. After she died in 1808, Sam Jr. married Mary (Polly) Fiske on the 1st of January, 1809. You have to wonder what the weather was like for their wedding day! Polly Fiske was born on the 29th of January, 1783, in Framingham. She was the daughter of Captain Richard Fiske and his wife, Zebiah Pond. Samuel Jr. & Polly had nine children.

Samuel Jr. added this store to the west end of the tavern (left of electric pole and notice roof condition change). He ran the public house, store and farm until his death on the 19th of February, 1823 at the age of 50. His widow Polly is thus identified with the Tavern on the 1831 map (page 53). She ran the tavern as a summer resort for boarders from the cities and she lived until the 13th of August, 1861 (age 78). In 1863, Samuel's will was probated and the estate was divided between each of the living children or grand-children. The land stretched all down Walcott Street and ran behind the buildings on Main. It included all the land which now abuts Ray Street (which didn't exist). This 72-acre property was comprised of the land leased to John Manning (and then John Barrett), as well as some of the adjacent common land (see page 11).

The Stone Tavern itself was assigned to two of Samuel and Polly's daughters: Susan Gilbert Valentine, who was married to Homer Tilton and lived in New York, and Ann Marie Valentine, who was married to Charles Winslow Claflin. Charles had become the innkeeper by 1855. His grandfather was Isaac Claflin, the owner previous to Valentine.

Samuel Valentine Jr. Estate appraisal:
"The Homestead, including the house, barns & outbuildings with about seventy two acres of land comprising upland, pasture, swamp and woodland, lying in one body are appraised at seven thousand seven hundred and thirty dollars; one other parcel comprising meadow and upland containing about six acres and not adjoining the homestead we appraised at the sum of one hundred dollars; and we have made partition of said real estate to the several heirs at law of said deceased and their assigns in manner following, that is to say. We first assigned to....(then each heir is listed with their lot described). The heirs were (as described in the appraisal):

Jane Sullivan, wife of James S. Sullivan of the State of Georgia, 1/10th part
Emeline Valentine, 1/10th part
Susan Tilton of New York City & Ann Marie Claflin, wife of Chas. W. Claflin
  2/10th parts (shares in common at their request)
Fanny Bixby of Boston,
  assignee of Samuel F. Valentine & George Valentine 2/10th parts
Eliza Farnsworth of Detroit 1/10th part
Fanny Bixby of Boston, 1/10th part
Mary Clark Jennison of Ashland, 1/10th part
Fanny Wadsworth Valentine, 1/30th part
Emma Kate Valentine, 1/30th part
George Albert Valentine, 1/30th part

The last three were children of John Tyng Valentine and Mary Wadsworth Claflin, sister of Charles W. Claflin. John died in 1852, or about 11 years before the probate of his father's will. Mary Jennison and Emeline were children of Samuel's first wife, Fanny Clark and were thus the eldest children. The others were children of Polly.

The tavern remained with Ann Marie after C. W. Claflin's death and is identified as such on a map of 1889. Their son Charles L. acquired the property after Ann Marie's death. He managed to reassemble much of the farm land with the Tavern. Apparently, he also inherited or bought out Susan Tilton's share.

Lawson Valentine at the Price Mansion

The eleventh child of Samuel and Elizabeth was Lawson (1792-1828). He married Mary Ann Price (1792-1881), daughter of Major William Price, on the 15th of December, 1818. Lawson was likely named for his uncle, Major Lawson Buckminster of Framingham. Lawson's mother, Elizabeth (Jones), had an elder sister Mary who married Lawson Buckminster in 1769. *His* parents were Joseph and Sarah (Lawson) Buckminster, so Lawson is a family surname. Joseph Buckminster's sister Elizabeth married John Wood, the father of the Woods of Woodville, Hopkinton. The various family relationships are outlined on the following chart:

Joseph & Martha (Sharpe) Buckminster (of Muddy River, now Brookline)

    Elizabeth Buckminster (1687-) m. John Wood (-1725)

        Joseph Wood (1722-1785) m. Martha Gibson (1721-1754)

            Hannah Wood (1750-1807) m. Samuel Haven (1751-1829)

                Fanny Haven m. Col. Joseph Valentine

    Joseph Buckminster (1697-) m. Sarah Lawson (-1747)

        Lawson Buckminster (1742-1832) m. Mary Jones (1750-1842) --

                                      |

Col. John & Elizabeth (Simpson) Jones, daughter of Savil Simpson |

    John Jones (1722-1797) m. Mary Mellen (1724-) |

        Mary Jones (1750-1842) m. Lawson Buckminster (1742-1832) --

        Elizabeth Jones (1751/2-1828) m. Samuel Valentine (1745-1834)

            Col. Joseph Valentine m. Fanny Haven

            Lawson Valentine m. Mary Ann Price

Lawson purchased much property in Hopkinton in addition to the Price lands which came to him through his wife and the will of Madam Price. He was a successful businessman in Cambridge and Boston. He was associated with William Parker & Co., paper manufacturers with mills in Sudbury and Watertown.

Tragically, Lawson had a stroke and died in 1828, at the early age of 35. His family never realized any return on his investment in the paper business. But the Price properties in Hopkinton continued to be held by his family. As mentioned earlier, sons Andrew and William inherited the homestead farm. They were both born in Cambridge, but moved to Ashland, shared the family farm and built additional houses. Their children were born in Ashland.

Mrs. Mary Ann (Price) Valentine married Isaac Peabody of Peterboro, New Hampshire on the 2nd of August, 1841, in Cambridge. They lived in Roxbury. Like her aunt, Mary Ann lived to the age of 89.

NOTES ON FANNY VALENTINE & HOMER TILTON

Lawson's sister Fanny was less than two years his senior. She married Homer Tilton of Framingham, who was in the provisions business. The marriage took place in Cambridge on the 22nd of October, 1817. Homer was born in Hopkinton in 1797 and he relocated his business from Framingham to New York City. Living in New York led his children to follow interesting careers. The two youngest children were Edward and Lawson.

Edward Lafayette Tilton was a popular, Broadway stage actor. He performed with Edwin and John Wilkes Booth (before John killed Abraham Lincoln). Edward married Mary E. Pentland. Her brother was the famous circus clown, Joe Pentland.[79]

Lawson Valentine Tilton was a steamboat operator. He was a captain employed by the Fall River Line and invested in the steamboat enterprises of Jay Gould and Jim Fisk.[80]

After Fanny died in 1850, Homer married her niece, Susan Gilbert Valentine, daughter of Samuel Jr. Homer was 58 and Susan was 40. This is the Susan who inherited the Stone Tavern along with her sister Ann (Valentine) Claflin.

---

[79] Obituary from The New York Times, March 20, 1887.
[80] Obituary from The New York Times, September 26, 1897.

Charles Valentine at the Price Mansion

The Price Mansion House was leased in 1821 to Charles Valentine, who occupied it until 1825. Charles was the youngest son of Samuel and Elizabeth (Jones) Valentine. He was born on the sixth of March, 1797. He married Isanna Chamberlain on the sixteenth of September, 1821. Her father was Moses Chamberlain (1766-1831), another man whose name appears often in the records of town events and development. He also owned property facing the Common. Her mother was Rhoda Mellen (1775-aft 1808). Rhoda was a second cousin to Charles Valentine.

The following is an excerpt from The Valentines in America 1644-1874 by T. W. Valentine, New York, 1874: "He (Charles) remained on the farm with his father a time; then went to the Framingham Academy. He then went to the center of the town of Hopkinton and established himself in business there." (Then he married Isanna Chamberlain.) "They went to live in the old Roger Price house, and their two eldest children were born there. He then removed to Cambridgeport, where he lived and carried on business in Boston. In 1826, he was of the firm Valentine & Bridges, until they dissolved, and he went in with Daniel Draper." He established Charles Valentine & Co. with his brother-in-law, Ambrose Chamberlain. "Charles was a shrewd business man, and carried on a very extensive business, both in Boston and at the West." But, like his brother Lawson, he died young, in 1850.

Charles and Isanna had twelve children. The two eldest sons were Lawson (1828) and Henry Chamberlain (1830). Lawson Valentine is credited with the creation of Valentine & Co. However, this firm was incorporated in 1832, when Lawson was 4 years old. His Uncle Lawson died in 1828. So, it was probably Charles who incorporated in 1832. Lawson (the younger) went on to build Valentine & Co. into a very successful paint and varnish company in Cambridge. Originally, they developed a varnish to protect the spars of wooden sailing ships. Today, the company is the core of Valspar Corporation, whose name is derived from "Valentine" & "spar."

After their factory in Cambridge burned, the business was relocated to Williamsburg, New York. Henry joined the firm about 1860. In 1870, the headquarters was established in Manhattan. Lawson Valentine hired chemist Charles Homer. This was a crucial decision in the development of the company. Charles Homer developed superior, smooth-flowing, varnishes. His brother was the famed artist Winslow Homer. Lawson Valentine became one of Winslow's principal patrons.

Lawson married Lucy Heywood Houghton in 1851. Lucy was born on the 7th of January, 1830 in Lancaster. Her third cousin (once removed) was the publisher and co-founder of Houghton & Mifflin and Co. and Mayor of Cambridge, Henry Oscar Houghton (1823-1895). Lawson invested some $200,000 in Houghton, Mifflin and Co.

Lawson and Lucy had three children:
Howard Lawson (1852-1855), Elmira Houghton (13 Nov 1855 Cambridge -), and Mary Campbell (15 Nov 1862 West Newton -).

Elmira married Nathan Trowbridge Pulsifer in New York City on the 13th of October, 1880. Eventually, he became president and director of Valentine & Co. and a director of Houghton, Mifflin & Co. Their son, Lawson Valentine Pulsifer graduated from Harvard University with a degree in chemistry. He joined Valentine & Co. and, with the approval of Charles Homer, developed the first clear varnish, named "Valspar."

In 1882, Henry Chamberlain Valentine succeeded his brother as president of the company. About ten years earlier, on the 14th of November, 1872, he had married Grace Cleveland Barrett, daughter of Samuel Barrett of Boston (not a close relative of Samuel Barrett of Hopkinton, but they were both ministers).

Henry and Grace had one son. His name was Langdon Barrett Valentine and he was born on the 12th of September, 1873. On the 25th of October, 1900, Langdon married Mary Hoe Harper in Manhattan. May, as she was called, was the daughter of Joseph Henry Harper and Mary Say Hoe. The marriage took place at the Harper home at 269 Madison Avenue. The wedding was the subject of a long article in the society column of the New York Times the next day.

The Valentine family lived at 13 East 36th Street, just east of Fifth Avenue. Next door, at number 11, was the luxurious townhouse of Robert Hoe. Langdon Valentine's wife May was the granddaughter of Richard March Hoe, inventor of an improved printing press which helped make possible the rapid and inexpensive production of newspapers. Richard became president of R. Hoe & Co., which was in business from 1805 to 1984. Robert Hoe took over after Richard's death in 1886. Robert III was instrumental in developing four-color printing. He also had the best collection of rare books in the country. After Robert III's death in London in 1909, 11 East 36th Street was replaced by a sky-scraper known as the Haviland Building. It still exists on the site. For many years it housed the headquarters of Valentine & Co.

The former Valentine residence at 13 East 36th Street, Manhattan, is the first house on the left. Two doors down was the famous, interior decorator Leon Marcotte & Co,[81] as seen by the sign near the top of the house. When this photograph was taken in 1912, the Hoe house had been replaced by the sky-scraper (the base of which is barely visible on the left) and the neighborhood had begun the transformation to the commercial scene so familiar to Manhattan visitors today. Surprisingly, the fourth building survives, but without its two-story bay window. It is on the corner of Madison Avenue and the J. P. Morgan Library & Museum is now just beyond.

[81] L. Marcotte & Co. and Herter Brothers were the premier interior decorators of the mid-nineteenth century. Examples of their work can be seen in rooms of Elm Park, masterpiece of the architect Detlef Lienau, in Norwalk, CT. (Lockwood-Matthews Mansion Museum), 295 West Avenue – open for tours).

Col. Joseph Valentine at 2 Hayden Rowe

Joseph Valentine (1776-1845) was the third son of Samuel Sr. and Elizabeth. Joseph married Fanny Haven (1780-1841) of Shrewsbury on the 3rd of November, 1799. They had seven children. Portraits of Joseph and Fanny used to hang in the Hopkinton Public Library, on either side of the archway at the back of the reading room. Colonel Joseph commanded infantry in Boston in the War of 1812. Early in September, 1814, the militia was called to the defense of the sea-coast, including Boston. The British Fleet lay off Boston Harbor. The infantry were attached to the first regiment under the command of Colonel Joseph Valentine, with Eliab W. Metcalf as Adjutant. Colonel Valentine was a delegate to the convention for the revision of the Constitution in 1820. He was president of The Society of Middlesex Husbandmen and Manufacturers in 1823 and 1824. He was president of the Massachusetts Agricultural Society in 1824. Col. Joseph was a Justice of the Peace and Representative to the General Court for many years. He was also president of the Trustees of the School Fund in Hopkinton. He purchased property in St. Louis. Joseph also had mill privileges on the Genesee River in Rochester, New York.

On the 17th of October, 1825, Joseph Valentine purchased the Price Mansion House from his brother, Lawson; Lawson's wife, Mary Ann (Price); and her sister, Olivia (Price) Hall. They had received it from Madam Price five years before, along with the rest of her remaining property in Hopkinton.[82] Joseph paid $4,700 for the (now) 16-acre homestead,[83] along with another 106-acre parcel known as the "Shay Place." The homestead lot extended along Main Street until it reached the property of Dr. Thomas Bucklin. Thus, on the 1831 map (page 53) there are only four houses between Hayden Rowe and Pleasant Street, namely the Valentine and the three Bucklin family houses (Bicknell – Bucklin - Davenport).

Joseph did not move into the Price Mansion right away. Instead, Benjamin Herrick was the next occupant. Benjamin was the son of Samuel Herrick and Elizabeth Flint. On the 21st of May, 1804, he married Puah Claflin, daughter of Ebenezer and Sarah Claflin. They had five children.

---

[82] The complete disposition of the Price properties on Saddle Hill, along the Sudbury River, and the Glebe land is beyond the scope of this book. C. W. Claflin purchased large parts of it. His son's estate at the Stone Tavern eventually included hundreds of acres of land stretching north toward Southborough. Much of this land later became part of the Hopkinton State Park.

[83] The Price family owned fifteen acres. It had grown by one acre, either by purchase or more accurate survey.

Soon after Joseph and his family moved into the Price Mansion, the old house burned, possibly by arson. Col. Valentine thus built his new house in brick on the same site. It is a classic Federal-style house with paired chimneys, arched brickwork over the second-story end windows and a Palladian window in the gable. This building still stands on the corner of Hayden Rowe and Main Streets.

Federal-style Valentine Mansion at 2 Hayden Rowe Street

This view shows the back of the barn and the Valentine Mansion with its gardens, which extended up Hayden Rowe, facing the Common (just out of view to the right). The white building to the left was then owned by Dr. Pratt, and was located where the new library would be built in 1895. The two houses in the foreground no longer exist. Beyond the Valentine Mansion can be seen the Congregational Church. To the left is the roof and enclosed, outside staircase of the Chapel Building,[84] then left of that is the Central Coffee House. Across Main Street from Dr. Pratt's are boot factory buildings of Claflin & Coburn and the rooftops of houses on Bird (later Claflin) Street. Beyond are farming fields. This photo was taken from the top of the Methodist Church on Church Street.

Though this is a later photograph, the Central Coffee House, the Valentine Mansion, the Chapel Building, and the Congregational Church are all shown on the map of 1831 (page 53). The following close-up photograph shows the quality of construction used for the 1830 church. It had a spire which was 142′ in height.

---

[84] At first, I wondered about the thin roof which seems to project off the west wing of the Valentine Mansion. But, it is actually across the street. This covered stairway is an obvious addition to the Chapel Building. It is clear in other photographs. The lower end of the stairway can just be seen in the photograph on page 81.

1830 Congregational Church

The sides of the building are sheathed with clapboards, but the front is smooth. This photo is taken from Hayden Row. Notice, above the horse shed behind the church, there is an unobstructed view of the hill behind. Notice too that Main Street is a gravel road with a tree and lamp post in the middle of what is now a busy intersection.

This view shows a corner of the Valentine Mansion. Notice the one-story wing of the house. The barn to the right was used as a livery stable. The snow-covered driveway of the barn extends up from Main Street.[85] Behind the Valentine Mansion can be seen the side and back of the Lee Claflin Mansion. In the distance to the right is the Methodist Church. Behind the church and facing Hayden Rowe is the roof of the Academy/High School. In the far distance, in the center, is the boot factory managed by Alonzo Coburn. This photograph was taken from the top of the Central Coffee House. Joseph Valentine was the largest investor in the Central Coffee House.

---

[85] The driveway was located roughly through the 1967 addition which connects the original library and the former church.

The Central Coffee House

A group of investors decided to build a hotel to replace the old Barrett house. This large and attractive, brick building was the result.

Close-up view of the Central Coffee House and its neighbors

On the third floor was a hall for dancing. It was later known as the Highland House, as it is identified here on the sign attached to the top of the second floor balcony. Thomas Barber was proprietor in 1850, C. W. Claflin in 1856, and F. N. Cobb in 1875. Next door is a building that had many uses. It is called the Chapel Building. It was built on the Congregational Church property. In 1875 it had a drug store, clothing store and a Y.M.C.A. It housed the library before the 1895 building was constructed. It is often referred to as the Callanan property.[86] The Greek-Revival-style with columns became popular in the 1830's.

---

[86] There were four Callanan families in town when these buildings existed. Thomas & Johanna Callanan had a son William who was born about 1853. Behind these buildings was a lot owned by W. Callanan.

The Central Coffee House Company, Hopkinton
Incorporated 1831

"We the subscribers severally agree to take and pay for the shares set against our names respectively in the Capital Stock of the Central coffee House to be erected in Hopkinton on that portion of the Parish land now offered for sale, together with the Barrett place, according to a plan to be hereafter agreed upon by a majority of said subscribers. The said Capital Stock to consist of fifty shares of one hundred dollars each and to be paid in such installments and at such times as shall be agreed upon by a majority of said subscribers at the first meeting, and the subscribers shall be at liberty to pay such a portion of the shares by them subscribed in labor and materials at such prices as shall be agreed upon by a majority of said subscribers at their first meeting, which first meeting shall be called when three fifths of the said Stock shall have been subscribed for. And Moses Chamberlain, Esquire is hereby authorized to call the first meeting by giving to each subscriber three days' notice in writing of the time and place of said meeting."   Dated: April 29, 1830
(Capitalization as in the original document.[87])

The first meeting was held at the "Adams and Claflin Tavern." Amaziah Claflin, Ezra Rockwood, and Jonas Phelps were chosen directors. Colonel Joseph Valentine was the largest stockholder with sixteen shares. Other investors included Dr. Jefferson Pratt and Lovett Walker. It was voted to purchase the Parish land at the average price of the cost to the Parish and to purchase Col. Valentine's Freeland land and house for $540.00. It was also voted to have the Treasurer take a bond from the Parish Treasurer to convey the Parish land in agreement to a vote by the Parish and to take a deed from Col. Valentine for the Barrett land.

Two parcels of land were purchased for the Central Coffee House. The first deed is recorded on page 521 of Vol. 18, Hopkinton & Upton deeds. Joseph & Fanny Valentine transfer "a certain tract known by the name of the Barrett Place, containing 144 rods" (39,203.86 sq. ft.), for $540.00. The lot was bounded to the west by land of Samuel B. Walcott, to the north by Samuel Valentine, to the east by the First Parish, and to the south by the Central Turnpike (Main Street).

The Barrett Place is called Col. Valentine's Freeland land because by the time Joseph acquired the property, it was owned by the widow Freeland, the former Nancy Barrett. Nancy married Thomas Freeland on the 5th of April, 1781. Thomas (bp. 13 June 1756 in Hopkinton) died on the 16th of August, 1805 at the age of 49. Nancy was born in 1761 so she was nearly 70 by 1830 (see pages 6, 8, 9).

---

[87] Pamphlet entitled "The Central Coffee House Company," Hopkinton Public Library collection.

The second parcel was transferred by the "Inhabitants of the First Parish" (Congregational Church) to the Central Coffee House for $142.00. This lot was about two thirds of an acre. The deed was signed by Moses Chamberlain. The first lot cost more because it contained the Barrett house.

If you combine the Main Street frontage of these two lots it stretches about 320-feet from the west side of the present Town Hall to the church. The total of the two lots amounted to about 1.5 acres and reached back about 223- to 240-feet (depending on which end) to Samuel Valentine's 72-acre property.

At the first meeting, the participants chose a committee of five to locate said Coffee House: Col. Joseph Valentine, Col. Nathan Adams, Arba Thayer, D. Eames, and John Gibson. These were large landowners in town. They subsequently voted "to have the Stockholders turn out and invite their neighbors to assist in preparing the place" (site). Then, it was voted to "build and erect…near the new meetinghouse, a Public House with such other buildings as may be thought necessary for the accommodation of travelers. The Company to be called and known by the name of the Central Coffee House Company."

"We agree to purchase the land of Abijah Ellis which The First Parish in the Town of Hopkinton voted to sell at a legal Meeting held for that purpose of the fifth day of April last past and also to purchase a lot of land of Joseph Valentine containing by estimation one acre with an old dwelling house standing on the same and known by the name of the Barrett place for the purpose of erecting said buildings for the same and for other accommodations." Matthew Metcalf – Clerk   Abijah Ellis – Agent

The two lots were purchased in July of 1831. In August, the property was mortgaged to raise $6,000. The estate of "James Perkins, late of Boston, merchant, deceased" was the investor. The money was to be paid back in five years at 6% per year, starting January 1, 1832. The new building was to be insured against fire for the total amount of the investment. Daniel J. Coburn[88] was listed as agent for the Central Coffee House Company.

---

[88] Daniel Jennings Coburn, 4 November, 1802 – 11 January, 1866, Hopkinton, Uncle of N. P. Coburn.

Here we are looking east toward the school at 1 Ash Street in the latter half of the 19th century. A door in the side of the Central Coffee House has a sign over it which reads "Billiard Hall." In the next block, shown on the left edge, there is a store owned by A. A. Sweet. It has an awning to shade the windows. This was a dry goods (department) store. (See the chapter entitled "The Merchants" for more on Alvan Sweet.) The Common is on the right, down towards the school. The Valentine Mansion is just out of view to the right.

After the death of Col. Joseph Valentine in 1845, the Valentine Mansion (and a portion of the land) passed into the ownership of William Claflin, who made it his home for several years. His business partner, Nathan Parker Coburn, was the next occupant (c. 1855), before building his mansion in Newton in 1864. An unnamed Catholic priest (possibly Thomas Barry, Pastor 1866-1870) lived there next and then it was purchased by the Hopkinton Bank. Dr. George Thompson had his practice there in the early 1900's. Although missing its front, columned porch, the building retains much of its former appearance. It still contains both residential and commercial space.

The Valentine Mansion and the Hopkinton Public Library
2013

An inventory of the estate of Col. Valentine contains a long list of real estate. The "Home Place with the Cottage" was valued at $12,600. By then he owned a one-quarter share in the Central Coffee House, worth $725 and twenty shares in the High School, worth $200. All totaled, his estate came to $43,664.49, dated the "eighth day of April, A. D. 1845."

Dr. Jefferson Pratt at 25 Main Street

Large Greek-Revival house of Dr. Jefferson and Harriet (Valentine) Pratt

This house faces Main Street some distance behind the Valentine Mansion. In contrast to the Federal–style Valentine Mansion, this house was built in the Greek-Revival-style, initially made popular by Thomas Jefferson and Benjamin Henry Latrobe. Industry brought prosperity to Hopkinton during the height of the style's popularity, so there are several fine examples near the Common. This one is the most grand and we will revisit it again in connection with the next owner.

Joseph and Fanny Valentine's eldest daughter, Harriet Jones Valentine, married Dr. Jefferson Pratt (1803-1883) of Belchertown in 1829. Dr. Pratt became another large landowner and investor in Hopkinton. He developed much of the acreage of the former Valentine estate. The Valentine property contained a "fine grove" of trees, known subsequently as "Pratt's Grove." When a new road was later cut through the property, it was thus given the name Grove Street. The property thus extended down Main Street past Grove. It was part of Samuel Barrett's forty-one acres. The western edge of Samuel's lot was not quite as far west as Pleasant Street. On the 1850 Census for Hopkinton, the value of Dr. Pratt's real estate is the largest listed ($22,000). Of course, the census taker was relying on what each person told him.

Jefferson and Harriet's younger daughter, Sarah Elizabeth (1836-1919), married, as his second wife, the wealthy John Crane Whitin of Whitin Machine Works in Northbridge. Whitin Machine was one of the largest manufacturers of textile machinery in the world. In 1872, John Whitin constructed a twenty-nine room mansion for Sarah as a gift. Sarah donated the land for the Hopkinton Library (1895) and also the adjacent Episcopal Church (1898).

Gothic-Revival-style mansion of John C. & Sarah Whitin in Northbridge (Demolished)

Episcopal Church of 1898   *Library of 1895*

These two buildings were connected in 1967 to form one of the nicest libraries in the area. The close proximity to Center School made it convenient to introduce young students to the joy of reading. The library was fortunate to have such qualified and caring librarians as Betty Strong, Jeanette Ellsworth, and Rose Leveille during and after this expansion.

Early view of the new library of 1895

Notice the two-story wing of the Valentine Mansion. By 1895, the house had been converted to a bank and the remaining land sold off and developed. The library building was the result of a challenge made by John Quincy Adams, a native of Hopkinton and, by then, a prosperous resident of Wheaton, Illinois. He pledged $4,000, if the remaining funds could be raised by a certain date. His cousin, James Adams Woolson, along with N. P. Coburn, Abram & Ann M. Crooks, and others, quickly raised the needed amount. A portrait of Ann Crooks is in the reading room of the library.

The building is exceptionally well constructed of cut-granite, with a clay tile roof. Fortunately, the original quarter-sawn oak interior has not yet been disturbed. The library was also built as a civil war memorial and has a large bronze tablet in the portico which lists the names of the soldiers from Hopkinton who did not return from the war.

Across Church Street from the library was the house of Miriam Valentine, who lived to the age of 92. She was born Miriam Rice Haven on the 3rd of November, 1801, in Shrewsbury, daughter of Moses and Dolly (Rice) Haven. Miriam married John Lowell Valentine (1802-prior to 1855) on the 25th of May, 1826. His mother, Fanny (Haven) Valentine was her aunt *and* mother-in-law. With John, she had six children: Frances Caroline, Henry Clay, Frederick Eugene, Eliza Jane, Ellen Maria, and Eliza Ann. The back of her house is pictured below. Henry inherited. The house was demolished by 1904. It was later replaced by an Arts & Crafts-style bungalow which was expanded into the current building on the site. In 2014, it houses the Pan Thai restaurant and other businesses.

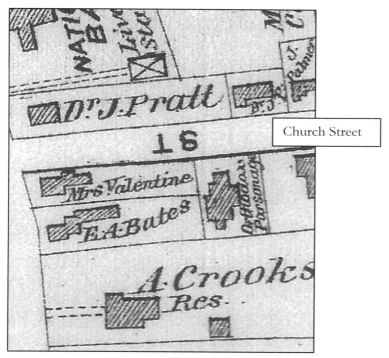

By the date of this map (1875), Dr. Pratt had sold his large house to Abram Crooks. He still owned two buildings on the other side of Church Street, as shown here.

At this point we have looked at development on three sides of the Common. On the north there is the Congregational Church of 1830, the burial ground, and the Stone Tavern. The west side is occupied by the Valentine Estate. To the east is the Tucker property between schools. On the south we have the Aldrich house. It occupies the eastern half of the south side, which leaves just the western half.

This early photograph was taken prior to 1882. On the far left edge, one can see a corner of the existing Valentine Mansion. The diagonal walkway through the Common remains. Otherwise, this scene has entirely changed. We will consider the events which caused such change in upcoming chapters.

You may recall that John Gibson purchased land on the south side. His brother Cornelius ended up with the east half. One of the Trustees for the School Fund, namely Moses Chamberlain, ended up with the west half. There is no deed to record either transaction. We will take a look at how the Chamberlain property developed, but first, we need some background on another family—one which would play an important role in the development of Hopkinton.

The Walker Family

Henry Walker lived to the age of 100. Contrary to popular opinion, many people lived to 80 plus in Colonial times. There was a higher mortality rate among children, so this lowered the overall life expectancy number. Good food, fresh air, and hard work promoted good health. Henry Walker Jr. was not so fortunate in this regard. He was born on the 15th of August, 1701, in Woburn and died in Cuba between 1740 and 1742. He married Elizabeth Frail on the 5th of January, 1737. The Frail family was one of the first lease-holders in Hopkinton. Their lease of 110 acres was located where a road headed north from Wood Street toward Saddle Hill. Members of the Walker family later lived at this intersection, which includes Proctor and Walker streets today. The genealogy of the Frail family has not been researched for this publication.

Henry and Elizabeth's eldest son was Solomon, baptized on the 3rd of June, 1739, in Hopkinton. He married Sarah Bullard, daughter of Seth and Sarah (Twitchell) Bullard of Sherborn, on the 18th of March, 1760. Solomon took part in the French and Indian War and was twice captured and wounded. After his escape, Seth and Sarah Walker went on to have a large family of eleven children. The eldest was Joseph Walker, born on the 26th of December, 1760, in Sherborn. He married Mehitable Gibbs on the 1st of January, 1784, in Hopkinton.

Joseph and "Hitty" had ten children. We will highlight three sons, the eldest being Lovett (1787), followed by his brother, Leonard (1789). A third son was Joseph Jr., born on the 18th of March, 1804. In 1828, he married Hannah Thayer Chapin, daughter of Eli and Libby (Thayer) Chapin. The Thayer and Chapin families were large. Members of each were prominent residents of Milford. Joseph Jr., like his father and older brothers, enjoyed early success. In 1829, we find Joseph Jr. and his wife living in Boston, where their first child, named Joseph Henry, was born. However, by the time of the Census of 1830, they were back in Hopkinton. Here, Joseph Jr. is listed with his father and brother Lovett. Leonard is listed elsewhere in town.

About 1818, Joseph Sr. came up with the idea of using wooden pegs to fasten the soles of boots. Stitching had been the preferred method. Glue had even been used for lightweight shoes. Nails had sometimes been used for work boots, but when these wore through, they were hardly comfortable!

The early cordwainers (custom shoe makers) took their equipment from door to door and made shoes for members of a family. Men like Joseph Walker in Hopkinton, and Arial Bragg (1777-1855), Rufus Chapin (1789-1840), and Lee Claflin (1791-1871) in Milford, started out on a small-scale, creating a "cottage industry" as they set up shop in small (say 12' x 16') sheds. Some, like Lee Claflin, started out in the leather tanning business, which his family had been in for generations. Men like these sometimes marketed their products by peddling finished goods. They might carry just six pair with them as they walked from place to place.

When Samuel Goddard,[89] also of Hopkinton, automated Joseph Walker's method of pegging shoes, it was revolutionary. Samuel Goddard was likely Samuel Brigham Goddard, born in Hopkinton in 1798, son of Samuel and Keziah (Pond) Goddard. Samuel doesn't often get the credit he is due.

The innovations of Joseph Walker and Samuel Goddard established Hopkinton as the founding town of the boot and shoe industry. These innovations made possible large factories, employing hundreds of workers. Factories were built in many area towns. Boot and shoe manufacturing would become a leading industry in Massachusetts in the nineteenth century. Marketing for the Hopkinton firms was done through offices in the Leather District of Boston.[90]

In 1826, Lovett and Leonard Walker set up business for themselves in Hopkinton, taking advantage of the new automation equipment. They were also, either the inventors of, or first to use, crimped forms for boot fronts, instead of sewed tongues.

---

[89] Samuel's grandparents were Ebenezer and Sybelia (Brigham) Goddard. Samuel's aunt Susannah was married to Phineas Howe, grandnephew of John How (page 10). Phineas and Susannah Howe were the grandparents of Brigham Young. That branch of the family moved from Hopkinton to Vermont and then to Utah.

[90] The Leather District is just southwest of South Station between the Financial District and Chinatown. It is bordered now by Atlantic Avenue, Kneeland Street, Lincoln Street, and Essex Street, but it used to cover more territory. The great Boston Fire of 1872 originated in this district.

This house at 28 Proctor Street is marked "L. Walker" on the 1831 Metcalf map. Lovett owned this farm on the corner of Saddle Hill Road. On the opposite side of Saddle Hill Road was the farm of Joseph Walker, which also bordered on Wood Street. These farms were both on what had been the 110-acre Frail lease. Lovett seems to have carried on the family farm. Both he and his brother Leonard died in Hopkinton (Lovett in 1859 and Leonard in 1863). In 1831, Lovett's daughter, Ann Maria married Albert Claflin, son of Amaziah and Ede, mentioned earlier.

On the 18th of June, 1836, Joseph Walker sold his farm to his sons Dexter and Joseph Jr. and to his son-in-law, Luther Eames. S. D. Davenport and Joseph Valentine owned adjacent property. On the Common, Joseph Jr. had a new house, but that was about to change.

Building 2 Park Street

It is easily the most altered structure in Hopkinton. Over the years it has undergone many transformations. Originally, it was a post and beam, two-story, five-room house of the typical "five-bay" arrangement, with a kitchen wing in the rear. A central hall was flanked by two rooms up and down. Two rear chimneys furnished five fireplaces and there was a full basement with granite foundation. When was it built?

As noted earlier, Moses Chamberlain was one of the members of the Trustees for the School Fund. On the 6th of October, 1823, Moses was in possession of the north-west corner lot, as he was the abutter when Willard Aldrich bought the adjoining lot from Cornelius Gibson on that date (page 59). Moses was born in Holliston on the 26th of October, 1766. He married Rhoda Mellen on the 10th of July, 1794. Rhoda was the daughter of Henry and Jerusha (Burnap) Mellen. Moses and Rhoda owned a farm on Hayden Rowe. Their house was where the tennis courts for the schools are located.

On the 31st of August, 1831, Moses died. His son, Henry Mellen Chamberlain was appointed executor. On the 6th of December, 1831, he sold the property at the Common to his third cousin, John Augustus Fitch (1803-1883), son of Deacon Elijah and Mary (Valentine) Fitch. John married Lucy Ann Howe, daughter of the third minister of the Congregational Church, Nathaniel Howe. The property is described in the deed as "a certain tract of land" containing 2 ½ acres and 36 rods, starting at the south-west corner of the Training Field, south on the highway leading to Milford, east on land of John Gibson, north on land of Willard Aldrich, and west along the Training Field. The purchase price was $485.00. Willard Aldrich owned the eastern portion of the school lot and now, John Fitch owned the west portion, adjacent to the Training Field (Common). John Gibson and Elijah Fitch owned the adjacent portions to the south, all part of the original 32-acre parcel. John Gibson (Jr.) owned much property in town at the time.

On the 31st of October, 1832, John A. and Lucy Ann Fitch sold part of the land they had received from the estate of Moses Chamberlain to Timothy B. Allen for $224.00. There is no mention of any buildings at this point.

Timothy B. Allen, *carpenter*, was married to Cerena Batchelor of Upton. He seems to have moved to Millbury later. On the 29th of October, 1833, they sold their property to Artemas C. Putnam and Jacob Fairbanks. John and Lucy Fitch also sold the rest of the lot they received from the estate of Moses Chamberlain to Artemas and Jacob. On the 31st of October, 1834, Jacob Fairbanks sold his share to Artemas (Artimus) Putnam. Artemas now owned the whole 2 ½ acres and 36 (square) rods.

On the 3rd of November, 1834, Artemas sold the property to William Smith. On the same day, William Smith mortgaged the property *"with a house"* back to Artemas for $1,500.00. Apparently, the original part of the house at 2 Park was complete by October of **1833** when sold by the Allen's. Certainly, by November of **1834** it was in existence. Next, on the 25th of August, 1836, William Smith, Gentleman, of Princeton, sold his remaining interest in the property to Artemas for $500.00.

On the 7th of October, 1835, Artemas sold a corner of the property to Joseph Walker Jr. for $175.00. On the 4th of November, 1836, Artemas, yeoman and Joseph, cordwainer, made adjustments to the property line. By then, Artemas legally owned the house built on the land he had already sold to Walker. Then in 1840, Artemas, ***housewright***, and Joseph, ***boot manufacturer***, made further adjustments.

On the 13th of December, 1842, Joseph Walker Jr. was declared bankrupt and Samuel B. Wolcott was appointed by the court to settle his debts. It may be that Joseph was taking advantage of the new bankruptcy provisions to liquidate his business in Hopkinton. The property was put up for sale at auction. Joseph moved to Worcester. Lee Claflin had moved his boot manufacturing operation to Hopkinton in 1839. Perhaps this had some impact on the profitability of the other firms in town.

On the 11th of May, 1843, Lee was the highest bidder at only $417.50 for the Walker land with buildings. Lee may have moved his family into the house. Since he owned so much property in Hopkinton, it is not possible to determine this for certain. However, it would explain why the house has been identified with Governor William Claflin. William would have been twenty-five years old in 1843.

Due to the Walker family's significant role in the development of the boot and shoe industry, the house has also been known as the Walker Mansion. Since the house has been altered greatly since 1843, we will interrupt our story to see what was happening around the rest of the Common before we see how it was transformed.

Artimus Conant Putnam

A. C. Putnam was at times a wheelwright and housewright, but also an investor and land speculator. He provided mortgage money for many real estate investments and thus, his name appears on many deeds.

Artimus was born on the 13th of November, 1805, in Wendell, Massachusetts, the son of Nathan and Rhoda (Gates) Putnam of Stow. His 5th great-grandfather, John Putnam (1579-1662), brought his family from England and settled in Salem. They had lived in Aston Abbotts, a small village in Buckinghamshire. The Conant name comes from the grandmother of Artimus, Mary Conant (1750-1824). Artimus is spelled "Artemas" in various deeds.

Artimus married Mary Pond Guy on the 4th of February, 1836 in Hopkinton. Mary was the eldest daughter of Ezekiel and Betsey (Johnson) Guy. Ezekiel (1774-1840) was from Dover and Betsey (1788-1858) was from Framingham. They had nine children, all of whom were born in Hopkinton, lived to adulthood, and married as follows:

Mary Pond Guy b. 6 September 1812   m. <u>Artimus C. Putnam</u> 4 February 1836

John Milton Guy b. 5 August 1814   m. Mary E. Carter 3 May 1838

Elizabeth Johnson Guy b. 11 April 1816   m. Isaac Burnap Valentine 3 October 1839

Charles Virgil Guy b. 13 November 1817 m. Susan E. Forbes 21 April 1845

Henry Rush Guy b. 26 July 1819   m. Mary E. McAllison 1 July 1846

Sarah Bucklin Guy b. 23 August 1822   m. <u>Samuel Crooks</u> 13 November 1844

Susan Isabella Guy b. 18 August 1824   m. William Valentine 1 November 1845

Emily Johnson Guy b. 29 October 1826   m. Samuel B. Forbes 1 September 1846

Ann Maria Guy b. 2 August 1831   m. <u>Abram Crooks</u> 28 November 1849

Therefore, Samuel and Abram Crooks were brothers-in-law to Artimus. The two Valentines were both sons of Captain Joseph and Patty (Burnap) Valentine.[91] The two Forbes were both children of Nahum and Polly Forbes.

---

[91] Captain Joseph Valentine was born the same year as Colonel Joseph Valentine. Capt. Joseph was the son of William and Elizabeth (Jones) Valentine. Capt. Joseph's father and Col. Joseph's father were brothers. Elizabeth Jones was the daughter of Anthony and Elizabeth (Alden) Jones. Her 3rd great-grandfather was John Alden of the Mayflower.

The Greek-Revival house (c. 1849) of A. C. Putnam, with former servants dwelling

According to a map of 1856 (see page 103), Artimus owned three houses here. Between here and the house at 2 Park Street, there was another house. It was later owned by John L. Pingry. Artimus also owned a house on Ash Street which stood opposite the east end of Park, facing the Common.

Mrs. Putnam's mother, Betsey Guy, lived across Hayden Rowe from 1846 until her death in 1858. The house was subsequently owned by the three Crooks brothers, John, Samuel, and Abram (see page 187). Abram Crooks lived next door, until he bought Dr. Pratt's house on Main Street.

The Claflin Family

Like the Price, Valentine, and Walker families, the Claflin family figures prominently in the history of the area surrounding the Common and Hopkinton itself. The Claflin family had been in Hopkinton for some generations and had married into the other large families in town. These relationships can get confusing. But by highlighting some of these relationships, I hope to provide some insight into the foundation of the boot industry which would have such an impact on Hopkinton. Various members of the Claflin family lived around the Common.

The family in Hopkinton began with Ebenezer and Hannah (Smith) Claflin. They moved from Wenham to Hopkinton. It is a family of Scot-Irish descent who were engaged in the business of tanning leather. Each of their six children was born in Hopkinton, starting in 1741.

Hannah, born 22 April, 1741, married John Hayden in 1759.

Ebenezer Jr. was born on the 14th of September, 1742. He married Sarah Tilton on the 18th of June, 1773. They had eleven children. The eldest daughter to marry was Sally (1780-1870). She married Dr. Thomas Bucklin on the 6th of January, 1799 in Hopkinton. Their large house stood where the old brick High School on Main Street now stands. Lee was another son and we will consider him in more detail when we pick up the story of the boot industry.

Dolly, born 1744, did not marry and lived to the age of 95.

Isaac, born 1748, married Mary Stimpson. This branch of the family will be discussed in detail next, since it is the branch most associated with 2 Park Street.

John, born 5 July, 1750, married Polly Sheffield on the 5th of April, 1770. They had a large family of nine children, all born in Holliston. One of which was Amaziah (1773-1886), whose daughter Ede married Joshua Tucker, mentioned earlier (page 55).

Aaron, born 1753, married Lucy Gibbs, daughter of Phineas and Mary (Mellen) Gibbs. Mary was a granddaughter of Henry Mellen and Phineas Gibbs was a grandson of John How. Lucy's sister Mehitable Gibbs married Joseph Walker Sr.

The following chart helps (at least a little) to show the complicated relationship between the Claflin, Bucklin, Davenport and Gibbs families:

EBENEZER CLAFLIN 1716-1793 & HANNAH SMITH 1720-1785
> 6 Children, including:

> 2. EBENEZER JR. 1742-1797 & SARAH TILTON 1755-1824
> > 11 Children, including:

> > 3. Sally 1780-1870 m. **Dr. Thomas Bucklin**
> > > 1 Child:
> > > Mary Claflin Bucklin m. **Samuel Daniels Davenport**
> > 7. Puah 1787-aft 1870 m. Benjamin Herrick   ↓
> > 10. Lee 1791-1871 m. Sally Adams, m. Polly Eames
> > > 3 Children: ↓
> > > > 1. William m.1st Nancy Harding
> > > > > Emma C. Harding Claflin
> > > > > 2nd Mary Bucklin Davenport
> > > > > Arthur Bucklin Claflin
> > > > > Adams Davenport Claflin
> > > > 2. Charles Lee (1829-1830)
> > > > 3. Wilbur Fisk m. Mary A. Streeter
> > > > > Clarence Augustus Claflin
> > > > > Adelbert Eugene Claflin

> 4. ISAAC 1748-1831 & MARY STIMPSON 1756-1825
> > 1 Child:
> > James 1790-1851 m. Susannah Wadsworth
> > > 7 Children: (See page 105)

> 5. JOHN 1750-1838 & POLLY SHEFFIELD 1750-1821
> > 9 Children, including:
> > 2. Amaziah 1773-1866 m. Ede Watkins
> > > Newel m. Mira (Mary) Rice
> > > > Celia Augusta m. **Daniel J. Coburn**
> > > Albert m. Ann Maria **Walker (dau. of Lovett)**
> > > Ede A. m. Joshua Tucker
> > 3. John 1775-1848 m. Lydia Mellen
> > > Aaron m. Mary Thayer
> > > Horace Brigham m. Agnes Sanger

> 6. AARON 1753-1813 & LUCY GIBBS 1761-
> > 2 Children, including:
> > 2. Winslow 1791-1815 m. Mercy Farrar

Samuel Daniels Davenport

A little background on the Davenport family is also appropriate at this point. Samuel was born in Mendon on the 28th of December, 1801 to Seth and Betsey (Godfrey) Davenport. The family came from Dorchester and one branch was in the furniture business, which is why a sofa is sometimes called a "davenport." Samuel married Mary Claflin Bucklin on the 25th of February, 1822 in Hopkinton. Mary was the daughter of Dr. Thomas and Sally (Claflin) Bucklin. Dr. Bucklin was successful in his profession and owned much property in Hopkinton. His house was on the site of the old brick high school on Main Street. Dr. Bucklin was born in Rehoboth on the 27th of September, 1772. He married Sally Claflin on the 6th of January, 1799 in Hopkinton. Next door to the west of their house was another house built around 1805-1810. It was a Federal-style house built in brick, in a typical symmetrical design, with a fan-lighted front door in the center and tall chimneys on either end.

S. D. Davenport became a successful boot merchant and manufacturer, with offices in Boston and a factory in Hopkinton. He invested in several Hopkinton enterprises and his name often comes up in Hopkinton records. He was a Justice of the Peace, along with his father-in-law, Dr. Bucklin, and Col. Joseph Valentine. As his fortune grew, Samuel decided to "modernize" his brick house in the latest Greek-Revival-style. The result is the house pictured below, located at 85 Main Street.

Davenport & Gibbs established the second or third largest boot factory in Massachusetts on Main Street at the corner of Mt. Auburn about the year 1840. On the following detail from a map of 1856, notice the "Gibbs Boot Shop" (of John Gibbs) and the "Davenport Block" on either side of Mt. Auburn Street. S. D. Davenport, Mrs. Bucklin, and Levi Bicknall (Bicknell) still lived in the same houses they did in 1831 (page 53), but they had been joined by several neighbors. By 1856, Sally Bucklin was a widow. Dr. Bucklin died in 1843. The Gibbs family was descended from Jacob and Martha (Howe) Gibbs. Martha was the daughter of John How and his homestead lot began at Mt. Auburn Street.

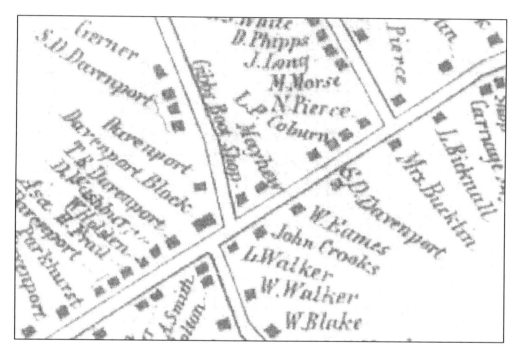

At the exhibition and fair of the Massachusetts Charitable Mechanic Association in 1837, the following award was given:

"S. D. Davenport & Son, Boston. Case of Boots. The Committee considered the manufacture of this case of best Kip Boots superior in finish and fully entitled to a Silver Medal. "

S. D. Davenport was also a director of the People's Mutual Insurance Co. They had offices in the Old State House on State Street in Boston.

Davenport Block with rear addition along Mt. Auburn Street

As an interesting side note, Samuel Davenport's aunt, Anna, married William Torrey in 1788. They had a son named Samuel Davenport Torrey (S. D.'s cousin). His grandson was the 27th President and 10th Chief Justice of the United States, William Howard Taft. The President's paternal grandfather, Peter Rawson Taft was born in Uxbridge in 1785.

Samuel's brother was Joseph Gibbs Davenport (1803-1862). He remained in Mendon. He married Mary Harding Daniels of Hopkinton in 1826. Their third daughter, Betsey (1831-1856) married Arthur Buckminster Fuller (1822-1862 Civil War), a Unitarian clergyman. Their grandson was R. Buckminster Fuller (1895-1983), the inventor and architect widely known for his design of the geodesic dome.

1856

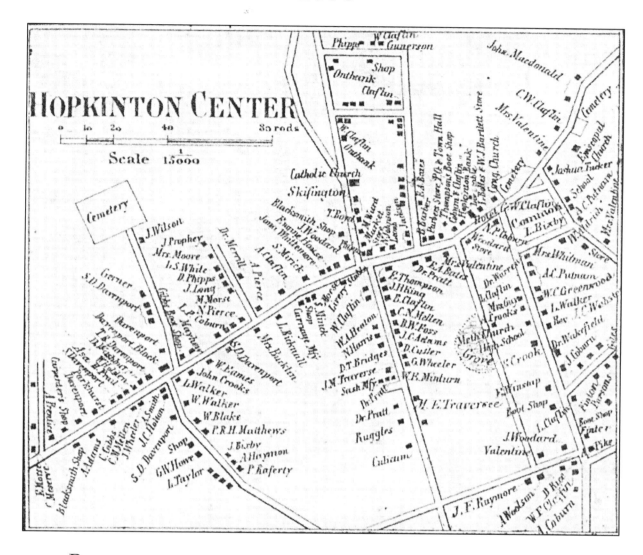

Between the map of 1831 and this one of 1856, the town has grown substantially. The industrial revolution had come to Hopkinton. For now, take note that Church, Grove, and Maple Streets fill the space between Hayden Row and Pleasant. Mt. Auburn leads to a new cemetery. Cedar and Walcott are new roads north of Main. A road that no longer exists runs in parallel to Cedar, starting across from St. Malachi's Catholic Church. N. P. Coburn is the owner of the Valentine Mansion. Next to N. P. Coburn we see L. Claflin, and then Mrs. Guy.[92] This would be Betsey, Mrs. Ezekiel Guy (1788-1858). Her son-in-law, A. C. Putnam has three houses across the street, including the two pictured earlier.

---

[92] The position of the little squares denoting each house is not precise. Lee Claflin's house is much closer to the Common.

Claflin & Whitman at 2 Park Street

As mentioned, Lee Claflin owned the house on the west end of what would later become Park Street, facing the Common. He likely lived there before building his new Greek-Revival house directly across from it on Hayden Rowe.

After owning the house at 2 Park for ten years, Lee sold it in 1853 to Joseph Whitman of Milford for $2,200.00. Joseph Whitman had been a Methodist clergyman in Milford. He went into partnership with Samuel Walker in Milford in 1850. Samuel was one of the very successful Milford manufacturers of boots and shoes. He was a nephew of Joseph Walker Sr. of Hopkinton. While serving as a Massachusetts Senator, Joseph Whitman worked as a cashier at the Hopkinton Bank. He did not enjoy good health and on the 8th of August, 1854, he died. Thus, Mrs. Whitman is shown on the corner of Hayden Rowe and Park on the previous map of 1856. On the 10th of February, 1857, Elenor Whitman was granted guardianship of her children. On the 9th of March, she sold her house to Charles W. Claflin and soon married N. P. Coburn.

Joseph Whitman

Isaac Claflin

The second son of Ebenezer and Hannah (Smith) Claflin was Isaac (1748-1831). He married Mary Stimpson (1756-1825). Mary's grandfather, George Stimpson, held one of the original leases. His 81+ acres were just east of the school lots and thus, just across the street from the Claflin family. Mary was also the great-granddaughter of Martha (How) Walker (1669-1721), sister of John How (1664-1740), whose house is pictured on page 10. Isaac and Mary Claflin had but one child, James, born on the 4th of July, 1790. Isaac was the innkeeper and farmer at the Stone Tavern until he sold the property in 1804.

James married Susannah Willard Wadsworth, daughter of Capt. David Wadsworth and Virtue Willard in August of 1812. Susannah was born on the 16th of August, 1793 in Barre and that is where they were married. They had seven children. She lived until 1890 and the age of 96. Eldest son, Thomas Jefferson Claflin married Mary Ann Holbrook and they lived in Boston. Daughter Mary Wadsworth Claflin married George Washington Valentine, son of Col. Joseph. After George's 1840 death in St. Louis, she married his cousin, John Tyng Valentine, son of Samuel and Polly. This family also lived in the Stone Tavern.

JAMES CLAFLIN (1790-1851) & SUSANNAH WADSWORTH (1793-1890)

1. Thomas Jefferson Claflin m. Mary Ann Holbrook
2. Mary Wadsworth Claflin m. George, then John Tyng, Valentine
3. Charles Winslow Claflin m. Ann Marie Valentine
    Emma Francis Claflin m. Edward Willard Pierce (d. 1871)
        Edward Winslow Pierce m. Emma Morse (Ash St. family)
        Winslow Claflin Pierce m. Emma Moore (4th cousin)
    Charles Leslie Claflin remained single
    Mary Valentine Claflin m. Arthur Osgood Young
        Charles Leslie Claflin Young
        Margaret Valentine Young
        Arthur Osgood Young (Jr.)
4. Martha Wadsworth Claflin m. Louis Putnam Hayward (4 Park)
5. Isaac Claflin m. Mary Watts Towne
6. Susannah Claflin m. Anthony P. Holbrook
    Evelyn and Elsie Holbrook each m. George I. Aldrich
7. James Fitzgerald Claflin m. Catherine Poole

Wadsworth & Claflin at 7 East Main

Next to the Stone Tavern is the house pictured below. It is known as the Willard Wadsworth house. Willard was born in Barre on the 20th of July, 1800. He was the younger brother of Susannah. It is easy then to understand how Charles Winslow (C. W.) Claflin came to live there since he was Willard's nephew. Charles married the girl next door. Ann Marie Valentine was the youngest daughter and ninth child of Samuel and Polly at the Tavern. Charles and Ann lived in this house just east of the Tavern after their marriage in 1844. He first worked as a farmer and bootmaker. C. W. is shown at this house on the map of 1856. Willard also owned the large stone house further east on East Main. Willard married Eliza Spring in 1832. Their daughter Frances married D. T. Bridges (see p 199) and their son Joseph married Meriam Woolson, first cousin of James Adams Woolson (see p. 186)

7 East Main Street

This house later became the home of the Luther Taylor family - see page 15.

C. W. Claflin & Co.

Charles Winslow Claflin, second son of James and Susannah, was born on the 4th of April, 1820. C. W. married Ann Marie Valentine on the 18th of April, 1844. C. W. is listed on the Census of 1850 as a bootmaker, but he was already doing business as C. W. Claflin Co. On the census of 1855, he is listed as the innkeeper of the Stone Tavern. On the map of 1856, he is connected with the Central Coffee House (labeled "Hotel"). He continued to farm the family land. Thus, on the 1860 Census, C. W. is listed as a farmer. But, he was in the coal business with A. C. Wellington in Boston by 1868 and in the lumber business in Hopkinton. Coal yards were soon added with yards located along the rail lines where they crossed Main Street. This is where Hopkinton Lumber is located today. The C. W. Claflin & Co. was organized in 1873. He began operations on Central Street in Worcester in 1875, along the rail lines of the Boston & Maine. Further expansion led to yards on Grafton, Albany, Ludlow, and Shrewsbury Streets. In 1883, offices were located at 133 Union and 415 Main in Worcester. Operations developed further in Boston, with offices at 55 Kilby Street.

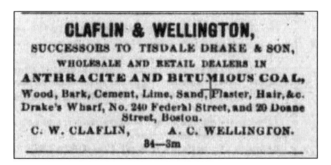

Advertisement from the Cambridge Chronicle, 1868

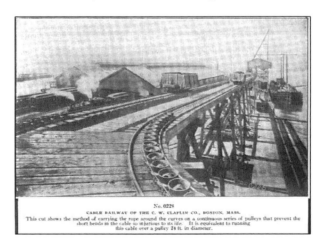

Cable railway and wharf of the C. W. Claflin Co. in Boston

Development continued through the aid of his son Charles Leslie Claflin; son-in-law, Arthur Osgood Young; and grandsons, Edward Winslow Pierce and Winslow Claflin Pierce. They were becoming the largest coal dealers in New England.

Charles W. and Ann Marie had three children: Emma Francis, b. 21 Feb. 1845; Charles Leslie, b. 16 Mar. 1851; and Mary Valentine, b. 3 Nov. 1855. Charles L. remained single. Emma Francis married Edward Willard Pierce of Foxboro in 1866. He died in New Orleans in 1871, leaving two sons: Edward Winslow, b. 19 Jan. 1867 and Winslow Claflin, b. 19 Sep. 1870.

C. W. and Anne's youngest daughter married Arthur Osgood Young of Somerset, Wisconsin on the 16th of January, 1890. His father, Stephen, was born in Maine and his mother, Sophia Minor, was born in New Brunswick. Arthur was born on the 3rd of April, 1860. So he was only about seven years older than his nephew, Edward Winslow Pierce. Arthur lived in Worcester, where he oversaw the wholesale and retail operations. Edward lived in Brookline and took care of the Boston wholesale operations. After the death of his father in 1884, Charles Leslie became the president of C. W. Claflin & Co. He was also the president of the Boston Wharf Coal Co., and eastern agent for the Delaware and Hudson Coal Co.

Advertisement from the Worcester Magazine of July, 1902

Arthur Young succeeded C. L. as president of C. W. Claflin & Co. and they merged with the Sumner Coal Co. The Claflin-Sumner Coal Company was chartered on the 1st of April, 1910 with offices in Worcester.

The company continued to prosper. This is a 1916 advertisement from Worcester.

In 1922, the Worcester Fuel Company consolidated with the Claflin-Sumner Coal Company. Meanwhile, Winslow Claflin Pierce was in charge of other coal companies. He succeeded C. L. Claflin as president of the Massachusetts Wharf Coal Co., organized 19 August, 1898, and the Framingham Coal Co., organized 3 May, 1902.

Winslow also ran the Hopkinton Supply Co. which was the families' new grocery store.[93] The existing building of 1906 is pictured here. It is a rare, pressed-metal building, listed on the National Historic Register. A store house was located on Hayden Rowe, opposite the end of Maple Street. It had previously been a storehouse for A. Coburn & Son. In 1912, William S. Morse[94] was in charge of the Hopkinton Supply Co. They advertised "Coal, wood, groceries, lime, cement, etc."

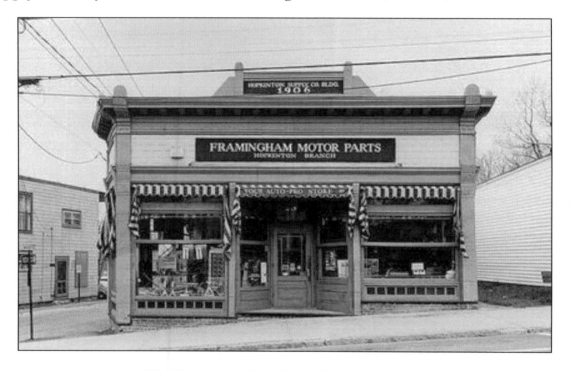

The Hopkinton Supply Co. building of 1906

The left side of this building became an A&P grocery store in 1928 (until 1954), while Edison (light co.) occupied the right side from this view (1928-1938). After 1938, the right side was used as a barber shop until 1954. In the 1970's it was the local auto parts store, as shown in this picture. In 2013 it housed a furniture gallery.

---

[93] Obituary from <u>The Boston Globe</u>, March 3, 1920, the death of Winslow Claflin Pierce.
[94] William Stearns Morse was a brother-in-law of Edward Winslow Pierce.

The Hopkinton Supply Co. building with an A&P grocery store and Edison business

A&P was known for the high quality of their products during the early part of the 20th century. Their display window here is well stocked. The building to the left on the other side of Walcott Street still exists, but without its third-floor hall. Compare this view to the previous photograph to see the change.

1939 - Framingham Coal Co. sheds

This building was located between Howard Street and the rail lines at Concord Street in downtown Framingham.[95] It was one of two coal sheds. The other was further west on the north side of Route 135 (Waverly Street), between Mellen Street and Waverly Court.

It is only natural that C. L. Claflin would have expanded in Framingham after his cousin expanded his boot manufacturing operations there. The factory was powered by burning a prodigious amount of coal. As you will see next, one of the coal sheds was serviced by a railroad siding which branched off the one leading to the boot factory.

---

[95] Image courtesy of the Framingham Public Library.

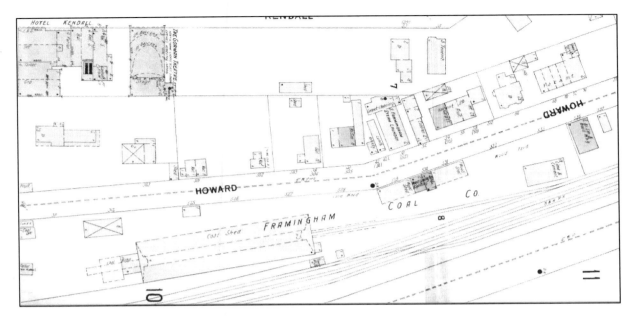

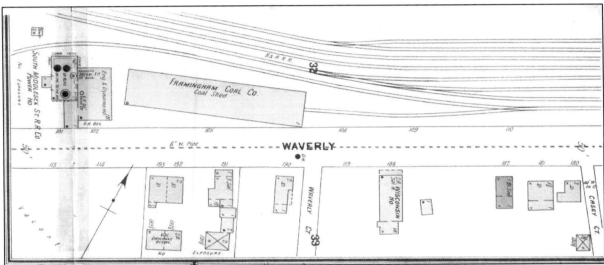

Two yards of the Framingham Coal Co., part of C. W. Claflin & Co.[96] Concord Street is along the left edge of the upper image. The H. H. Richardson-designed passenger station is just to the west, on the opposite side of Concord Street. The lower image shows the power station for the street railway (trolley) just to the left (west) of a second coal shed. This one was close to the shoe factory of Wm. Claflin, Coburn & Co. The railroad spur just above the power station led to the factory on Mellen Street.

As business increased, Charles W. and Charles L. increased their property holdings in Hopkinton. C. W. was one of the directors of the Hopkinton Railroad.

---

[96] Insurance maps, Sanborn Map Company, New York, courtesy of the Framingham Public Library.

Hopkinton Railroad Company

The Hopkinton Branch Railroad Company was incorporated in 1854. "Lee Claflin, Silas Mirick, and Erastus Thompson, their associates and successors," were made a corporation. Originally, it was to run from "a point near the centre village of Hopkinton, then running to the sand banks, near Indian Brook, thence to the station house of the Boston and Worcester Railroad, at Cordaville...." It needed to be constructed within three years. Well, this did not happen. So, they tried again and the Hopkinton Railroad Company was incorporated on the 17th of June, 1870. It opened for public use on the 24th of December, 1872 and ran from Ashland, crossing West Union, then under East Main, around the north side of Hopkinton Center, across Main again and then south along the west side of Hayden Rowe to Milford.

According to a report ending the 30th of September, 1875, the track ran for a total of 11.59 miles and there were fifteen grade crossings and one bridge. Only two of the crossings had gates or flagmen. Lovett H. Bowker, Erastus Thompson, and C. W. Claflin were the directors. The cost for the bridge, masonry for abutments, and grading was only $177,856.45. When you see the huge volume of earth moved and the existing cut-stone, abutment remnants, this seems like such a small amount. Total cost was nearly $297,000. In 1875, they managed a profit of nearly $7,000., but interest on the principal was over $9,000., which ate into their surplus, leaving only $420.35 at the end of that year.

In 1880, the railroad was called the Hopkinton, Milford & Woonsocket. But it was never a great success. Though the expenditure was lamented and criticized in later years, it must be remembered that the builders envisioned long-term industrial growth in Hopkinton. For C. W. Claflin, it meant that he could ship in coal to feed the five large boot manufacturing factories. As can be seen in several of the pictures of Hopkinton at the time, there were few trees. The first leaseholders generally had a wood lot. Now, coal was more convenient for heating and cooking.

The industrial growth which justified building the railroad was cut short by a series of devastating fires. This led to a reevaluation of Hopkinton as an industrial center. The year after the fire of 1882, the bank foreclosed on the railroad company.

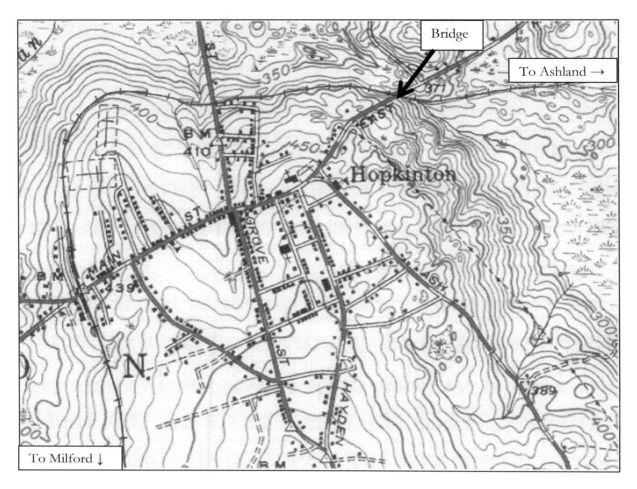

Path of the Hopkinton Railroad

Though it circled the hill, it was still necessary to climb from 330-feet, where it crossed by the Little Cedar Swamp, to 430-feet as it reached Main Street at grade. From there it continued to climb past 470-feet on the way to Milford.

The one bridge carried East Main Street over the existing gorge near Wilson Street. The tracks continued up the hill, crossing Cedar Street just below C Street, then continuing around Mt. Auburn Cemetery and across Main Street again, this time at grade, just above Wood Street. Here was located the small passenger station and the buildings of C. W. Claflin. They can be seen on either side of the tracks on the next map and in the pictures which follow.

Map of 1899 showing the railroad crossing Main Street east of Wood Street

117

The passenger station has been restored and is now located at Ice House Pond on West Main

Passenger station and one of the C. W. Claflin buildings facing a rutted Main Street

118

The steam engine is from the Civil War period, perhaps built just a little later than the similar one shown here. This one was built in 1858 by The Portland Company, Portland, Maine, for the New Brunswick & Canada Railroad. Not many pictures have survived from when they were shiny new like this one.

"The Shamrock" No. 4
The Portland Company, 1858

George Draper of Hopedale[97] saved the railroad after foreclosure. In May of 1884, he deeded it to the Milford and Woonsocket Railroad. It later became known as the Franklin & Ashland Branch of the New York, New Haven, & Hartford Railroad. The railroad leading from the train station on Main Street to Milford continued long after the rest of the line was torn up. It remained in operation until a bridge in Milford burned and it was deemed impractical to replace. The right of way into Hopkinton was still intact until the land was sold by the N.Y., N.H., & H. Railroad in the 1970's. Housing development off Hayden Rowe now interrupts the route. In Milford, you can follow the old rail bed on the new bicycle path. In Hopkinton, parts of the rail bed are less disturbed, especially where a nice trail (now called "Central Trail") leads from Main Street to the schools on Hayden Rowe. When the Hopkins School and adjacent fields were constructed, the access roads cut through the rail bed twice, without taking advantage of this very scenic walking/running path. It is still there, but it was inexplicably difficult to find each end until recently.

Since the rest of the line has been abandoned longer, it is mostly in poorer condition. However, from Cedar Street to the site of the bridge at East Main, there are some pristine sections, as shown below.

---

[97] George Draper was head of the various Draper companies of Hopedale. Focusing on looms for the cotton textile industry, Draper became part of the "Big Three" textile machinery makers in the Blackstone Valley, along with Crompton & Knowles of Worcester, which focused on looms for wool, and Whitin Machine Works in Whitinsville, which largely made spinning frames and cotton preparation machinery.

The bridge at East Main Street just west of Wilson Street (looking south)

Site of the former bridge (also looking south)
From here, the trains would have been heard loud and clear at the Common.

A narrow drainage channel in cut-granite

Heading uphill toward Cedar Street

Sections below the Mt. Auburn Cemetery are still quite impressive. There, a wide swath cuts through the woods in a sweeping curve where steam engines once thundered up the grade.

C. W. Claflin at 2 Park Street

Once he had the capital from his profitable business ventures, C. W. began to expand his house at 2 Park in the Greek-Revival-style, in keeping with his neighbor and cousin, Lee Claflin. The rear ell was expanded, raised to two levels, and given a gambrel roof. At some point, a remarkable room was added to the front of the house. It measures 18'3" x 22' and projects from the second floor, supported entirely by fluted columns (and the front of the original house). In the corner of this room is a fireplace with its brickwork and chimney, also supported by these columns! Fortunately, C. W. was in the lumber business and had access to large beams, which have carried this load for some one hundred and fifty years. The rear ell benefits from this same access to large beams. Recent restoration work uncovered the fact that the load-bearing walls of the gambrel-roofed wing no longer reached all the way to the ground floor! In one place, a tenon at the end of a beam, which once was inserted into a post, is instead pinned and suspended from above as seen here:

Large beams above the second floor have suspended the load for decades. This method allowed rooms on the first floor to expand outward. Additions were wrapped with porches. As styles changed, the son, C. L., added elements in the Queen Anne-style. The result was the impressive, albeit unusual, house pictured next.

Walker-Claflin Mansion as expanded by Charles L. Claflin
2 Park Street

In that the core of the house is an earlier structure with lower ceilings than those of a typical late-Victorian era house, the scale is uncommon. It results in comfortable rooms of a practical size. The tower on the right (partly obscured by trees) featured an open, covered, viewing platform at the fourth floor level. Looming in the back is the tall, gambrel-roofed, barn/carriage house. Bedrooms occupied its second level by the time this photo was taken. Glimpses of the east wing can be seen through the trees to the left. Behind the house to the right can be seen a small, one-story portion of the J. L. Pingry house and the side of the A. C. Putnam house beyond. This picture was taken between 1904 and 1910. The photographer was standing on the north side of Main Street. This image has been cropped and enhanced to focus on the house. Extremely good emulsion used for film in this period, coupled with modern editing software, has made possible a view of the house not seen in many years.

The Claflin house, as viewed from Hayden Rowe after 1892. The shadows of the trees make you think of a nice, warm, summer day. Below the chimney can be seen a small portion of the gable end of the original house. Through the porte-cochere on the right can be seen a sliding barn door. At one point, the wing to the right was nearly as large as what is pictured here. Some of this can be seen in the picture on the next page.

After 1904

The "X" marks the English elm tree planted by Madam Price. Under the tree and to the left was located the first school. 4 Park can be seen behind the elm tree and the gable end of 6 Park is beyond. When a house was built behind 4 Park in the 20th century, the street numbers were revised (4 became 6 and 6 became 8).

When owned by the Claflin family, the house was occupied by the family and a servant or two. In 1860 there were ten residents. In 1870 there were only six. In time, the house was expanded to provide guest rooms. The Claflin and Valentine extended families were large.

C. W. Claflin died on the 13th of October, 1884. The probate documents for his estate reveal the extent of his wealth. His personal estate, which included C. W. Claflin & Co. of Hopkinton, Boston, and Worcester, as well as farming tools and three cows at the Stone Tavern, amounted to $35,114.39. Additionally, his real estate included the "home place," valued at $4,000, with twenty-two other parcels, for a total of $16,135.00. His wife, Ann Marie, died on the 23rd of March, 1892. In the probate of her will in 1894, her interest in the Stone Tavern was divided between her three children.

As family fortunes increased, Charles L. Claflin acquired sole ownership of the Stone Tavern and proceeded to reassemble much of the 72-acre farmland which had belonged to his great-grandfather Isaac Claflin and his grandfather Samuel Valentine.

This photo is taken from the front porch of the Claflin house. We are looking through the large circular east porch or "piazza" toward the side of the house at 4 Park, with its Victorian bracketed and hooded rear doors. This view is from about 1911 when Edward Pierce was still in control and the house was at or near its largest. This view also gives a tantalizing glimpse of the east wing (barn portion). A portion of shingled roof is barely visible. Other photographs exist, but they are poor reproductions. If originals can be discovered and enhanced, these may reveal further details of the parts of this house which no longer exist. School photographs were sometimes taken on the Common, with the east side of this house visible in the background.

A study of the construction of the house raises more questions than it provides answers. The plan of the front portion of the house is symmetrical. The windows and fireplaces were symmetrically placed on either side of a central hall (since widened on one side). The floor plan indicates a building which was meant to measure 33'x15', with a 13'x14' kitchen wing behind the western of the two rear chimneys. However, unless it is an earlier building moved to the site and then altered, it may have been redesigned while under construction and the frame design lengthened to match a wider foundation.

The lower façade of the house is framed by pilasters with matched boards in between. From the outside edge of one pilaster to the outside edge of the other, it measures 30'8." A tall baseboard also runs between the pilasters. Beyond each pilaster is a 12" section of clapboard and a 17.5" wide, plain corner trim after the Greek-Revival-style. The original porch did not extend all the way to each end of the building. Instead, it stopped at the pilasters. Take note of the ceiling in the picture below.

Porch ceiling, showing the end of the original porch, with pilaster detail below

The original porch ceiling may have been higher. When the room was added to the front of the building, it was set at a height which allowed for the same floor level as the existing second story rooms. The porch ceiling was designed to allow for the front door height, which seems to be original when viewed from inside the house.

Ceiling modification to allow for the door height
These pictures were taken before recent restoration work was completed.

By 1875, C. W. Claflin had added the rear, gambrel-roofed wing over the original kitchen wing on the south side. It measured 20' by 20', but was subsequently widened on the first floor toward Hayden Row by 5' and toward Ash by 4.5', then 6', until it was as wide as the front portion of the house. About this time, a large gambrel-roofed barn was added as well. This is all reflected in this sketch from the map of 1875. The house is relatively square and the barn is the center of three more additions to the rear of the house. By then, the main portion of the house measured 35'6" wide by 37' deep. It is thus the largest of the four connected squares at the corner of the Common below.

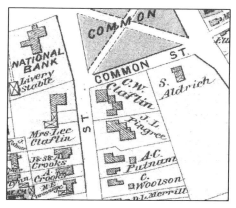

1875 map detail

The J. L. Pingry house had been built between that of C. W. Claflin and that of A. C. Putnam to the south. The Lee Claflin house is across Hayden Rowe. In 1875, the former Valentine property on the corner was only as wide as the Common.

The Pingree property was added to the Claflin lot as we shall see. Therefore, we should consider the family. According to "A genealogical record of the descendants of Moses Pengry, of Ipswich, Mass" by William Morrill Pingry, John L. Pingry/Pingree was married to Jane Young of Hopkinton and (John) "went into shoe business at Hopkinton, Mass.; is overseer. Has accumulated a good property." His distant (4th) cousin Samuel Hoyt Pingry worked for Claflin, Coburn, & Co. It may be that John did too.

John Pingry was born in 1834 to Jasper and Adeline (Bryant) Pingry of Denmark, Maine. Jasper was originally from Rowley, Massachusetts. John's wife Mary Jane was the daughter of David and Miranda (Coburn) Young. They were married in Holliston on the 6th of January, 1857. Little else is known about John and Mary Jane.

However, at the age of fourteen, John's younger brother, Hazen Stuart (b. 30 Aug. 1840), moved from Denmark to Saco, Maine, where he worked at a cotton factory. Two years later, he moved to Hopkinton and worked several years as a cutter in one of the boot factories. In 1862, Hazen enlisted in the Union Army and served with the 1st Massachusetts Heavy Artillery regiment. He was at the second battle of Bull Run and at Spotsylvania Court House. In May of 1864, he was captured and sent to prisons at Lynchburg, Virginia, and Salisbury, North Carolina. He was then taken to the infamous Andersonville Prison and then to Millen, Georgia, where he escaped by pretending to be John Phelps during a roll call for a prisoner exchange in November, 1864. Phelps was too sick to come to roll call. Pingree was present at Appomattox Court House for the surrender.

After the war, he moved to Detroit. In 1866, with Charles H. Smith, he established the Pingree & Smith Shoe Co. In March of 1887, a fire destroyed the entire factory. But they were able to recover and by 1889 were employing over 700 workers. By the 1890s, they were the leading Western shoe manufacturer.

Hazen Pingree was elected Mayor of Detroit (1889) and Governor of Michigan (1896). In 1900, Detroit was described as "one of the cleanest and most beautiful cities in the Union" – not what one would write in 2014!

In 1901, after an African safari trip with his son, Hazen was in London when he became sick with peritonitis. King Edward VII (who Hazen was said to resemble) even sent his physicians to assist. As Hazen's wife and daughter were preparing to leave New York for the voyage to London, they learned that he had died.[98]

Hazen Stuart Pingree (1840-1901)

[98] Image and other material on Hazen Pingree, with quote regarding Detroit from: Cyclopedia of Michigan, Historical and Biographical, Comprising a Synopsis of General History of the State, and Biographical Sketches of Men Who Have, in Their Various Spheres, Contributed Toward Its Development, (Western Publishing & Engraving Co., New York and Detroit, 1900), pp.144-146. Circumstances of his death: Don Lochbiler, "The Shoemaker Who Looked Like a King," The Detroit News, June 11, 1998.

C. W. Claflin at 4 Park Street

C. W. Claflin set off a portion of his lot and constructed another house at 4 Common (Park). He sold this house to his brother-in-law, Lewis Putnam Hayward on the 4th of October, 1882 for $2,800.00. When Lewis died in 1897, his widow sold it back to her nephew, C. L. Claflin, for $2,600.00 (see page 105 for the family relationship).

4 (now 6) Park Street

It is an Italianate-style house. The current porch is a later version. Lewis P. Hayward worked for A. Coburn & Son, boot manufacturers.

C. L. Claflin at 2 Park Street

Charles Leslie Claflin continued to redesign the house, adding elements shown in the previous pictures. In the 1890's, C. L. Claflin added the towers to the house. Another addition was to the front porch (if not the porch itself). An elaborate vestibule had a single front door framed by narrow windows and two three-part bays. Looking from the front of the building, the vestibule was in turn framed by the double columns on the front of the porch.

In this extreme, zoomed, detail view (from the photo on page 124), it is possible to see part of the vestibule. We see the narrow, double-hung windows with paneling below and about half of the centered, front door. This photograph was taken from Main Street over one hundred years ago.

All the additions led to a very unusual roof. The east side of the rear gambrel roof was cut back at an odd angle. It is difficult at this point to determine why. The roof was covered with wooden shingles and a lower portion of it still exists in the attic, with a higher roof above. The gable roof on the left (east) side was redesigned after the east tower was removed. The roof of the front addition was originally designed as shown in the detail below and was probably susceptible to ice backup and leaks. In a redesign, the peak was extended back to meet the main roof. The current roof design can be seen in the aerial photo. Note too that the large circular porch on the east side, both towers, and the rear half of the house have all been removed.

West side detail

In memory of his parents, C. L. donated this Victorian cast iron fountain for the Common. Originally of three levels, it no longer works and is in need of restoration. Trees falling during the 1938 hurricane and later vandalism damaged the fountain. C. L. left money to the Town to aid in its upkeep. Until a few years ago, a factory was still making cast-iron fountains of similar design.

The Claflin Fountain in 2013

In addition to all the family businesses and farms, Charles L. became the president of the Hopkinton National Bank. He was a trustee of the Hopkinton Savings Bank and president of the local Board of Trade. He was a director of the Quinsigamond National Bank. Somehow, he also found time to be a Hopkinton Selectman.

This next view is another taken from the Methodist Church on Church Street. At the far left can be seen another small portion of the John Pingree house. A large purple beech tree now occupies the site. C. L. Claflin purchased this house from John L. and Mary J. Pingree on the 26th of November, 1900. At this point, C. L. owned three adjacent houses, as well as his third of his mother's half interest in the Stone Tavern across the Common. He also purchased lots from Amy Perkins at the foot of Park Street across Ash (see page 63). This was in addition to the other properties inherited from his father, which were scattered around town. To the right of the Pingree house is the large Greek-Revival of Artimus C. Putnam. The barn behind it was replaced with a garage.

The house in the center foreground was the Methodist parsonage (see page 156). The house to the left exists. It was owned by Abram Crooks. Also notice the line of trees along Ash Street and the open space between there and the houses on Hayden Rowe in the foreground. This is all part of land which was owned by Willard Aldrich - the backyard of 6 (now 8) Park Street. On Ash Street, the white house in the center was owned by J. A. Woodbury. On the right edge is the home of Fisher Hemenway. The view beyond Ash Street is also unobstructed. This means the view from the towers on the Claflin house must have been spectacular.

In 1900, the architectural firm of Barker & Nourse, in operation from 1879 to 1904, in Worcester, drew up a conceptual set of plans for further expansion of the Claflin Mansion at 2 Park.[99] It called for a radical transformation into a larger, Queen Anne-style house with large gables on the third floor extending forward toward Park Street. The west tower would have remained. A new 46'x19' kitchen wing extending to the east was proposed. The second floor would have contained two new bedrooms and a large billiard room with fireplace.

Conceptual Plan of 1900 recreated and corrected by the author

Instead, the south wing, which included the gambrel-roofed barn, was expanded. Rooms were built in front of the Hayden Rowe side of the barn and they extended around the south side. Much of the barn was incorporated into the living space of the house. However, barns were not typically built on foundations extending below frost level. This may partially account for the fact that these structures no longer exist.

A plan view of 1904, shown on page 138, corresponds with the conceptual plans of 1900 (minus the proposed additions). A porte-cochere is shown in dotted lines projecting off the southwest corner. It is the same length as the wing shown to the right. According to the 1900 plans, the porte-cochere and the wing were fifteen feet long. The barn was thirty-six feet long. If accurate, the conceptual plans called for moving the barn west so the front would be in line with the west edge of this fifteen-foot wing. The width of the barn (or "stable" as labeled on the 1900 plans) was not

[99] The Barker & Nourse plans used to be in the treasure room at the Hopkinton Public Library, but may have been moved to the Hopkinton Historical Society.

shown. It was approximately 20-24' wide. A one-floor extension on the south side of the barn apparently had replaced an earlier building shown in the 1875 sketch.

The missing wing extended 15' to the south (measured from the face of the building on the left side of this picture) and included a one-story portion to the east. When this part of the house was demolished, it was partially replaced by a two-story porch shown here, which utilized some of the columns from the front porches. This picture was taken prior to restoration. Part of the one-story east portion of the former wing is visible in this view. It is the part with the door. Its roof was an extension of the side porch. That part of the building once extended to the right, along with the two-story wing, where it met the wall of the barn. The door shown above was therefore originally an interior door. This section was modified again after 1904.

Expansion after this point is more difficult to determine. On the following pages are some maps which show some of the changes. Other than the pictures included here, no documentation or photographic evidence seem to exist. It may be that the barn was moved against the wall shown under the porch in the above view. That seems to be what is shown in two of the photographs. A comparison of the following plan views from 1904 and 1910 indicates a change that is no longer discernible by physical or photographic evidence.

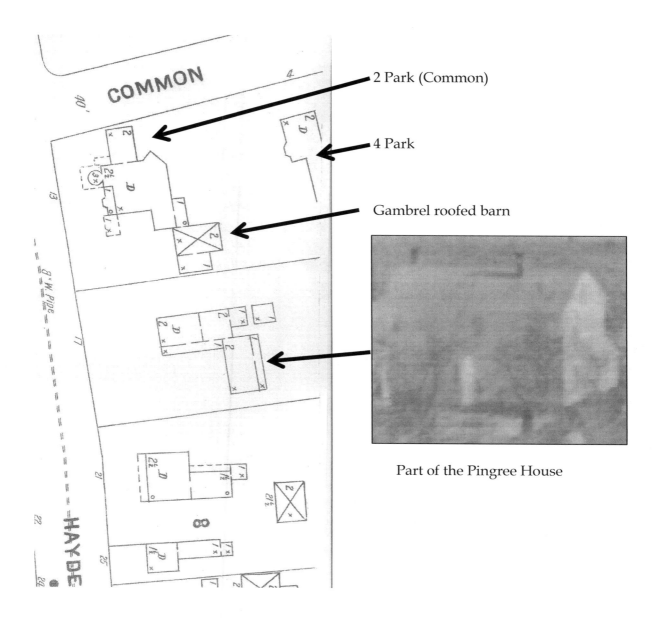

2 Park (Common)

4 Park

Gambrel roofed barn

Part of the Pingree House

This drawing from 1904[100] shows the gambrel-roofed barn (the part with the x) attached to the south wing of the Claflin house at 2 Park. The plan depicts the second floor of the house and only part of the porches below. To the south is the Pingree house, also owned by C. L. Claflin. Below that are the two houses and barn of Artimus C. Putnam. Also, note that Park Street was still named Common in 1904.

---

[100] Insurance map, Sanborn Map Company, New York, March, 1904, courtesy of the Hopkinton Public Library.

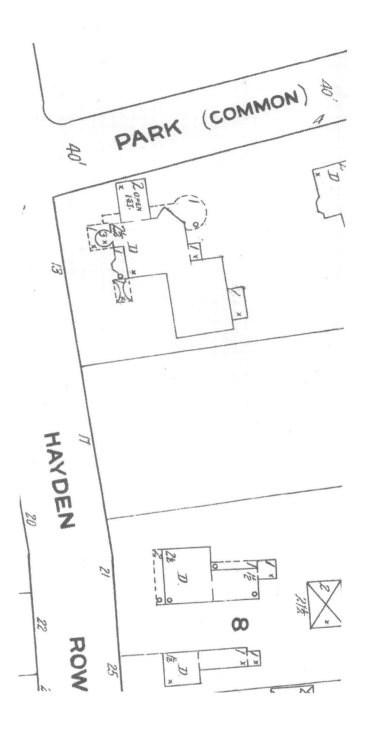

Here, from 1910, additional expansion has taken place.[101] The south wing has been extended across in front of the barn, in addition to other changes. The Pingree house is gone. It burned down and was not replaced.

---

[101] Insurance map, Sanborn Map Company, New York, August, 1910, courtesy of the Hopkinton Public Library

Hayden Row Street, from Church Street, Hopkinton, Mass.

In this photograph we are looking down Hayden Rowe toward the Congregational Church of 1883 on Main Street. On the right is the Putnam house and beyond it you can see the massing of the C. L. Claflin house on Park. This image is not of sufficient quality to enhance the details, but it is possible to pick out a few. Just to the right of the closest, white, electric pole is the end of the porte-cochere. To the right of that is the large south wing of the house. This has to be part of the Claflin house because the front portion of the Pingree house was only one floor (by then) and the roof gable faced the street. The rear portion of the Pingree house (as shown in the small fuzzy photo on page 138) would be too far back behind the Putnam house for us to see it in this view (see page 135 for the relationship of the Putnam and Pingree houses).

On the left edge of the photograph is the house formerly owned by Abram Crooks. Behind it is its similar neighbor. Notice that the main roof of each house has not yet been extended down in a curve to cover the porch, as it does today. However, the attractive bay window of the Abram Crooks house is present. It had different and longer windows, with shutters at that time.

C. L. Claflin & W. C. Pierce at
4 Hayden Rowe

In 1892, C. L. Claflin, along with George McConnell of Boston, purchased property on the west side of Hayden Rowe from Sarah Whitin. This was part of what had been the gardens of the Valentine Mansion. You will recall that she donated land for the library about this time. Another part of the garden, next to Lee Claflin's house, was sold earlier to Erastus Thompson. His son, Edwin D. Thompson had constructed a new house on the lot—a house we will consider later. Edwin sold some land between his new house and the Valentine Mansion to C. L. and George, who combined it with the land from Sarah Whitin to create a lot large enough for another house.

On the 18th of November, 1892, the new building lot was sold to C. L. Claflin's nephew, Winslow Claflin Pierce, who was just 22 years old. Winslow built the beautiful Queen Anne-style house at 4 Hayden Rowe pictured here:

The W. C. Pierce House circa 1892/93

Vintage photograph showing the E. D. Thompson house on the left and the W. C. Pierce house on the right. Both were built facing the Common between the Valentine Mansion and the Lee Claflin Mansion. A corner of the Park House can be seen on the right edge, beyond the brick Valentine Mansion.

As discussed earlier, Winslow Pierce became the president of the Boston Wharf Coal Co. Though also president of the Hopkinton National and Hopkinton Savings banks, he must have decided to move to Brookline (like his brother), in order to be closer to Boston. In any event, he sold his new house at 4 Hayden Rowe to his uncle, C. L. Claflin, on the 14th of January, 1895. If you compare the architectural details of this house with additions made to 2 Park Street pictured on page 125, you should see some similarities. The flared shingling of the third floor of each tower on 2 Park imitate the shingle detailing of 4 Hayden Rowe. The porch stairs added to the porte-cochere on 2 Park imitate the front stairs of 4 Hayden Rowe.

On the 5th of May, 1898, C. L. Claflin sold 4 Hayden Rowe to Webster W. Page. Webster had been a bookkeeper for S. & A. Crooks & Co. He later worked as a cashier at the Hopkinton National Bank. He became the Treasurer of the Hopkinton Savings Bank. Webster was born in July of 1839 and his wife, Henrietta, in England, in May of 1840. The house is a particularly fine example of late Victorian architecture. It remains in superb condition with few exterior changes.

2 Park Street in Later Years

After the sudden and unexpected death of C. L. Claflin during cancer surgery in 1905, the family erected this memorial tomb in Pine Grove Cemetery in Milford. Charles was only 54.

C. L. Claflin's sister, Emma Pierce, continued to live in the main house with two servants to help maintain it. It must have been no easy task to take care of such a large house. She stayed until her death on the 15th of July, 1917.

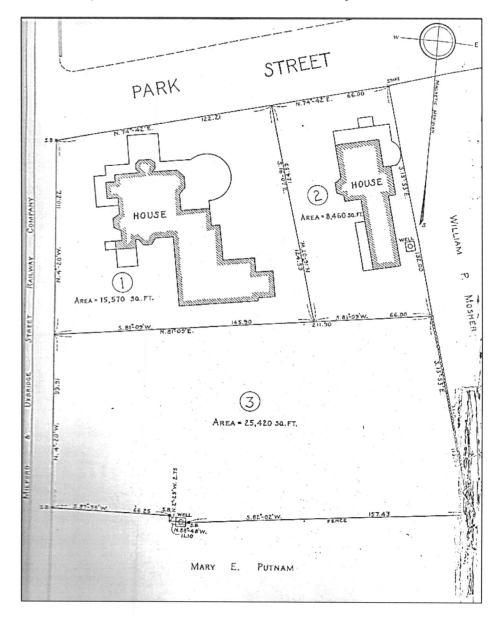

It wasn't until the 25th of November, 1919 that the will of C. L. Claflin was probated. In 1920, when Winslow C. Pierce died, his brother, Edward W. Pierce ended up with sole ownership of 2 and 4 Park. In 1923 he had the property surveyed and the resulting plan is pictured here. It shows the first floor and porches when the houses were at their largest. William Mosher and Mary E. Putnam were the abutters.

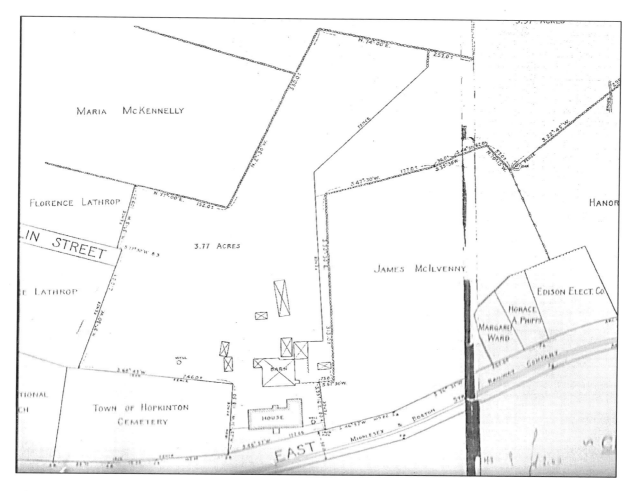

This is a continuation of the plot plan of the Charles L. Claflin Estate shown on page 13. It shows the Stone Tavern property, some parts bounded by stone walls. Several barns and outbuildings were part of the property. The Willard Wadsworth house next door was then owned by James McIlvenny. Florence Lathrop owned the land on either side of Claflin Street, which, by then, stopped at the Claflin property line. Maria McKennelly owned a large lot to the north, which had also been part of the Tavern property before it was divided among the Valentine heirs.

Emma Pierce's son, Edward W. Pierce, married Emma Morse on the 11th of February, 1892. Emma's brother was William Stearns Morse. He received the larger of the two lots which C. L. had bought from Amy Perkins on Ash Street (see page 63). The smaller lot, which had once belonged to A. C. Putnam and later to George Ellard, remained in the estate after the death of Charles, but since the property all ended up with Edward and Emma, it was eventually combined with the larger lot.

Emma and William S. Morse were the children of Charles Henry (1832-1899) and Priscilla Almena (1838-1899) (Stearns) Morse. In a very convoluted way, they were related to Willard Aldrich Morse, who had owned the property previously. Priscilla was the granddaughter of Cornelius and Patience (Aldrich) Gibson who had owned the land at 8 Park Street (see page 59).

In February, 1920, the coal trade weekly "Saward's Journal" reported that the C. W. Claflin Co. had "been incorporated in succession to the business of C. W. Claflin & Co., the well-known Boston wholesale house." Arthur O. Young was president and Edward W. Pierce was treasurer. It mentions that the business was founded in 1848.[102]

Arthur and Mary Young erected a house in Worcester on Institute Road. It is the large Shingle-style house pictured below, somewhat obscured today by vinyl siding. The Pierce brothers both lived in Brookline—the most exclusive suburb of Boston. In Brookline they could take advantage of the horse-drawn, and later electric, trolley system to get to their Boston office.

Worcester home of Arthur Osgood and Mary Valentine (Claflin) Young

---

[102] "Saward's Journal: A Progressive Coal Trade Weekly," Volume 2, Feb. 21, 1920, edited by Frederick William Sayward.

In 1924, Edward sold 2 and 4 Park to George Caim and Carlotta Blair (McDonnough) Minard. They had been married in Bath, Maine on the 17th of June, 1902. George was born in Boston and Carlotta in San Francisco. In the 1920's, George was a teacher in Manhattan, New York. In 1925 they mortgaged the property to a private individual named Porter for $1,000. The following year they mortgaged it again for $8,000 to the Framingham Cooperative Bank. The tax valuation determined on the 1st of April, 1929 shows a value of $7,500 for the main house as compared with its neighbor at 4 Park with a value of $3,000. The Pingree lot is empty, but with land included, the combined property had a valuation of $13,200. 1929 was the year of the stock market crash.

Foreclosure in 1930 led to putting the house at risk for many years while it was owned by the bank. On the Census of 24 April, 1930 there are renters occupying the house, namely: Robert Merrill and family, Sadie P. Coburn, and Sadie B. Polley.

On the 20th of July, 1932, the directors of the Framingham Co-operative Bank voted to sell "The Minard Real Estate" at Park and Hayden Rowe Streets to William H. & Susan E. Arms of Newton. But this deed did not include the house at 4 Park. Three years later, on the 20th of May, 1935, the property was once again seized by the bank for mortgage default.

On the 21st of September, 1938, Hopkinton felt the effects of another destructive hurricane. It caused significant damage in town, including toppling the steeple of the Congregational Church across the Common. With the towers on this house sticking up in the air, damage to the house was also likely. Though of high quality finish work, they were essentially sitting on the roof. One corner of the east tower was supported by the porch below. Access to the third floor rooms of these towers was through unfinished attic space.

The house continued to be rented while it was owned by the bank. The 1940 Census shows that it was occupied by a family of ten by the name of McKenny. They had two servants. They were running a rest home. There were twelve, mainly elderly, lodgers, for a total of twenty-four residents.

In 1943, the Bank found a buyer in Phil H. & Marjorie C. Clow of Hopkinton. By the time they sold the property in 1945, the house had been reduced to its present size. It went through a few more owners, until finally, in 1955, it became the property of the Dockstader family, who have owned it ever since.

The newly restored Walker-Claflin Mansion at 2 Park Street

Lee Claflin at 8 Hayden Rowe

Across Hayden Rowe from 2 Park was another Greek-Revival house. It was constructed just south of the Valentine Mansion on land that had also been part of Samuel Barrett's lot. It was built for Lee Claflin and dates from the same period as the house of Artimus Putnam just up the street. Based upon Lee's sale of the Park Street house in 1853, it is likely that his new house was ready for occupancy in that year. It is not as far down Hayden Rowe as drawn on the map of 1856 (page 103). It was built in the form of a Greek temple, considered the purest of the Greek-Revival forms.

Originally, a carriage house/barn extended the wing on the left. The construction is of the highest quality. The roof is slate. Lee maintained this as his residence for the rest of his life. He chose to stay in Hopkinton, while his son William moved to a large, new house in Newton. Wilbur built a large Italianate further south on Hayden Row. Lee's was a relatively modest house, which belied his considerable fortune. It is sometimes written that William built this house for his father. However, this was the time when Lee was building his Academy and the Methodist Church, so it is more likely that he had his new house constructed at the same time. His son may have encouraged him to move from the more modest house (at the time) across the street.

As seen from the Common

Though his cousin Charles across the street had considerable success in business, Lee would have even greater success. With the aid of his sons and their partners, he established a boot and leather company which, in time, came to be one of the largest and most revered in the industry.

Lee Claflin was the youngest son of Ebenezer Jr. and Sarah (Tilton) Claflin. He was born in Hopkinton on the 19th of November, 1791. His father died when Lee was only five. He was sent to live with a local farmer, where he worked long hours. As a teenager, Lee decided to learn the tanning trade, which was a family tradition. The only tannery of which he knew anything was that of a Mr. Warren of Framingham, which seems to have been one of the best at the time. Before Lee reached the age of twenty, he was foreman of the business.

Not content with his situation, Lee decided to go into business for himself in the North Purchase[103] section of Milford in 1815. In those days, it took a long time to realize a return on investment in the tanning business. One had to have capital to keep going while waiting for profits. Due to his reputation for integrity and good business sense, Lee was able to borrow money from his friends. Then, he fortuitously married Sarah (Sally) Watkins Adams on the 9th of December, 1815.

On their wedding day, Sally's father, Elisha Adams, gave her a packet containing $1,000. A few days later, he gave Lee the same amount. Upon learning that Lee had debts, he gave another $1,000 and a loan for an additional $1,000 (which he

---

[103] The North Purchase derives its name from a purchase of Indian land by the Town of Mendon prior to the existence of Milford.

never asked to be repaid). Now the business had the capital it needed.[104] The next year Lee and Sally built the house currently numbered 179 Purchase Street in Milford. It is pictured below.

1815/1816 was a particularly difficult time to start a business, or build a house for that matter. There was a large volcanic eruption in Indonesia in 1815. It dramatically affected the climate, especially in New England and Europe. There were wide swings in temperature. Crops failed and grain prices shot up. This was also the year of the "Great Gale" mentioned earlier. In spite of these conditions, Lee and Sally were successful and soon started a family.

Sally Watkins Adams was born on the 25th of April, 1792 in Hopkinton, the sixth child of Elisha and Sarah (Watkins) Adams. Agriculture had been the dominant business in Hopkinton, until the establishment of the boot and shoe factories. The Adams family was very successful and prosperous. Sally's older sister, Eda (1788-1839), married James Rix Woolson on the 4th of May, 1826, in Hopkinton. Their son James Adams Woolson was born on the 22nd of December, 1828. He would continue a financial role in the Claflin enterprise, eventually becoming a banker and the third senior partner of Wm. Claflin, Coburn & Co, the successor to Lee Claflin & Co.

Lee and Sally had three children, all boys and born in Milford: William, 6th of March, 1818; Charles Lee, 1st of September, 1829; and Wilbur Fisk, 11th of March, 1831. Charles died in 1830, leaving just two sons, both of whom became partners with their father.

After the birth of their first child, Lee decided to take the risk of making boots by hand, utilizing his leather. Gradually he began to employ others to make them. In

---

[104] The Hopkinton Light, Vol. 2, No. 3, December, 1895.

1819/20 he formed a partnership with a Mr. Bailey. Lee would work all day and then head off to Boston or Providence in the evening with a load of boots packed in barrels and boxes. The next day he would sell to individuals in the street, and eventually to merchants. He was a pioneer in growing the boot and shoe business.

Once he was well established, Lee took an even greater risk by going to St. Louis. His product had to be carted to Boston, put on a ship to New Orleans, and then transferred to a riverboat for the trip north to St. Louis. Banks were not yet established in St. Louis, so boots were exchanged for raw hides, salt pork, hams, and lard. These were then transported back East and sold for profit.

Unfortunately, Sally died in 1834. Lee Claflin then married Polly Jones Eames on the 8th of March, 1836 in Milford. She was the daughter of Phineas and Izzanna (Jones) Eames.[105] Izzanna's father was Nathaniel Alden Jones, who was related to Col. Joseph Valentine's wife and a descendent of John Alden of the Mayflower. Her mother was Lois Claflin, who was a first cousin of Lee's father. The relationships do get complex.

Lee moved his business to Hopkinton in 1839 and John Goldsmith purchased the Milford operation.[106] The first factory in Hopkinton was managed by Lovett Bowker. It was located in the village of Hayden Row and became known as Bowker & Phipps.

Through the 1840's, Lee Claflin & Co (which included Bowker & Phipps), grew rapidly. It took hard work and considerable risk to build the business. James A. Woolson and Wilbur F. Claflin were brought into the business as partners. Offices were at 158 Congress Street, Boston. Meanwhile, Lee's eldest son William went to St. Louis to continue developing operations there. S. D. Davenport was also working in St. Louis at that time (but not for Claflin). By 1854, Lee Claflin & Co. had offices at 17 and 19 Hide and Leather Street in Boston.

On the next page is a detail map of Hayden Row from 1856. In addition to Bowker & Phipps, we see the boot shops of F. B. Mansfield and the Loring family. Also, Lowell Claflin had gone into business with Stephen Barnard.

---

[105] The original, very large, Eames grant was next to that of both Thomas Valentine and Savil Simpson, in what is now Ashland.

[106] Ernest A. Bragg, The Origin and Growth of the Boot and Shoe Industry in Holliston and Milford, Massachusetts, 1793-1850, (Boston, 1850), page 19.

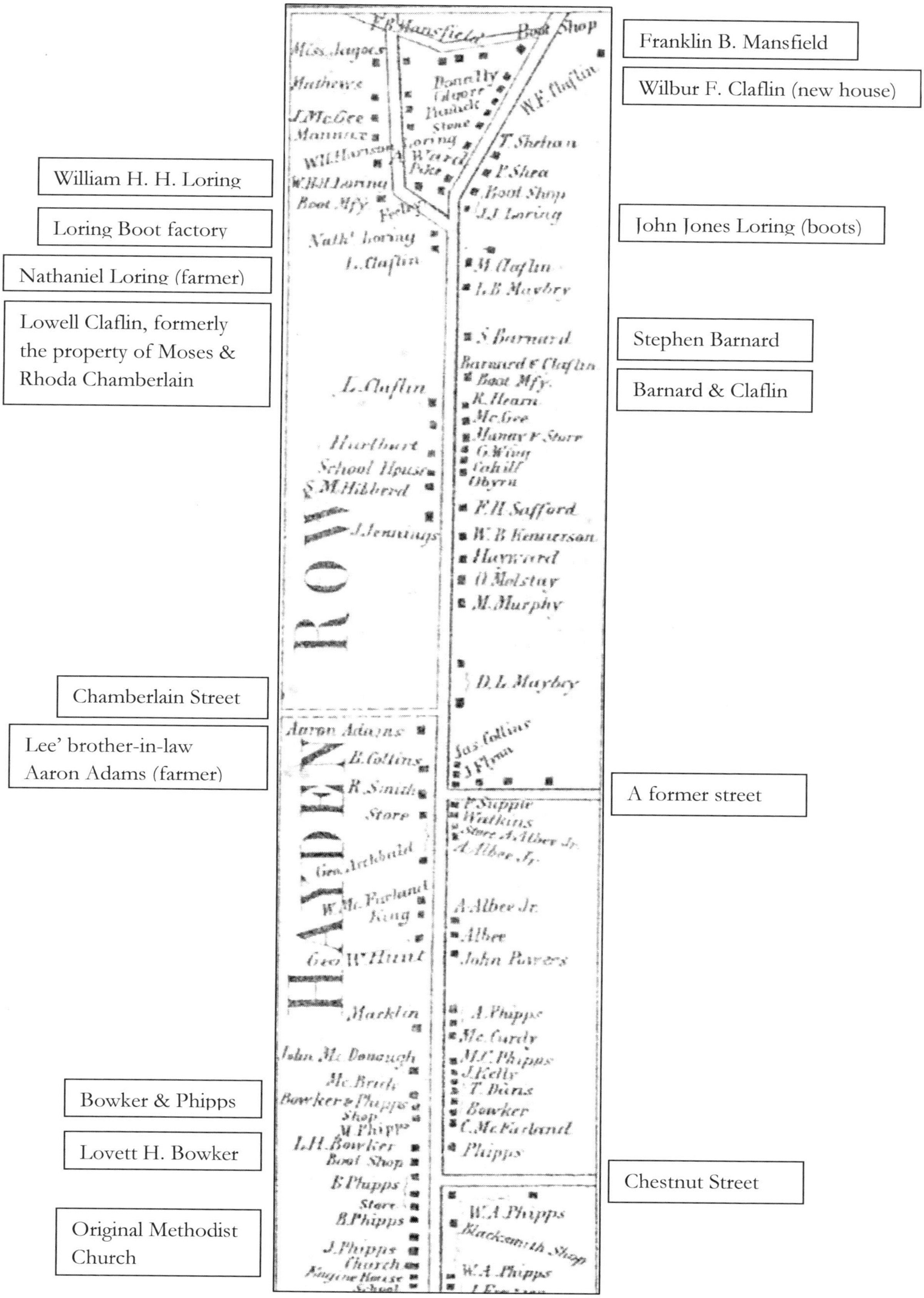

Franklin B. Mansfield
Wilbur F. Claflin (new house)
William H. H. Loring
Loring Boot factory
John Jones Loring (boots)
Nathaniel Loring (farmer)
Lowell Claflin, formerly the property of Moses & Rhoda Chamberlain
Stephen Barnard
Barnard & Claflin
Chamberlain Street
Lee' brother-in-law Aaron Adams (farmer)
A former street
Bowker & Phipps
Lovett H. Bowker
Chestnut Street
Original Methodist Church
F.B. Mansfield
Boot Shop
W.F. Claflin
T. Shehan
P. Shea
Boot Shop
J.J. Loring
Nath' Loring
L. Claflin
M. Claflin
L.B. Maybry
S. Barnard
Barnard & Claflin
Boot Mfy.
R. Hearn
McGee
G. Wing
Cahill
L. Claflin
Hurlburt
School House
S.M. Hibberd
J. Jennings
F.H. Safford
W.B. Kennerson
Hayward
M. Murphy
D.L. Maybry
ROW
Aaron Adams
B. Collins
R. Smith
Store
Geo. Archbald
W. McFarland
King
Geo W. Hunt
HAYDEN
Marklin
John McDonough
McBride
Bowker & Phipps Shop
M. Phipps
L.H. Bowker
Boot Shop
B. Phipps
Store
B. Phipps
J. Phipps
Church
Engine House
School
P. Supple
Watkins
A. Albee Jr.
A. Albee Jr.
A. Albee Jr.
Albee
John Powers
A. Phipps
McCurdy
M.C. Phipps
J. Kelly
T. Burns
Bowker
C. McFarland
Phipps
W.A. Phipps
Blacksmith Shop
W.A. Phipps

Lee was very interested in encouraging education. He soon established an Academy on Hayden Rowe, on property he had purchased a little south of his home. We will pause here to look at a map from 1875. Even though it is dated after his death, it indicates the land he owned. The Valentine property is now the "National Bank." If you follow the line south along Hayden Row, as indicated, you can see his original lot. Dr. Pratt had owned all the adjacent lots behind Claflin's house. This probably constitutes the extent of the original, eastern property line of the 16-acre lot of Morris, Price, and then Valentine.

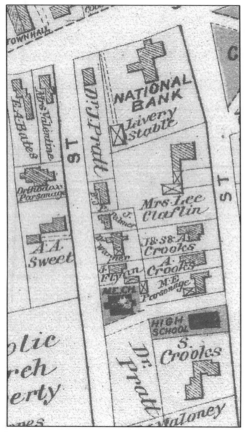

Property from here

To here

Main Street is at the top, with Church on the left and Hayden Rowe on the right. Note that the properties facing Hayden Rowe were then owned by Claflin or Crooks, both families of Scottish descent and business associates. There is a lane running between the "High School" and the parsonage and past the church to Church Street. In 1858, Lee and Polly deeded the church property to the trustees of the church. In the deed is a description of the bounds which includes "one hundred and eighty feet along the Academy lot." This is because the High School of 1875 was Lee's Academy in 1858. Even before 1858 it was alternatively known as the High School. Shares were sold to invest in the "High School." An image of the first stock certificate is shown next.

This certificate was issued in 1841, appropriately to Dr. Thomas Bucklin who had been one of the Trustees of the School Fund since its formation in 1820. He invested $550.00 for 22 shares. Lee Claflin was treasurer and Samuel Davenport witnessed the document as clerk. Samuel B. Walcott, John C. Webster, and Dr. Bucklin were appointed by the Massachusetts legislature as members of a corporation to be called "Hopkinton High School." The school was the Academy, built prior to 1856 on land owned by Lee Claflin. The three members of the High School Corporation were made up of a physician (Dr. Bucklin), a lawyer (Samuel Walcott, see page 226), and a minister, John C. Webster.

John (or Jessie) Webster was the pastor of the Congregational Church from 1838 to 1864. He was at the Andover Theological Seminary, where he graduated in 1832. There he met George Thompson, MP, visiting from England. He was considered by the seminary to be an agitator for his anti-slavery views. Webster was rebuked by his professors for walking arm-in-arm with A. A. Phelps. Phelps was a co-worker with Thompson at the time. He was also in Hopkinton from 1830 to 1832 (see page 54). J. C. Webster became the president of the American Church Anti-Slavery Society. He lived on Hayden Rowe and eventually moved to Wheaton, Illinois.[107]

---

[107] Rufus Blanchard, <u>Du Page County, Illinois</u>, (Chicago: O. L. Baskin & Co, Historical Publishers, 1882).

The Claflin family were Methodists, but they also held ardent, anti-slavery views. Lee had spent time in New Orleans and St. Louis, where he would have seen the slave trade in person. As we will see, William Claflin was also disgusted by what he saw after he moved to St. Louis.

The Academy

Notice that the Academy was very similar in style to the Lee Claflin Mansion to the north. It dates from about the same time. The Academy was a noted school of learning. Students came from Boston and other, more distant, locations. A portion of the Methodist parsonage can be seen to the right and more fully in photos taken at a later date and shown next.

Here we have the old Academy, remodeled as the "Hopkinton High School." This photograph was taken on February 24th of 1891. It must have been cold to stand still for the photographer because there is a stiff wind blowing from the south, as evidenced by the flag flying from the top of the school. The school is standing in the middle of what is now Church Place. St. John's Catholic Church is in the background and the Methodist is hidden from view. Its parsonage is clearly seen to the right. The house on the left edge still exists at the corner of Hayden Rowe and Church Place. Incidentally, that house was built on a lot sold by Lee Claflin to Nathan Coburn on the 2nd of September, 1845. Its northern boundary is described as "by land of Hopkinton High School ten rods and twenty four links" (180'). It was in 1851 that the Academy officially became a *free* high school, but it continued to be known as "The Academy" for years.

M. E. Parsonage, Hayden Rowe Street.

Hopkinton High School

Here is how the High School looked shortly before it was moved. The photo was probably taken after 1900. Notice that several panes of glass are broken. In 1895, a new and much larger High School was built on the site of Dr. Bucklin's mansion on Main Street. It was designed by Barker & Nourse of Worcester and constructed in 1894/1895. Baker & Nourse also designed a proposed expansion of 2 Park Street (page 136). The school of 1895 can be seen behind the Davenport house on page 201.

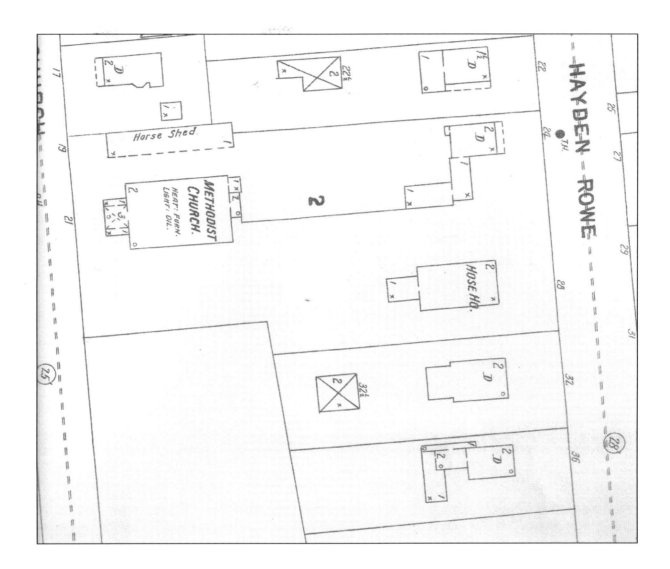

This map is from 1904.[108] The parsonage is facing Hayden Rowe behind the Methodist Church. Compare the previous pictures to the plan view. By 1904, the old school was being used as a "Hose House," presumably for the fire department. A few years later it was moved back toward Church Street and the front was then the back of the building.

[108] Insurance map, Sanborn Map Company, New York, March, 1904, courtesy of the Hopkinton Public Library.

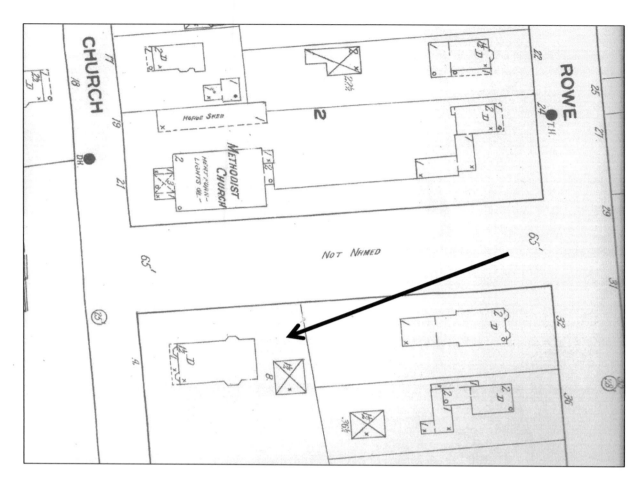

On this map of 1910,[109] the school has been moved to Church Street on what had been a vacant lot and a new, 65' wide street, not yet named, had been created where it stood. This road became Church Place. The school was remodeled once again, this time into an apartment building. Later, it became a parish hall for the Catholic Church.

It is interesting that when Lee deeded the property to the trustees of the Methodist Church (of which he was one), he made four stipulations. He reserved all the odd-numbered pews for himself. The even-numbered pews and the parsonage were to be rented by the trustees for the support of the minister. The property was to remain debt free or it would revert to him. Finally, Lee reserved for himself "the five horse sheds now erected on said premises." The horse sheds are located on the map above. The house shown in the lower right of the map also still exists. The lot was sold by J. C. Webster to N. P. Coburn in 1845. Coburn sold both this lot and the one above it, purchased from Lee Claflin in 1843, to Sam Crooks in 1855.

[109] Insurance map, Sanborn Map Company, New York, August, 1910, courtesy of the Hopkinton Public Library.

The Methodist Episcopal Church of 1855 on the left and as modified on the right

This building provides for an interesting study in architectural modifications. It is one of the few buildings with enough pictures to see a progression. It is also the building from which some early photographs were taken, as we have already seen. The owners were willing to make significant changes. The image to the left shows how it looked when first constructed. Each corner of the building and of the steeple is crenellated, as is the front gable. The first floor on this side is set in and is not sheathed in clapboards like the rest of the building. In the view to the right, the steeple has been moved forward and widened at the base. This was probably done during the first renovation, which reportedly cost $1,600. In the next photo, architectural detailing has been simplified and a contrasting paint scheme adopted (c. 1900). And finally from 1906, the sides have been modified and clapboards cover the lower section.

Notice the horse sheds in the fourth view. The site of the church is now the backyard of a newer house at 18 Hayden Rowe. The lot is still the same as shown on page 160 from 1910, including an 8' jog on one side, which originally accommodated the horse sheds.

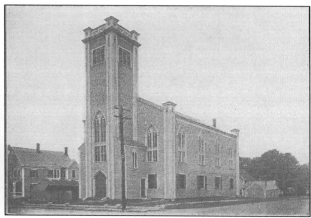

Gas light on the left -- Electric pole on the right, but horse shed remained

The Methodist Church was torn down after the congregation dissolved in May of 1918. The church property was sold by the trustees to William D. Mosher on the 18th of July, 1922. The parsonage was replaced by a house which closely resembles in scale its older, northerly two neighbors. The new house was owned by the Mosher/Moshier family.

18 Hayden Rowe, built c. 1925

Hon. Lee Claflin c. 1868

This is not the typical image of a "titan of industry." He didn't make a show of his wealth, but quietly gave away much of it throughout his lifetime by generous gifts to poor individuals, by supporting causes in which he believed, and by donations to large institutions.

Lee was president of the Hopkinton Bank and the Milford Bank. He was an original stockholder of the Exchange Bank, chartered April 12, 1847. He was the founder of the Hide & Leather Bank in Boston and its president from 1857 to 1860. With Lovett Bowker and Edwin Thayer, he incorporated the Hopkinton Savings Bank in 1867. He was one of the three founders of Boston University and the founder of Claflin University, Orangeburg, South Carolina. Claflin University was established as the first African-American college. Lee was also a trustee of Lawrence University, Appleton, Wisconsin and a trustee and major benefactor of Wesleyan University, Middletown, Connecticut. Its first president was Willbur Fisk, for whom Lee named his son.

Lee died on the 23rd of February, 1871, at the home of his son William, in Boston, as the result of an accident. He was struck while walking. His grave monument is in the Pine Grove Cemetery in Milford.

After the death of Lee, Polly Claflin continued to live in the house on Hayden Rowe. By 1889, her son, William Claflin was the owner. By 1906, it was occupied by Dr. Edgar Andrew Briggs, a dentist (d. 4 Jun. 1927). His office was at 2 Hayden Rowe. While William had ownership, he tore down the carriage house and built a duplex house next door to the family home. The duplex house is pictured next. It was built between 1875 and 1889. The south end of the Lee Claflin Mansion can be seen to the right.

10-12 Hayden Rowe

Wilbur Fisk Claflin

Wilbur Fisk Claflin suffered from diabetes and retired January 1, 1880 to his beautiful residence in Hopkinton, where he lived until his death at the age of 54 in 1885. The house (1854) is located at 65 Hayden Rowe opposite the end of Pleasant.

This side of the house faces away from Hayden Rowe. The left portion of the house, which contained servant's quarters, was demolished, as well as the carriage house, a separate building off view to the right. Originally, this property extended from Hayden Rowe to Ash and contained more than thirty acres. The grounds are now considerably reduced, but the house retains its setting. From the belvedere on the top of this house one can see Boston and much of the coastline of Massachusetts.

"Did you know that the Bunker Hill Monument, dome of the State House, Minot's Ledge Light, Miles Standish Monument and sunrise on the ocean can all be seen from Hopkinton?" – The Hopkinton Light, Vol. 1, No. 1, 15 October, 1894.

Wilbur married Mary A. Streeter on the 10th of October, 1853. She was born in Vernon, Vermont in 1832. Wilbur and Mary had three children. Clarence Augustus, born 16 October, 1854, in Cambridge; Ernest Lee, born 12 June, 1859, in Hopkinton; and Adelbert Eugene, born 24 January, 1866, in Hopkinton. After Wilbur's death, Mary moved to Newton, where she lived until her death in 1898.

Boston and the Blue Hills from Hayden Rowe about 1945 before the forest grew back

William Claflin

It was the keen desire of his mother that William Claflin have a college education. After attending Milford Academy, he entered Brown University in 1833. He was negatively impacted by the death of his mother the following year. His health suffered and, on the advice of the family doctor, he moved to St. Louis, where he could take over for his father. William took advantage of the expanding West and quickly became very prosperous. At first, he engaged in business with Seth P. Carpenter of Milford. He married Nancy Harding in Louisville, Kentucky in 1840. In that year, he set up a wholesale boot and leather business with John How (1813-1885), a prominent man in St. Louis and onetime Mayor. The firm was named How and Claflin. In 1845, Robert Cook of Philadelphia joined the firm under the name of How, Claflin & Cook, in business until 1851. In that year, Mr. How took the hide and leather business and William Claflin went into partnership with John A. Allen under the name of Claflin, Allen & Co. This firm lasted until 1884, when Mr. Allen died. It was then reorganized into the Claflin-Allen Shoe Co. which continued until 1888. Meanwhile, the hide and leather business continued under John How until his retirement, when management was transferred to Samuel Hoyt Pingry (1810-1886). When Mr. Pingry died in Boston, at the age of 75, he had been with the house of William Claflin & Co. and its successors for nearly fifty years.[110]

While in St. Louis, William became familiar with the evils of slavery. This issue disturbed him greatly. When he had become well established, he decided to take action. He went to a slave auction and purchased a husband, wife, and child, and promptly set them free—much to the outrage of the local populace. They began to boycott his business. William later became a Free Soil Party candidate from Hopkinton. Party members opposed allowing slavery in the western territories.

William and Nancy had one child, Emma C. Harding Claflin, born on the 25th of December, 1841.[111] Nancy Claflin died in January of 1842, probably from complications of childbirth.

By 1845, William was one of the wealthiest citizens of St. Louis and he decided to return to Hopkinton where he had found a new bride. William and Mary B. Davenport were married on the 12th of February, 1845. She was the daughter of S. D.

---

[110] See page 129 for information regarding John L. Pingry and his connection to Samuel.
[111] Emma married Charles Warren Ellis in Newton on the 5th of November, 1862.

Davenport. William acquired the Valentine Mansion upon the death of Col. Joseph in March. He soon began building up manufacturing capacity in Hopkinton.

The following detail of a map from 1856 shows the location of the Claflin-Coburn buildings. By then, N. P. Coburn owned the Valentine Mansion.

Cedar and Walcott Streets are north of Main in this view. Grove, Church, Hayden Rowe, and Ash are south.

Two buildings on the west side of Grove are labeled "W. Claflin." One of these is the original meetinghouse which was moved from the Common to the Valentine Estate for use as a barn.[112] About 1845, William Claflin began using it for his factory. Business prospered and, opposite the end of Church Street, is his factory of 1850—the "Coburn & Claflin Boot Shop." Nathan P. Coburn became a partner in 1854 and his

---

[112] Edgar Homer Grout, "Boyhood Days in Hopkinton, Massachusetts in the 1870's," 1950.

168

name is listed first, at least on this map. In 1853, the Crooks brothers moved into the old building on Grove Street. It was still owned by William Claflin, so his name appears on the map.

How do we know that this is the correct location on Grove for the old meetinghouse building? There is more evidence than the previous map of 1856. In the 1940's, Edgar H. Grout looked into the matter.[113] Edgar lived on Grove Street in the house marked "B. W. Foss" on the previous map.[114] He says that Gardner Woods built a house on the old foundation of the factory on Grove Street, just north of the Charles Parmenter house. It was an unusually deep foundation. In 1900, Gardner P. Woods lived at what was then numbered 14 Grove. By comparing maps of 1856, 1875, 1899 and c. 1907, one can see that one of the two blocks labeled "W. Claflin" on the previous page is on the same lot labeled "G. P. Wood" in 1907. The house and its neighbor were torn down when Colella's Supermarket expanded their building and parking lot.

In this hazy detail (it is a very early photo!), we see the Central Coffee House hotel on the right. Also included in this view are some early factory buildings of William Claflin and Nathan Coburn. They are the dark, three-story buildings on the far left. The white building in the foreground is the Woodard Store. Willard Woodard was also an early boot manufacturer. His wife was a cousin of Nathan Coburn next door. The building which housed the store was owned by Dr. Jefferson Pratt. His daughter donated the land to be used for the new library. Willard and Hannah Woodard moved west to Ohio to continue manufacturing. They settled in Cleveland.

---

[113] Ibid. The Grout family lived at 19 Grove Street from 1868 to 1951.
[114] On the map of 1875, H. Grout is living in the house marked B. W. Foss in 1856. In 1875, the King and D. Cutler families were still living in same houses as in 1856, so it is easy to see which house became Grout's.

As business prospered, Claflin & Coburn continued to expand. In the next photograph we see a new building on the same site and many of the workers they employed.

The 1850 boot factory of Claflin, Coburn & Co.

On the 29th of March, 1876, fire was discovered in a storehouse behind this building. It spread to the factory and the livery stable behind the Central Coffee House (now called Highland House). It is surprising that the Town Hall, pictured on the left edge above and noted below, did not burn as well. That would come later!

J. & B. Mahon Mrs. Barber   Town Hall   Claflin-Coburn   Livery Stable

The previous view is from the Methodist Church. The Town Hall and factory are centered in this view. The intersection is of Church and Main. The Highland House is just out of view to the right. We can see the livery stable. The white building with the porch is not labeled on the following map of the same time period (c. 1875). It is not the newer building with A. A. Sweet's store, pictured on page 84. The Hopkinton National Bank was located about there, before it moved into the Valentine Mansion. It also may have been a store. After the fire, the post office was located there.

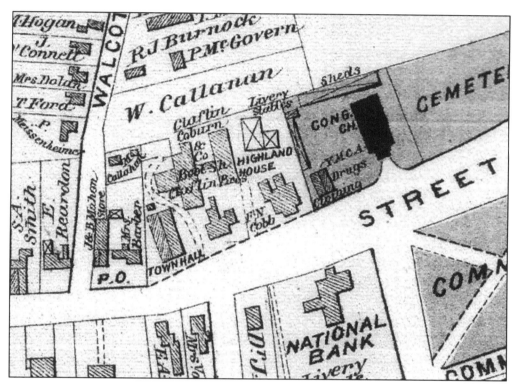

This 1875 map detail shows how close the buildings were. On the corner of Walcott is the store of J. & B. Mahon, then a house labeled "Mrs. Barber." The next building is the first Town Hall, followed by the white building from the previous photo and the three buildings pictured on page 81, including the 1830 Congregational Church.

Five hundred workers were temporarily out of a job when the boot shop burned. But the company quickly established operations in the Mansfield factory on the corner of Pleasant and Hayden Rowe and also in the box mill on Grove.[115] They had the means to rebuild and an even larger factory was constructed on Main Street behind the Town Hall in May of 1876. We will take a look at that factory shortly.

---

[115] The boots were shipped in wooden boxes. With such a high demand, it was another business opportunity.

William and Mary Claflin had five children:

Charles Lee (16 Nov. 1847 Hopkinton – 2 Jan. 1848)
Agnes Elizabeth (31 Jul. 1849 Hopkinton – 30 Jan. 1869 Rome, Italy)
Arthur Bucklin (10 Aug. 1852 Hopkinton – June 1900)
William Davenport (16 Nov. 1858 – 23 Oct. 1863 Newtonville)
Adams Davenport (7 Feb. 1862 – 1933 Newtonville)

In 1855, William and Mary moved to their new home in Newton. The mansion was well suited for entertaining. Here, William and his wife hosted the leading literary and political figures of their day, including Oliver Wendell Holmes, Harriet Beecher Stowe and Henry Ward Beecher, John Greenleaf Whittier, Horace Greeley, James Freeman Clarke, and President & Mrs. Rutherford B. Hayes. Some of their associates, like the Beecher's and Whittier, held ardent anti-slavery views. Unlike those families in Massachusetts who derived their income from the textile industry, which was dependent on southern cotton, the Claflin family had no such conflict. They also came from Hopkinton, where both the Methodists and Congregationalists had long been involved in supporting the anti-slavery movement. William was also a close friend of Henry Wilson of Natick, a fellow shoe manufacturer and abolitionist, who served as Vice-President during the second term of Ulysses S. Grant.

William and Mary Claflin continued to own much property in Hopkinton. They added a duplex dwelling next to the family home on Hayden Rowe, after demolishing the attached carriage house/barn. But their new location in Newton brought them closer to the social scene in Boston and their real-estate interests west of the city. They also maintained a residence in Boston.

Mrs. Claflin was a trustee of Wellesley College from its foundation and of Boston University from 1878 to 1896. In 1876, she founded a society for the aid of young college women. She was the author of several books. Mary died in Whitinsville, Northbridge, in 1896.

William served in the Massachusetts House of Representatives from 1849 to 1852. He was elected to the Massachusetts Senate in 1859 and became its president in 1861. He was Lieut. Governor from 1866 to 1869 and Governor of Massachusetts from 1870 to 1872. He was a member of Congress from 1877 to 1881. He was president of the New England Historic Genealogical Society and of the Massachusetts Club. William lived in Newton until his death on the 5th of January, 1905. His tomb is in the Newton Cemetery and is similar to three other Claflin tombs in Milford.

Governor William Claflin

Governor William Claflin   *"The Old Elms" in Newtonville*

The Old Elms was a country estate once known as Brooklawn. This Italianate house of 1855 was located in the middle of a large park. It replaced an earlier house of General William Hull, the Governor of the Michigan Territory. His ancient house was moved in 1846 to a new location. The estate was first owned by Thomas Mayhew, who was granted the entire island of Martha's Vineyard and became its Governor. The estate had also been owned by Royal Governor Simon Bradstreet. Today it is the site of the Newton North High School complex.

Governor Claflin and an Elm planted by Joseph Fuller (1652-1740) which was still standing in 1900, thus "The Old Elms"

In the middle of a large park with many elm trees

The park-like estate replaced by Newton North High School fields
The house was moved and is visible – the largest white one in the distance

Same doorway in 2013

The Claflin heirs moved the house to Elm Road when the estate was first developed for schools, as indicated on the following map. The house now contains apartments. Since this photograph was taken, it has lost some of its porch detail and a fire escape mars the principal façade—but it is fortunate to have survived at all.

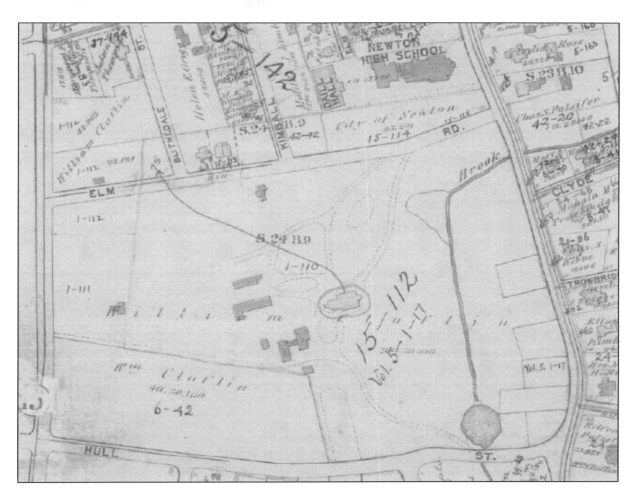

1895 Newton Atlas[116]

The house was in the center of the estate with many out-buildings which included a stable. William Claflin owned a large lot across the street to the left which even had a factory building. He owned many other parcels around Newton. Several of these were developed for housing.

The success of the company was not all due to the entrepreneurial skills of the Claflin family. Other partners played a significant role. N. P. Coburn oversaw production at the various factories and J. A. Woolson was responsible for much of the financing. The Crooks brothers directly managed one of the largest factories in Hopkinton.

---

[116] Historic Maps of Newton, Newton City Atlases, 1895. Plate 16, courtesy of the City of Newton, Massachusetts, www.newtonma.gov/gov/it/gis/historic_maps.asp.

Nathan Parker Coburn

N. P. Coburn was born in Sugar Hill, Gunthwaite, (Lisbon), New Hampshire on the 6th of February, 1817. He came to Hopkinton in about 1836 at the age of 19. He began a modest boot manufacturing business, married Lucinda Morey in 1838, and had one daughter, Emma Lucinda, about 1845. When Lee Claflin moved his business from Milford to Hopkinton, Mr. Coburn came into association with his firm (about 1843). In 1854, his name was added to the firm, to be known as Claflin, Coburn & Co. Nathan was a selectman in Hopkinton throughout the Civil War. He owned 2 Hayden Rowe at the time. On the 13th of February, 1856, Mrs. Coburn died. About 1857, Nathan married Elenor (Wheeler) Whitman, widow of Joseph Whitman. Recall that she sold 2 Park Street in March of 1857. In 1864, they moved to a new home in Newton. They also resided at 63 Mount Vernon Street, Beacon Hill, Boston.

Mrs. Elenor W. W. Coburn died in Newton on the 6th of December, 1877. On the 20th of December, 1878, Nathan married Eleanor J. Haynes (Merrill) Silsby, widow of Ithiel Homer Silsby. Mr. Silsby had leased and operated the United States Hotel and later the large Winthrop House hotel at the Boston Common, corner of Tremont and Boylston, which was consumed in a spectacular fire in 1864. He died in 1874. Mrs. Coburn died on the 12th of December, 1890.

Nathan remained a senior partner when the Boston firm of Wm. Claflin, Coburn & Co. was established in 1877 and until the last day of December, 1891, when the firm was dissolved and he retired at the age of 74. Nathan married once again. His new wife was only 49 when they married in Springfield on the 18th of May, 1892. Mrs. Coburn was born Sarah Frances (Fanny) Carpenter in Chicopee Falls.

Nathan was the eldest of eleven children. Three brothers were Alonzo (1821-1902), Benjamin Franklin (1827-1891) and Daniel J. (1835-1902). All three were boot manufacturers in Hopkinton.

Nathan Parker Coburn

N. P. Coburn

His mansion in Newton

In this grainy photo we can just make out the manicured grounds, greenhouse and carriage house of his Newton estate. It was located in Kenrick Park, with an additional entrance on Waverly Street. His factory in Framingham was also located on a street named "Waverly."

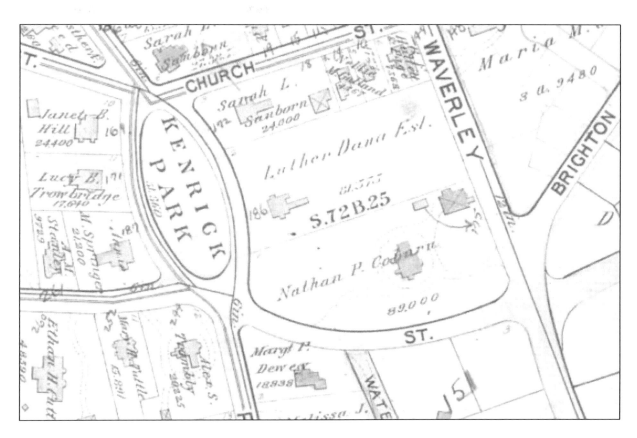

Nathan P. Coburn Estate in Newton[117]

After the property was sold to Loren and Helen Towle in 1910, the house was demolished and replaced by a very large brick mansion. It proved too big to survive the effects of the Depression and the introduction of the income tax. The Coburn house might have survived, since it was more in scale with its neighbors. The outbuildings and greenhouse were retained for the new house. One of the outbuildings was later turned into a house and it is the only one standing today. The property has been divided into smaller housing lots.

[117] Ibid. Plate 2.

Nathan donated $50,000 for the establishment of the N. P. Coburn Library at Colorado College in Colorado Springs, Colorado. The president of the college was a friend. Nathan also contributed to the Hopkinton Library.

N. P. Coburn Library at Colorado College, 1894-1963
Andrews, Jacques & Rantoul of Boston, Architects

Nathan Coburn died on the 25th of August, 1894. Notice of the probate of his will was printed in the Newton Graphic in the issue of September 7. It said: "It is estimated that Mr. Coburn left a fortune of nearly half a million dollars. Mr. Coburn provided liberally for his wife and relatives, and the list of private bequests covers many pages of foolscap." He established several charities for the poor, for orphan girls, and for the education of young men for the ministry. He donated $15,000 to the Newton Cottage Hospital (now Newton-Wellesley Hospital) for the establishment of the Coburn wing. Colorado College received an additional $10,000 for library books. James A. Woolson was one of the executors of his estate.

N. P. Coburn was buried at Mt. Auburn Cemetery in Cambridge. His tomb is paired with that of his third wife's husband, I. H. Silsby.

I. H. Silsby & N. P. Coburn

James Adams Woolson

James A. Woolson was the grandson of Nathan Woolson, a prosperous farmer in Hopkinton. One hundred elm trees from the farm were chosen for Boston Common. In 1846, James was given the position of boy clerk in the store of Lee Claflin. He became a partner in 1857. When he died in 1904, he was still a stockholder in the F. Brigham & Gregory Company, the direct descendent of the original Lee Claflin & Co. In addition to his position as one of the senior partners of Wm. Claflin, Coburn & Co., Mr. Woolson was a director of many banks, including the Shoe & Leather Bank, and the First National Bank of Cambridge. He was vice-president of the Boston Five Cents Savings Bank. He was a relatively modest man who did not make a show of his philanthropy. Nevertheless, his will made provision for $625,000 to benefit Boston University—this at a time when the entire endowment was just over $2,000,000.

James Adams Woolson

His mansion in Cambridge (existing)

The Woolson monument, Mt. Auburn, Cambridge

The Crooks Brothers

They were sons of Samuel (1792-1873) and Emeline (Stearns) (1795-1864) Crooks. Do you remember Cornelius and Mary (Aldrich) Gibson from 8 Park Street? Their eldest daughter, Mariah, was Emeline's sister-in-law (Mariah Gibson was married to Emeline's brother, Alanson Stearns).

Samuel and Emeline Crooks lived in the village of Woodville in Hopkinton where they had three sons:

> John 29 May 1819 – 1 Jan. 1905 m. Emily M. Parker
> Samuel 17 Dec. 1821 – 7 Feb. 1893 m. Sarah Bucklin Guy
> Abram 29 Mar. 1826 – 19 Aug. 1892 m. Ann Maria Guy

Samuel's grandfather John was born in Hopkinton about the year 1726. John's father, also named Samuel, was one of the early leaseholders.

John of 1819, though the eldest son, seems to have been content to work in the boot shop. He was still working in 1900, at the age of 81. In that year, he listed his occupation as that of "shoe operative, cutter." Perhaps he lived longer than his brothers because he did not have the added stress of running the business. After his first wife Emily died in 1878, John married again. His new bride was Sarah L. Matthews (1840-1913), daughter of Orlando and Carrie from New York. She was 43 and he was 61 at the time of their marriage. The wedding date was the 23rd of June, 1880.

If you take a look at the map of 1856 on page 168, you will notice N. P. Coburn on the corner of Hayden Rowe and Main. Below Coburn are L. Claflin, then Mrs. (Betsey) Guy, then A. Crooks, then the Methodist Church and the High School, and then S. Crooks. According to a map of 1875, Mrs. Guy's house was owned by the three Crooks brothers and is labeled "J & S & A Crooks." Next door, the house is still labeled A. Crooks. These last two houses are pictured on the next pages. Another of Mrs. Guy's daughters lived across the street (see page 97).

14 Hayden Rowe

"Mrs. Guy" in 1856 and "J. & S. & A. Crooks" in 1875
(John, Samuel, & Abram Crooks)

Samuel Crooks purchased this house from the Guy estate in 1859. Next door, Abram Crooks had a very similar house, but it is turned ninety degrees to the street. Betsey Guy (widow) purchased this lot in 1846 for only $200.00, so before the house was built.

16 Hayden Rowe

The dormers and curved porch roof on these houses are early 20th century modifications. Both houses on this page were built about the same time.

Samuel Crooks

Samuel Crooks Junior's Italianate house, 28 Hayden Rowe, Built prior to 1856

Abram Crooks

Abram Crooks purchased this Greek-Revival house at 25 Main Street, built for Dr. Jefferson and Harriet Pratt. This and the previous picture give evidence of the success the brothers had in business. This was due in part to their association with Claflin-Coburn.

Wm. Claflin, Coburn & Co., Boston

On the left is Wm. Claflin, Coburn & Company's Boston warehouse and store. It was located at 136-138 Summer Street. This was the site of the home of Daniel Webster, which is pictured to the right, as it appeared about 1850.[118] The location is just up from where Bull's Tavern had stood. Daniel Webster's house was replaced by an elegant block of stores known as The Webster Buildings. These were destroyed in the great Boston fire of 1872. The Claflin, Coburn building was subsequently constructed of iron using the latest fire-proof methods. However, on Friday, the 17th of January, 1890 the building went up in flames due to an electrical fault. It was rebuilt in a similar style. Very tall buildings cover this area now.

The three senior partners were William Claflin, N. P. Coburn, and James A. Woolson. Other partners ran many different companies which were all part of this larger consortium. Included were the companies in St. Louis.

---

[118] Image of the Wm. Claflin, Coburn & Company headquarters from King's Handbook of Boston, Fourth Edition, (Moses King, Publisher, Cambridge, 1881). Image of Daniel Webster's house is available at the Boston Public Library, Print Department and from numerous online sources.

Operations also included a tannery, located in the town of Becket, Mass. There, William was in partnership with Henry Addison Bidwell and J. W. Wheeler, with the firm name "Bidwell, Wheeler, & Claflin." They built and conducted a store at Becket, and carried on an extensive lumber business and tannery business. They cut hemlock timber, using the bark for the tannery and the lumber for building purposes. Exhausting the hemlock in the surrounding area, the firm moved to Caroga, New York. For over thirty years they made upper leather of such superior quality that boots of Claflin & Coburn became famous all over the country, especially in St. Louis and in the West and Southwest.

Several factories were located in Hopkinton. First, there was that of S. & A. Crooks & Co., begun by Samuel and Abram Crooks in 1849. Samuel and Abram became very successful after starting out in the J. Walker shop on Hayden Rowe. In 1853, they moved into the old meetinghouse on Grove Street. In 1860, they moved to the Davenport Block, which had been a factory of Davenport and Gibbs, mentioned earlier. The first part was built about 1840 and we are looking at only two of the five parts. Main Street is in the foreground. The sign under the eaves says Davenport Block

Davenport Block of S. & A. Crooks & Co.
(Before a large addition on Main Street)

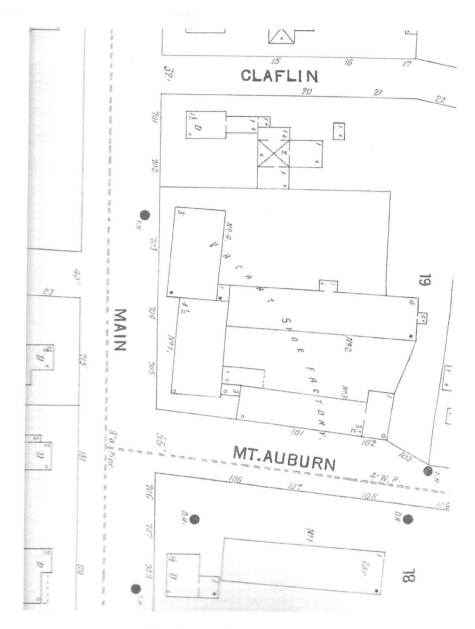

The Crooks factory buildings

Behind the colonial house ("Mayhew House" c. 1745, which still remains on the site, though moved back from the road), there was a part of the Crooks factory (building "No. 1").[119] It had been removed by 1910. Parts of the factory on the other corner survived at least until 1910. For many years it was the site of Terry's gas station, repair shop and Terry Oil Co., and is now Main Street Service Center. Claflin Avenue is at the top of this plan, not to be confused with Claflin Street and Claflin Place.

---

[119] Insurance map, Sanborn Map Company, New York, March, 1904, courtesy of the Hopkinton Public Library.

The Mayhew House is all that remains. Main Street Service Center can be seen to the left, on the site of the Davenport Block. This property was all owned by William Claflin when the S & A Crooks & Co. factory was in operation. The Crooks factory remained after other parts of Wm. Claflin-Coburn & Co. moved out of Hopkinton. In fact, to meet growing demand, a new factory was constructed at Meserve Street, near the corner of Wood and Main for Crooks, Root & Co. After the factory closed in 1901, Andrew Fyrberg & Sons used the building for a few years. By 1910, it was called "Imperial Shoe."

The sign on top of the building reads: "Crooks, Root & Co. Boot & Shoe Manufacturers"

Production at Wm. Claflin, Coburn, & Co. also included the factory of A. Coburn & Son in Hopkinton. It was managed by Alonzo Coburn and his son, Charles Henry Coburn. Again, Alonzo (1821-1902) was a younger brother of Nathan P. Coburn. This had been Wilbur F. Claflin's factory, before his retirement.

Buildings of A. Coburn & Son on Hayden Rowe

The scale of the building can be better appreciated in the view below.

After this building of 1859 burned on the 27th of August, 1889, a new, wooden factory was built on the site. It was built to face 90 degrees from this one (100'x80' with a 27'x30' annex, 4 floors).

After the Coburn operation moved out of town in 1895, the factory became home to Andrew Fyrberg and Sons in 1903, before this firearms company moved into the abandoned Crooks, Root & Co. factory at Meserve Street. The next occupant was the Hermina Silk Mill. In 1912 it was home to Lawson Pink Food Products Co. Then, in 1918, Seamans & Cobb Thread Mills moved here from Framingham. In more recent years, it was renovated for use by General Packets, Inc. (1958-1969). The little sugar packets you get at a restaurant were made there.

In 2013 the building contains first-class office and warehouse space. Though covered in brick and missing its top floor, there is still an old shoe factory underneath. It faces Hayden Rowe near the corner of Maple and opposite the end of Fenton.

Next is a picture of the factory, taken about 1910. Beyond the factory to the right one sees a portion of the Benjamin Franklin Coburn house. B. F. Coburn (1827-1891) was another brother of Nathan and Alonzo. He married Sarah Elizabeth Wentworth[120] of Great Falls, New Hampshire in 1858. After Benjamin's death, the house became the property of J. Cunningham. It had deteriorated by the 1960's (losing much of its red paint in the process), and was burned for practice by the fire department.

Hermina Silk Mill

---

[120] Sarah Wentworth was a descendent of Giles Cromwell, first cousin to Oliver Cromwell.

SEAMANS & COBB THREAD MILL

34 Hayden Rowe

The next page shows it remodeled and encased in brick.

Last remaining Claflin-Coburn factory

Alonzo Coburn's Italianate house, 52 Hayden Rowe (c. 1844-1848)
The garage on the left is a recent addition to the carriage house

The largest factory was that of Bridges & Co. It was constructed after the fire of 1876 destroyed the Claflin-Coburn factory of 1850 on Main Street. It was under the management of Daniel Thurber (D. T.) Bridges of Hopkinton. Daniel was the eldest son of Luther Rockwood and Hannah (Stearns) Bridges. His wife, Frances Ellen, was the daughter of Willard Wadsworth.

Bridges & Co., Main Street, with Claflin Street behind

This is the Bridges & Co. building lost in the fire of the 4th of April, 1882. It existed for less than five years. This firm, like the others, came under the umbrella of Wm. Claflin, Coburn, & Co. The shape of the rear portion of this building can still be seen in the woods behind "Bill's Pizza and Restaurant" and the Town Hall. The bridge connected with the Post Office on Main Street. The Post Office building was between the Town Hall and the Highland House.

After the fire of 1882, only the brick foundation and chimney remain

In those days, it was possible to react quickly to property loss. William Claflin and N. P. Coburn already owned property in Framingham, adjacent to the mainline railroad. Claflin, Coburn & Co. began building their new factory right away in 1882, on the corner of Waverly and Mellen Streets. At first called Bridges & Co., it was renamed Gregory & Co. when Bridges retired and William Gregory took over. D. T. Bridges retired on the 1st of January, 1890.

In 1856, D. T. & Frances E. (Wadsworth[121]) Bridges lived on Grove Street. Then, in March of 1864, Mary S. Davenport (second wife of S. D.) sold her house to Bridges. The house still stands just west of the old high school of 1894. The brick high school (now offices) is on the site of Dr. & Mrs. Thomas Bucklin's mansion. The Davenport Mansion used to be larger. A kitchen and dining wing and a porch extended further out the back and there was a separate barn behind. The foundation of the barn remains.

---

[121] Frances was the daughter of Willard Wadsworth (page 106). Her brother, Joseph, was married to Meriam Woolson, first cousin of James A. Woolson (page 186). As James was a senior partner of Wm. Claflin, Coburn & Co., Bridges & Co. was not only a subsidiary, but it was run by his relative, Daniel T. Bridges. Also, Daniel's aunt was Emeline Crooks, so Samuel and Abram Crooks were his first cousins.

S. D. Davenport / D. T. Bridges House, 87 Main Street

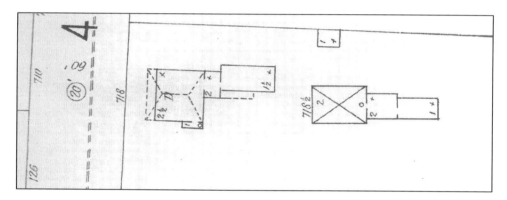

This plan view of 1904 shows what it looked like. The building to the right was the carriage house/barn.[122]

On the 28th of January, 1886, D. T. Bridges sold the property to Priscilla (Stearns) Morse, wife of Charles H. Morse, for $6,000. Priscilla was Daniel's first cousin. Daniel's mother Hannah was another sibling of Alanson and Emeline (see page 64). She sold the property to Horace & Helen Fenn in 1906. By 1910, it was known as the Spillane Lodge. Overnight guests were accommodated there by successive owners in the early 1900's.

---

[122] Insurance map, Sanborn Map Company, New York, March, 1904, courtesy of the Hopkinton Public Library.

Here is a section of a hand-drawn "bird's eye view" by O. H. Bailey, of the Gregory, Shaw, and Co. factory in Coburnville, South Framingham, as it appeared in 1898.[123] The rear section was 240-feet long. The row of ten double tenements on the southwest side of Coburn Street was owned by N. P. Coburn. Another row of houses was owned by William Claflin on Claflin Street to the east. Coburnville had its own school and general store. The Coburn House, a hotel, was on Mellen Street (probably the large building opposite the factory as shown on Mellen Street above). The street names are all misspelled on this drawing.

[123] O. H. Bailey & Co., Lithographers and Publishers of Boston, 1898.

The double line leading to the factory is the railroad spur which crossed the intersection at Fountain Street. The heavy, dark line to the right is a division between maps and not the railroad.

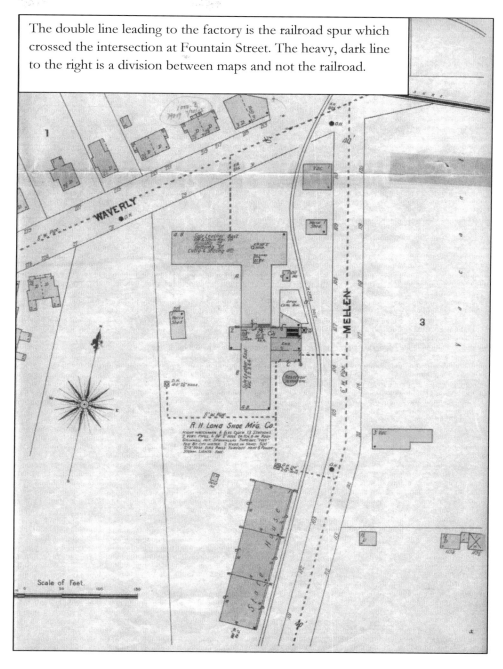

The factory layout from a map of 1903 to compare with the previous view[124]

[124] Insurance map, Sanborn Map Company, New York, 1903, courtesy of the Framingham Public Library.

These are some of the ten houses built by N. P. Coburn on Coburn Street in Coburnville in the 1880's. When new, these houses all looked alike. Some have been modified more than others, but it is easy to see they were built at the same time.

GREGORY, SHAW & CO., SHOE MANUFACTORY.

This is another view from the O. H. Bailey map. This view is looking from the corner of Mellen and Waverly streets. To the right of the chimney is a brick firewall which extends above the roof. They were taking more precautions against fire! But, on the 24th of April, 1885, the company had yet another fire. The firewall saved the rear portion and they rebuilt again. Notice too, the lettering on the front of the building. It says:

Established 1815 – Gregory, Shaw & Co. - Salesroom 136 Summer St Boston

(1815 was the year Lee Claflin began his business in Milford.)

N. P. Coburn directed operations of the factories and under his able management they were a prolific source of revenue for the company. When he too retired at the end of 1891, the following changes took place: the factory at South Framingham was renamed Gregory, Shaw & Co.; the Crooks factory in Hopkinton would be called Crooks, Root & Co.; and the A. Coburn & Son factory in Hopkinton would now do business under the name of Coburn, Gauss, & Co, with separate offices at 13 High Street, Boston. William T. Gauss (1851-1928) moved from St. Louis in 1889. In 1898, the boot industry was in decline and he moved his family to Colorado Springs where he had mining investments. William F. Gregory (b. January, 1849) had been a partner since 1877. He was in St. Louis in 1880, then in Hopkinton, Framingham, Newton (1900) and then back in St. Louis (1910). Oliver B. Root (b. March, 1847, Vermont) was admitted as a partner in 1882. D. T. Bridges moved to Framingham, where he had a house on the site of Marian High School.

Business boomed for a decade. Crooks, Root, & Co. even built the new factory in Hopkinton on the corner of Wood and Main, pictured earlier. Then, in 1893, there was a financial panic which lasted for four years. This had a negative impact on the boot & shoe industry, like most other industries. The Framingham factory ran on a shortened work week for five years.[125] In January of 1895, the Coburn, Gauss, & Co. operation was relocated to Wolfeboro, NH. In June, 1901, the Crooks, Root & Co. factory in Hopkinton closed. This was the last active Claflin-Coburn factory in Hopkinton. In September, 1901, the Gregory, Shaw & Co. merged with the F. Brigham Co. of Hudson. They moved the machinery to Hudson and closed the Framingham factory, which was put up for sale. William Hartwell Brigham of Hudson became the new president of the firm. It continued to be a privately held company with assets in 1903 of $412,286.64.[126]

F. Brigham & Gregory Factory, Hudson, Mass.
Published by C. E. Sexton.

F. Brigham & Gregory Co. was located on South Street in Hudson until about 1970.

---

[125] Stephen W. Herring, Framingham – An American Town, (Framingham Tercentennial Commission, 2000).

[126] 1903 assets as reported in the United States Investor, Vol. 15, (Boston, New York, and Philadelphia, July 9, 1904).

In 1902, Richard H. Long, formerly of South Weymouth and Belchertown, purchased the vacant factory in Framingham in order to expand his shoe business. He had opened 120 retail shoe stores around the country and demand was growing. He became the first shoe manufacturer to establish an eight-hour work day, and have unions.[127] Then, in 1909, he built a 500-foot long, reinforced-concrete factory on the other side of the railroad tracks. It was highly praised for its design and working conditions.

R. H. LONG SHOE FACTORY, FRAMINGHAM, MASS. *Fountain St.?*

The concrete factory still exists. After WWI, Long went into the automobile business as R. H. Long Motors Corporation. First, he bought the Bela Body Company and moved it to Framingham. That factory later became part of Dennison and was located further east from the one pictured above. They built bodies for the Franklin Motor Company. The shoe business was interrupted by the war and, rather than rebuild his clientele, R. H. Long decided to build the "Bay State" automobile in what had been his new shoe factory. It was marketed locally in New England. Like many new industries, consolidation and competition forced the continued need for large amounts of capital. Even many of the strongest companies folded after 1929. The "Bay State" didn't make it that long. The company, with its Fountain Street factory, was bought by the Luxor Cab Manufacturing Company in 1925.

---

[127] The Framingham Evening News, 12 September, 1918.

R. H. Long's shoe factory of 1909 became his automobile assembly plant
Now known as the Bancroft Building, Fountain Street

In the foreground there are fewer tracks than in the previous view, but they remain well used. Today, this is a route of Amtrak and the MBTA Commuter and CSX Corporation freight lines from Boston to Worcester. The building now houses many companies.

When his auto business failed, R. H. Long reorganized as the R. H. Long Motor Sales Company. He opened a Cadillac dealership in front of the old Claflin-Coburn factory, which he still owned. Founded in 1927, it is the oldest, continuously-run, family-owned, Cadillac dealership. When it relocated to Southborough, the service facility was torn down and replaced by a drug store. What else?

Judging by the cars in the showroom, the old Claflin-Coburn factory was still around in the mid-1960s. By then, it was over 80 years old.

Former showroom of R. H. Long in Framingham
(The new pharmacy is in back)

Erastus Thompson

Erastus was born on the 24th of April, 1815, in Paris, Maine, son of Ira and Sophia (Drew) Thompson. Ira and "Goshia" had gone from Middleboro to Maine, where all of their eleven children were born. Erastus was the seventh child, so he looked elsewhere to find employment. His elder brother, Arad, went north and became very successful in Bangor, Maine. Erastus headed back south and was equally enterprising. He began business in Hopkinton in 1846 as Thompson, Bales & Barker in an upper story of the old Central Coffee House. He then had a shop behind the Town Hall as shown on the map of 1856 (page 168). The successor, Erastus Thompson & Co., had offices at 4 High and 121 Summer Street in Boston and a factory in Hopkinton on the corner of Main and Grove. They were known for the durability of their products.

Factory of Erastus Thompson & Co.
Corner of Main and Grove

This factory was similar in design to that of Alonzo Coburn and built in two stages. The part with more windows is the newer section. By then, they were more concerned about providing additional natural light. Colella's Supermarket is now located on this corner.

The other side of the factory with the adjacent Phipps Livery Stable

Another view of the stable with its very large Greek-Revival detailing

The following rare photographs provide a glimpse of life in a boot factory. They were taken inside the Thompson Factory. The names of the workers are unknown.

Wooden boxes are stacked here, ready for wholesale delivery. Boots were shipped to the wholesale office with about twelve pair per box.

Here we see work stations lined up in front of the windows which provided natural light. A drive rod runs along the ceiling to which belts could be attached. Light bulbs in reflective fixtures also hang from the ceiling and a hot air pipe is visible. The factory produced its own steam power from a coal furnace. Finished boots are stacked in racks.

These look to be dress boots. Nevertheless, they have a substantial sole and heal.

Looking Up Grove Street

In this view, the Thompson factory has been reduced to the basement and first floor only and opened up for use as a car barn for the street railway. The following plan view[128] shows the car barn and adjacent livery stable from the same direction. Just

[128] Insurance map, Sanborn Map Company, New York, March, 1904, courtesy of the Hopkinton Public Library.

right of the stable is a building labeled "Hardw." Hitchings Hardware (1961-2010) maintained the same use for this building. Though the store was small, Mr. Hitchings seemed to have everything. Hiller's Cleaners now has a new building on the site. It incorporates style elements from the old building.

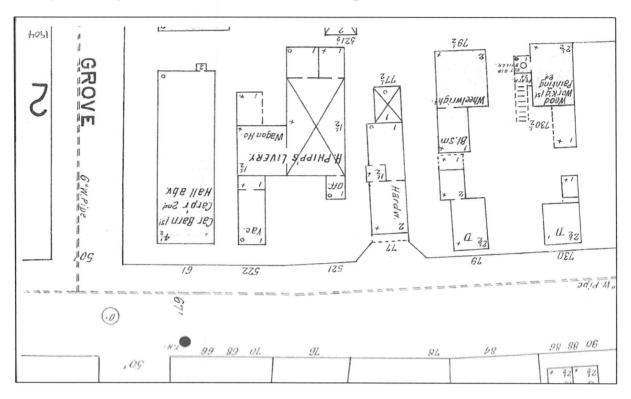

Erastus Thompson married Catherine Wheelock Oakes on the 14th of May, 1843, in Hopkinton. They had five children:

Charles E. Thompson (1845-1886) m. Adelia M. LORING (1845-1926)
Edwin (Eddie) Davis Thompson (1848-1905) m. Mary Greene BARTLETT
Clarence A. Thompson (1852-1898) m. Mary B. SAWYER (1855-)
Katie S. Thompson (1855-1857)
Franklin O. Thompson (1858-aft 1940) m. Mary A. CROOKS (c. 1860-)

Erastus Thompson at 43 Main Street

Erastus Thompson built this Greek-Revival house of simple lines, located at 45 Main Street. It was close to his new factory on the corner of Grove Street.

When Erastus built a new house next door, he sold this house to William Burrage Coburn. William had a meat market in the small building in front of the house. It is now a gourmet coffee shop.

William was the nephew of Nathan P. and Alonzo Coburn. He was born in Medway on the 4th of November, 1846. He married Mary Elizabeth Thayer (1848-1909) on the 31st of December, 1867.

Erastus Thompson at 35 Main Street

Erastus Thompson built this Greek-Revival house at 35 Main Street. It too was built on what had been part of the 16-acre Valentine estate on the Common.

Franklin (Frank) grew up in this house on Main Street, which is next door to that of Abram & Ann Marie Crooks. Frank married their daughter Mary on the 10th of October, 1883. Frank and Mary owned the house at 35 Main after his father's death. With the decline in boot manufacturing in Hopkinton, Frank too looked to the growing coal industry of the C. L. Claflin family. Enjoying better health than his siblings, Frank was still alive in 1940 at the age of 82. He was living in Brookline then and listed his occupation as "coal dealer."

Erastus Thompson Monument

Erastus died in 1885. His monument is near that of Lee Claflin in the Pine Grove Cemetery, Milford, Massachusetts.

E. D. Thompson at 6 Hayden Rowe

E. D. Thompson House, c. 1875

This Italianate house was built for Edwin Davis Thompson on land that Erastus had purchased earlier from the Valentine Estate. Edwin D. Thompson married Mary G. Bartlett on the 1st of December, 1874. They had three children. 6 Hayden Rowe was constructed for them sometime between 1875 and 1880. With his eldest brother Charles, Eddie continued the boot manufacturing business, but then Charles died in 1886. Erastus Thompson & Co. closed about 1892. Edwin held the position of clerk for C. W. Claflin & Co. in 1896. By the time of his death in January, 1905, he was the local coal dealer for the same firm. Coincidently, Edwin was 56 that January. Charles L. Claflin was two years younger when he died that September.

By 1898, 6 Hayden Rowe was owned by Fred A. (1861 -) and Mable L. (1871-) Wood. Fred Wood held the position of Treasurer of the Hopkinton Savings Bank, like his next-door neighbor, Webster Page.

On a map of 1910, Mrs. Mary Thompson is shown as the owner of the Valentine Mansion. The Bank had moved into the Park House building by then. In 1920, Dr. George Thompson and his family had moved into the Valentine Mansion, but they were not related to Erastus and Mary Thompson.

Besides working in the same industry, there is an interesting connection between the Thompson and Claflin families. Clarence A. Thompson (1852-1898), the third son of Erastus and Mary, married Mary B. Sawyer (no date found). Mary's elder sister, Alma M. Sawyer married Clarence A. Claflin (1854-1899) on the 12th of June, 1877. C. A. Claflin was the son of Wilbur Fisk Claflin who built Spring Hill Farm, pictured on page 165. Across Hayden Rowe from this house was an equally large house.

Clarence Augustus Claflin

Clarence Augustus Claflin

C. A. Claflin was a boot manufacturer like his father Wilbur. His factory was on the south side of Pleasant Street, at the corner of Hayden Rowe. It was of similar style to the Thompson and the Coburn factories, but smaller. Curiously, C. A. Claflin & Co. was not listed as part of Wm. Claflin, Coburn & Co. It is also shown as a separate company on the bird's eye view map of 1880. Claflin's large house (then 78 Hayden Rowe), was in the middle of a "2 Acres, ¼, and 10 Rods" lot (100,732.1 sq. ft,) on the opposite corner of Pleasant and Hayden Rowe. A detail of the bird's eye view is shown on the next page. It shows a section of Hayden Rowe south of the Common (refer to the map on page 11).

In this view,[129] we are looking west with Hayden Rowe in the center. The Common is out of sight to the right. In the lower left, we see the artist's depiction of Wilbur F. Claflin's Spring Hill Farm. Across Hayden Rowe is his son's factory and house on either side of Pleasant Street. To the right is a smaller house which served as the Catholic parsonage for some time. Next, to the right, is the house of Alonzo Coburn. Then, almost in front, is the former school house moved from the Common by Lee Claflin. It was then considered part of A. Coburn & Co. After Maple Street are the factories of A. Coburn & Co. The boot factories were powered by steam engines fueled by coal, thus the smoke.

Moving right, the next house was owned by B. F. Coburn and then there is the house of Samuel Crooks - in the upper right corner of this view. The unlabeled street in the foreground was proposed but never constructed. The street labeled Claflin is now Holt. The southern part of the old 32-acre School Lot is thought to have extended to Pike Street. So, from Pike to the right, we are looking at part of what had been one lot fronting on the Common. To the left of Pike, the land had all been part of James Wilson's 53 ¾-acre lot. Most of the other side of Hayden Rowe in this view had been part of the 40-acre Ministerial Lot (see the map on page 11).

The large Italianate house at what was formerly known as 78 Hayden Rowe was originally built for Franklin B. and Eliza B. Mansfield. Like Lee Claflin, Franklin Mansfield had early success. As noted earlier in connection with the map of 1856, F. B. Mansfield had a boot shop and then factory on the corner of Pleasant. Each company had a specialty which set them apart from the competition. If C. A. Claflin

---

[129] Detail of "Hopkinton, Mass.," O. H. Bailey & J. C. Hazen, Publishers, Boston, 1880.

didn't just purchase the factory, but also continued Mansfield's business, it would explain why his company was not part of Wm. Claflin, Coburn & Co. The type of boots produced may not have fit in with their market.

F. B. Mansfield was in business at least until 1871, when he took out a mortgage for $6,000. He had begun assembling the acreage for his house with multiple purchases, starting in 1853. Included with these deeds is one from the Congregational Church which relinquishes any claim on the land (so there would be no cloud on the title). So, they believed that the ministerial lot had extended to Pleasant Street. On the map of 1856, Franklin's house was behind his factory on Pleasant Street. His new house was constructed about 1860, across Pleasant Street from his factory. Franklin sold the new house to Edward F. Wiswall for $10,000 on the 2nd of February, 1874. This price indicates that the house was indeed as large as depicted on the previous bird's eye view.

Edward Wiswall was born in Boston about 1829. His father Elisha established Wiswall & Co., dealers in lumber in Dorchester. Like C. W. Claflin & Co., they expanded into coal. Sons George and Edward went into business with their father. In 1870, Edward listed his real estate assets at $59,000. He came to Hopkinton for just a short time before moving to Needham. Perhaps he was associated with C. W. Claflin & Co.

On the 2nd of July, 1877, Edward F. and Lizzie M. Wiswall of Needham sold the property to Clarence A. Claflin for $8,000. After his father Wilbur died in 1885, C. A. Claflin moved his family to Omaha, Nebraska. C. A. Thompson is listed in the directory of 1886 at 78 Hayden Rowe. But he didn't own the property. In that their wives were sisters, it is not difficult to see how that came about. C. A. Claflin was on an extensive expedition for the purpose of establishing mercantile trading posts throughout Alaska when he died at Nome on the 12th of October, 1899. His wife Alma came back from Omaha and was living in Winthrop when she died in 1904. Burial was at the Pine Grove Cemetery in Milford, like most of the Claflin family.

Clarence had a mortgage on the house and, after the move to Omaha, payments were not made. An auction by the Hopkinton Savings Bank (Webster W. Page, Treasurer) was held. Clarence's brother Adelbert E. Claflin of New York was the high bidder at only $3,403.00. Adelbert sold the house to Daniel J. Coburn on the 22nd of August, 1893. Daniel assumed a mortgage and back taxes. Then, in December, there was a transfer to Charles P. Wonderly and back to Celia A. Coburn, Daniel's wife. This was probably a private financing arrangement.

Daniel Jennings Coburn (1835-1902) was a younger brother of N. P. Coburn (see page 180). He married Celia Augusta Claflin (1839-1912) on the 21st of November, 1860. Celia was the daughter of Newell and Mira (Mary) Rice Claflin (see page 99). Celia did not continue to live at 78 Hayden Rowe for long after her husband's death in 1902.

On the 19th of March, 1903 the house was purchased from Celia Coburn by Andrew Fyrberg when he moved his firearms business to Hopkinton from Worcester. Andrew was born in Sweden in 1853. He produced guns for Sears, Roebuck, & Co. After 1908, the family moved back to Worcester. The Fyrberg family had apparently developed a fondness for Hopkinton. When Andrew died in 1936, he was buried in Hopkinton, as were other members of the family. The house at 78 Hayden Rowe was sold by Andrew Fyrberg to Nellie M. Hewitt of Buffalo on the 12th of September, 1911. Nellie's husband, Paul A. Hewitt (retired),[130] was listed there in the 1912 directory.

The F. B. Mansfield Mansion, 1860-1936, formerly at 56-62 Hayden Rowe[131]

---

[130] Paul Anson Hewitt married Nellie May Thompson of Hudson, NH on the 28th of April, 1892 in Hudson, NH. He was born in St. John, NB, about 1850, the son of William and Francis (Wright) Hewitt. Nellie was the daughter of John and Lizzie (Marsh) Thompson of Hudson, NH. John Thompson was from Bridgewater, MA. and was not closely related to the other Thompson families of Hopkinton.

[131] Detail of "Hopkinton, Mass.," O. H. Bailey & J. C. Hazen, Publishers, Boston, 1880.

The property was sold by Hewitt to Levi and Annie L. Diamond of Brookline in 1914. Starting at the end of 1917, there were a number of transactions and mortgages involving Diamond to Samuel Lebowich, Lebowich to Mary E. MacDonough of Hopkinton and back to Lebowich. Then, in 1919, from MacDonough to Arthur N. and Ethel M. Bruerton of Malden "for consideration paid." They gave a mortgage to the Henry Wilson Co-op Bank of Natick in the amount of $7,000.

The next transfer was to Mary A. Allen, wife of Silas G. Allen, along with Carolyn N. Boliver, all of Southboro. Mortgages to Bruerton in 1922 totaled $8,000. Several more transactions and transfers culminated with a default to the Henry Wilson Co-op Bank and a determination by the bank to sell the property at auction on the 4th of Nov., 1927.

The buyer was Samuel M. Berger of Malden. His assessment in 1928 was as follows: House - $6,000, Barn - $2,200, Land - $1,800 = $10,000; Tax: $280.00. In 1929, the assessment was the same, but the tax went up to $330.00. But then, in 1930, for some reason, the house valuation was reduced to $4,000, while the barn and land stayed the same. In 1931, the property transferred to Nathan Hyman. Nathan defaulted on his mortgage in May of 1931. He sold to Sophie Siden of Everett, but soon, the property was put up for auction again. George Frye was the high bidder at only **$800.00**. Meanwhile, the property assessment plummeted with the house valued at only $1,000, but the barn at $1,500. The land value stayed the same. Clearly, something had happened to the house. It was more than the effects of the Great Depression. The house at 2 Park Street was still valued at $7,500. The value of the house came up a little the next year to $1,200 and stayed stable through 1935, when it was sold to Paul M. Keaney. Paul had two other properties on Main Street. In 1936, the value plunged further to $500.00 for the house and $1,500 for the barn. In 1937, the assessor's records just list "Building" and a value of $500.00 and that decreased to $300.00 by 1940.

The house may have been reduced in size in 1930. In 1935 it must have suffered significant damage, or the owner decided to tear it down. Did it have a fire?

The street has since been renumbered.[132] Four 1940's Capes were built on the site along Hayden Rowe and a fifth house on Pleasant. The F. B. Mansfield house was one of the largest houses (if not the largest) to be built along Hayden Rowe (including Wilbur Claflin's across the street, Samuel Crooks', Alonzo Coburn's and C. L. Claflin's). It is the only one not to survive.

---

[132] 78 Hayden Rowe is now 58 to 64 Hayden Rowe and 85 Pleasant Street.

The Fire of 1882

This is the first Town Hall and to the left is the store of Mahon Bros. The L. H. Wakefield (former S. B. Walcott) house is tucked out of sight between these two buildings. It is visible in the next view. The Town Hall included storefronts. In the picture below, E. A. Bates & Co. is on the left and A. A. Sweet & Co. is on the right.

All three buildings burned in the fire, which started in the back of the Town Hall

This is all that was left of Mahon Bros. store shown in the previous photo. It stood on the corner of Walcott Street, which, in this view, is filled with debris. All the buildings from Walcott Street to the cemetery were lost to fire this time, including the 1831 Central Coffee House (Highland House) and 1830 Congregational Church. Of course, the new Bridges boot factory went up in flames at the same time. Damage was estimated at $400,000, making it the worst of several bad fires. The Hopkinton Supply Co. building (shown on page 110) took the place of the second Mahon Bros. store in 1906, after the next fire.

Walcott Street was named for Samuel B. Walcott, Esquire. While his house remained until 1882, a store had been built on part of the same lot. Samuel Baker Walcott was born on the 7th of March, 1795, in Cambridge, the son of Jabez and Mary (Baker) Walcott. He studied law and graduated from Harvard in 1819. He married Martha Pickman on the 6th of January, 1829, in Salem. Martha was born on the 24th of November, 1802, in Salem. After moving to Hopkinton, they had eight children between the years 1830 and 1842. Samuel was a Selectman in Hopkinton from 1831 to 1836. Son, Charles Folsom, graduated from Harvard Law School in 1860 and became a Colonel in the Civil War. He settled in Cambridge where he practiced law.

Samuel B. Walcott, Esq. was a noted attorney, but not just in Hopkinton. His reputation was such that Fletcher Webster (1813-1862), son of the famous statesman Daniel Webster, studied law with Samuel in Hopkinton and with Daniel in Boston, after graduating from Harvard in 1833. Fletcher went on to practice law in Illinois, where he met Abraham Lincoln. He was killed at the 2nd Battle of Bull Run in 1862.[133]

The Walcott property on Main Street eventually came into the family of Thomas Barber. It was this development which led to expansion of the retail trade, as we shall see in the next chapter. The merchants of Hopkinton were continually challenged by the need to recover from devastating losses to fire.

Devastation – 1882 – North Side of Main Street
In the distance:
Tavern's Barns, Cemetery Pines, Ash Street Schools, Price House, Valentine Mansion

---

[133] Thomas Wentworth Higginson, <u>Harvard Memorial Biographies</u>, Vol. I, (Cambridge, MA: Sever and Francis, 1866).

The Merchants

In the nineteenth century, the commercial center spread down the hill to the west and today it is oriented around the intersection of routes 135 and 85. However, several stores, two banks, and the post office used to be located close to the Common—still within the original lots of Samuel Barrett. As we have seen from some of the pictures, the merchants included E. A. Bates and A. A. Sweet. Who were these men and how were they connected to Thomas Barber?

Thomas Barber was born on the 10th of April, 1798 in Milford, the son of Hamblet and Rhoda (Ware) Barber. He married Emily Elizabeth (Betsey) Rockwood on the 7th of March, 1818. She was born on the 13th of June, 1800 in Hopkinton, the daughter of Nathan and Joanna (Day) Rockwood of Hopkinton. The couple lived in Newton and Cambridge, before moving to Hopkinton. Between 1819 and 1843, they had thirteen children, most being born in Newton. By 1850, Thomas and Betsey were the innkeepers of the Central Coffee House. However, Thomas died in 1852.

His father, Hamblet Barber was in Hopkinton in 1790, then during the next two decades in Holliston, according to census records. He married a widow, Rhoda (Ware) Clarke (d. 25 Dec. 1824). In his History of the Town of Milford,[134] Adin Ballou calls Hamblet "an ingenious shoemaker." He lived to the age of 83, (July, 1834). He was thus born about 1751, in England. The following excerpt[135] is of interest, but would benefit from supporting documentation:

> "Hamblet served as a British Officer in General 'Gentlemen Johnny' Burgoyne's army during the Revolutionary War. Burgoyne was defeated, and Hamblet was captured by the Colonists during the Battle of Saratoga in upper New York in the fall of 1777. Hamblet was paroled into the custody of a Massachusetts militiaman, named Ware, who had fought for the American cause at the Battle of Crown Point, New York. In 1778 he married the eldest Ware daughter, Rhoda Ware (Clarke), who was then a young widow with an infant daughter."

After the war, with a talent for shoemaking, it is interesting that Hamblet settled in the area which would become the cradle of the boot and shoe industry. The Barber children (of whom there were twelve) married spouses surnamed Claflin, Davenport, and Adams, among others. Not everyone became bootmakers. Thomas

---

[134] Adin Ballou, History of the Town of Milford, Worcester County, Massachusetts, From Its First Settlement to 1881, (Boston: Franklin Press, Rand, Avery, & Co., 1882).

[135] Website of Jeffrey La Favre, www.lafavre.us/genealogy, original source not cited.

was the youngest son and he chose a profession which would support the growing industry.

Section of the map of 1856 shown on page 103

Walcott Street is across the top of this view. The first three black squares from Walcott along Main represent the store and house of (then widow) Betsey Barber, followed by the Post Office and Town Hall building, as we saw in the previous pictures. By then, Eliakim A. Bates store was behind Barber's on Walcott and his house was next to Dr. Pratt's across Main. Eliakim was married to Thomas and Betsey's eldest daughter, Johanna Day Barber, in 1841. "A Brief History of Hopkinton," 1915, lists the buildings destroyed in the fire of 1882. With regard to Mahon Bros. store, it says: "remembered by older residents as "Bates Exchange." So, apparently, Bates took over the Barber store after 1856. The business was later moved to the Town Hall building.

Another daughter of Thomas and Betsey Barber, born in Newton, was Emily Elizabeth (1831-1896). She was married to Homer Gibbs, son of John and Fanny

(Pierce) Gibbs of Hopkinton. In 1870, Homer worked in one of the boot shops. Homer and Emily later lived in Framingham.

Thomas Barber Jr., born 1829, also in Newton, had a very tragic end. He died by drowning on the 4th of July, 1849, while having a picnic on an island in North Pond in Hopkinton. He went fishing with five friends and decided to try swimming for the first time. His friends were unable to save him when he got into trouble.[136]

Sarah Jane Barber was born in June of 1839 in Hopkinton. She married Lucius H. Wakefield in Hopkinton on the 1st of May, 1860. Lucius was an attorney, like Samuel Walcott. He is the L. H. Wakefield identified with the Walcott house at the time it burned. Like Samuel, he also taught law. One of his students was William Henry Harrison Allen, B. K., A. B. (1829-1893). William was a "student-at-law" in 1856, at Hopkinton. He went on to be an Associate Justice of the Supreme Court of New Hampshire.[137] L. H. Wakefield also had an office at 7 Court Square, Boston.[138]

Lucius Henry Wakefield was born on the 28th of August, 1825 in Salem or Colchester, Connecticut. His parents were Tubal Cain and Rosella/Isabella (Greenwood) Wakefield. Tubal was the pastor of several Baptist churches in Connecticut. He reportedly died in Woodville in 1868, but was buried in Oxford. He was born in Dudley in 1794. His wife was born in Sutton in 1797. She died in Charlton in 1861.

On the Census of 1880 for Hopkinton, Betsey Barber was living in the house on Main, along with the Wakefield family of her daughter Sarah. She was 80 years old. After the fire, the family moved to Framingham, where they lived on Irving Street.

E. A. BATES

Eliakim A. and Johanna D. (Barber) Bates lived on the "safe side" of Main Street – "safe" in the sense that this side of the street did not repeatedly burn. Their house was located between the Pratt/Crooks Mansion and the home of Miriam Valentine.

E. A. Bates was often a Selectman in town, serving off and on from 1851 to 1870. The act to incorporate the Hopkinton Bank on the 28th of April, 1853 included three officers. They were Erastus Thompson, Eliakim A. Bates, and S. D. Davenport. Eliakim represented Hopkinton and Ashland in the 1876 Massachusetts House of

---

[136] Elbridge Luthur Rockwood, A Historical and Genealogical Record of the Descendants of Timothy Rockwood, Boston, 1856 (published by the compiler).
[137] "Psi Upsilon Fraternity," 1888.
[138] "The Boston Directory," 1873.

Representatives. He was born on the 30th of June, 1817, in Bellingham, the son of Ezekiel and Sabra Bates. Eliakim and Johanna had five children: Theodore Sedgwick, b. 24 Mar. 1845; Ella Jane, b. 1 Apr. 1850, d. 8 Feb. 1852; Jennie Sabra, b. 2 Apr. 1853; Thomas Barber, b. 3 Feb. 1855, d. 26 May 1860; and Lizzie M., b. c. 1859, d. 12 Mar. 1879.

After his first wife died (before 1865), Eliakim remarried. His second wife was Ellen M. Tonne. He died on the 7th of August, 1878 in Hopkinton.

E. A. Bates' house

The house is similar to the one next door, which was owned by Miriam Valentine at the time.

Bates/Crooks House

There is a house on the site today. The style elements of Carpenter-Gothic indicate the late Victorian period (thus, after Bates). However, from the back it appears to be the same house shown in the photograph above. It simply may have been remodeled to reflect changing tastes in architecture. Sometime after E. A. Bates died, the house was purchased by Abram Crooks for his son Arthur and his bride, Myra Adams. It was probably in conjunction with their wedding in 1889. For many years, this house was the home and office of Dr. Joseph Annunziata and his family.

A. A. SWEET

Alvan Able Sweet was born on the 9th of March, 1832, in Plainfield, Windham, Connecticut. He was thus about fifteen years younger than E. A. Bates. On the 10th of November, 1856, he married Marion Eliza Fiske in Milford. Marion was born on the 15th of November, 1835, in Medway. She grew up in Bellingham and Milford. Her brother was named Hamblet Barber Fiske and he was born two years after Marion. You may now recognize the name Hamblet Barber as Mrs. Bates grandfather, who also lived, at times, in Milford (see page 228).

Marion and Hamblet Fiske were the children of James J. and Rebecca (Prouty) Fiske of Milford. James Fiske was a "dealer in dry goods and groceries, retail" in Milford.[139] So Alvan's father-in-law was in the dry goods business in Milford. Likely, there would have been advantages for Alvan to open a similar business in neighboring Hopkinton. His father-in-law also must have had a regard for, or connection to, the Barber family, since he named his son Hamblet Barber Fiske. Hamblet (or Hamlet) came to work as a clerk in the store in Hopkinton.[140]

By 1870, A. A. Sweet was enjoying success in business. On the census of that year, Alvan, age 38, listed real estate valued at $9,000 and personal property of $6,000. In addition to his wife and two children, there were a servant and three clerks from his store living at the house on Church Street, pictured on the left edge below. It was an easy walk to his store on Main Street. The house next door now has a gable roof.

---

[139] 1870 Federal Census for Milford.
[140] 1865 Federal Census for Hopkinton.

The A. A. Sweet house at 10 Church Street is a fairly typical example of the Second-Empire-style with its characteristic mansard roof, introduced in America by the European-trained architect Detlef Lienau. Hopkinton has few examples because growth was slowing by the time the style became popular. The Sweet house later became the home of Dr. W. A. Phipps. It remains today, but without its matching carriage house shown in the lower right below.

Sweet/Phipps Carriage House

Notice the unobstructed view to the northwest in this picture. The large barn in the center went with the Pratt/Crooks house on Main Street. Erastus Thompson's house is just behind it and his factory (without the addition) on the corner of Grove Street can be seen.

At the time of his death on the 14th of January, 1904, in Newton, Alvan Sweet's occupation was still listed as that of merchant. His former partner, S. A. Knowles, was still in Hopkinton.

S. A. KNOWLES

Seymour Augustus Knowles was born on the 27th of July, 1849, in the new town of Ashland. His parents were both from New Hampshire. From the age of fourteen, he worked in shoe factories. In 1867, he went to work as a clerk in a general store in Ashland. In 1875, he formed a partnership with A. A. Sweet under the name of Sweet, Morse, & Knowles. After he bought out Sweet's interests, the firm was known as Morse & Knowles and then, S. A. Knowles. I have not discovered which Morse was involved. In 1874, Seymour married Bertha Ella Howard and they had one child, Walter E. Knowles. In 1903, Seymour married Grace E. Hemenway of South Framingham.[141]

MORSE & KNOWLES.

Dry Goods at Prices Never Known Before.

Now is the time to stock up for winter.

GOOD 40 INCH SHEETING FOR 6 and 6 1-2 Cts.

We offer another bale of those Extra fine and heavy 40 inch Cottons at 7c; never been old under 8 cents.

ALL OUTINGS AND PERCALES

that have never been offered under 12 1-2 cents and are sold for that in most places, for 10 Cents a Yard.

ONE LOT FALL SKIRT PATTERNS 25 CENTS EACH.

We shall offer BLANKETS at 25 per cent less than last year.

BARGAINS IN HOSIERY AND UNDERWEAR. MANY AT 3-4 REGULAR PRICE.

GREATEST VARIETY AND LOWEST PRICES IN BOOTS AND SHOES.

Call and Examine.

Morse & Knowles.

---

[141] William Richard Cutter, <u>Historic Homes and Places and Genealogical and Personal Memoirs Relating to the Families of Middlesex, Massachusetts</u>, Volume 1, (New York: Lewis Historical Publishing Company, 1908).

Seymour's house is located on Church Street, but on the opposite side from his partner, A. A. Sweet. It is the house just behind the Public Library at 9 Church Street. Like his partner, Seymour suffered the loss of his business to fire, first in 1882 and again in 1900. He died in Hopkinton on the 23rd of September, 1914 at the age of 66.

S. A. Knowles House

This house once had richer detailing, now obscured by siding. For example, just above the brick foundation there was a wide banding of wooden trim. Though the parts of the foundation which show are brick, below ground it is composed of large cut-granite blocks. The house was built with central heat and there is one fireplace.

Detail of original trim, as seen on the north side

Out of the Ashes

The Bridges Block & the Town Hall

New construction replaced the old Federal-style buildings destroyed in the fire of 1882. To the left is the Bridges Block which housed a number of stores, including one which apparently sold furniture. It was built on the site of the old Walcott house. Just beyond is the new Mahon Bros. store on the corner of Walcott Street. On the opposite corner we can just see a building that still exists, but without its top floor.

To the right of the Bridges Block was the new, dark-colored, Stick-style Town Hall. It was on the same site as the previous and current Town Hall. Out of view to the right was the small Braithwaite Building. Beyond the Braithwaite Building was the Stick-style Highland Block, with its Mansard roof shown on the next page.

The Highland House (formerly called Central Coffee House) was replaced by the Queen Anne-style Park House shown to the right of the Highland Block. Between the buildings is a lane leading to a new livery stable behind. Poles to support the electric lines for the new street railway are evident in this view.

The Highland Block & the Park House

Under the awning to the left was the store of S. A. Knowles. It is at the same location as A. A. Sweet's dry goods store (page 84). On a map of 1889, A. A. Sweet is shown as the occupant of the Highland Block. E. B. Clifford was the proprietor of the Park House to the right (east). The Hopkinton National Bank owned the building and had their office in the section to the right. A drug store and the post office were on the first floor. The Masonic Lodge moved to the upper floors after the Highland Block burned.

Since these buildings were all constructed at the same time due to the fire, they comprised a harmonious ensemble. Each was rich in texture and detail. They reflected the latest tastes in architecture. These late nineteenth-century buildings would have been difficult and expensive to maintain, but they must have presented a colorful scene when new. It was also a much more grand and substantial streetscape than what exists today.

Just east was the fifth large building in this harmonious row. It too reflected the architecture of the times.

The third Congregational Church

We are looking down Hayden Rowe toward Main Street, with the Common on the right. The watering trough is in the center of Hayden Rowe at the intersection. One rail of the street railway can be seen on the right side of the road. The Park House was just to the left when this photograph was taken. The large elm trees contributed to a welcoming, shady, and peaceful scene.

The Park House survived the next great fire of March 19, 1900. The Highland Block, with the dry goods store of S. A. Knowles, was not so fortunate. The building was only eight years old. The same was true for the Bridges Block, the second Town Hall and the Braithwaite Building. Mahon Bros. were also burned out again.

The sign was about all that was left of S. A. Knowles' store, but the Park House looks unscathed
A new addition was constructed on top of the bank as seen below

One of the Business Buildings at the Center.

The next view is from the Common after rebuilding had taken place. Note the trolley and the same watering trough from the previous view of Main Street. The photo of the adjacent church is contemporary, but is taken from another angle. It was an elaborate, Gothic-Revival-style building with Stick-style elements.

S. A. Knowles remained in the same location. His store still has an awning, but the building was not restored to its original look. Sadly, the Park House too was eventually destroyed by fire, in January of 1941. Today, the Masons have a small Colonial-style building on the site. The building which housed S. A. Knowles later had a drug store. It was remodeled in brick and is now The Middlesex Savings Bank. The building which became Brown & Smith's can be seen just east of the new brick Town Hall of 1902. Bill's Pizza and Restaurant now occupies the site of Brown & Smith's.

The buildings in the last few photographs show that there was still a lot of money available to support good architecture and quality craftsmanship. The third Town Hall, shown here, was constructed in brick and it survives today. The exterior trim and windows were restored in 2012.

Hopkinton had been expanding rapidly[142] and though the series of three, devastating fires in 1876, 1882, and 1900 slowed the pace, the engine of progress was still running. When it finally slowed to an idle, the town was left with a streetscape that still surprises. As the population dwindled to less than 2,300 by 1920, it was all the more striking. Here was a sleepy little village with these remarkable buildings. A visitor looking up Church Street in 1920 would have also glimpsed the enormous, granite, Catholic Church across from the old Methodist. This too was unusual for a small town.

1907 Skyline

Pine Trees Congregational Town Hall   *Methodist Catholic*

---

[142] Between 1850 and 1860, the population increased by 54.9% to 4,340. In 1880, it was 4,601, but by 1920 it was only 2,289. It didn't recover to 1880 levels until the late 1950's. In 2012, the population was over 15,000.

In September of 1938, the scene across Main Street from the Common changed once again. On the afternoon of September 21st the winds continued to increase. A hurricane was a new experience for everyone.[143] There were not the advance media warnings of today and the dash to the store for bread, milk, and batteries. One eyewitness was Dorthea Thompson. She lived in the Valentine Mansion at 2 Hayden Rowe. She was born about 1922, so she would have been about 16. Reports had been circulating about the swaying of the steeple on the Congregational Church, accompanied by groaning sounds. Dorthea left her window for a few minutes and suddenly she heard and felt a tremendous crash. The 125 foot, slate roofed, steeple had toppled. It crashed right through the middle of the building. The walls left standing were so buckled that the building was condemned and subsequently torn down. Crowds gathered to see the spectacular damage. They also came to witness the fallen pine trees in the cemetery. These had stood for over 100 years. Remember, there were unobstructed vistas from on top of the hill at that time. These pine trees had reached great height and were reportedly visible for 30 miles—suddenly, in an afternoon, they were gone.

6 Main Street - John Warren Lodge

Site of the Park House

2 Main Street - 4th Congregational Church

The Korean Presbyterian Church in 2014

---

[143] A major hurricane had not hit this area since the "Great Gale" of 1815.

The Walker Family

Continued

What happened to Joseph Walker Jr. after he went through bankruptcy? Was this the end of his business success? By no means! Just a few years after Lee Claflin moved his operation to Hopkinton, Joseph Walker Sr. and Jr. moved to Worcester. This was in 1843, just after Joseph Jr. went bankrupt. In Worcester, Joseph Jr. formed a partnership with a Mr. Barber, known as Barber & Walker. They built a factory on Lincoln Square next to the rail lines.

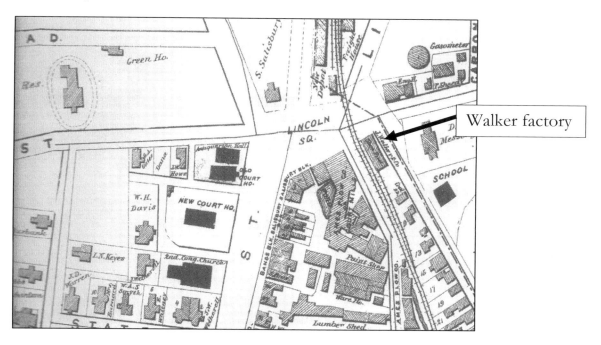

Walker factory

Just before entering Lincoln Sq. on what is now Route 9 (from the right in this view), you would have crossed the two railroad tracks shown here. If you looked left, just before crossing the tracks, you would have seen the J. Walker and Co. factory. Notice they had their own railroad siding like Claflin in Framingham.[144] Joseph Jr. appears to have continued to make boots to order. Joseph Sr. died in Worcester on the 9th of January, 1852, at the age of 91. Hitty preceded him on the 26th of September, 1849. She was 83.

---

[144] Also notice the Salisbury Mansion in Lincoln Square. This house was saved from destruction when it was moved west to the other side of the large house circled by a driveway (another Salisbury house). Both still exist and the Salisbury Mansion is open for tours under the direction of the Worcester Historical Museum.

Joseph Henry Walker was admitted to the firm of J. Walker & Co. in 1851 upon coming of age. Prior to this he had worked in the factory and kept the books after working hours. His brothers, George Moore Walker and Andrew Chapin Walker were likewise admitted in time. George became a soldier during the Civil War. In 1862, Joseph H. left the firm and established his own business on Eaton Place. George joined him in 1864, after the war, and the firm was named J. H. & G. M. Walker. Subsequently, they built a factory on Front Street and one on Eaton Place in Worcester.

But in 1870, they moved to a new factory on Water Street and G. M. soon retired. Samuel D. Davenport Jr. took his place. The factory was doubled in 1879. Boston offices were at 115 Pearl Street. Their specialty was the very popular "Walker Boot" advertised here.

J. H. & G. M. WALKER,

MANUFACTURERS OF

WALKER

STOGA,   **BOOT**   VEAL KIP,

☆

DRESS & CALF BOOTS,

MADE FROM

WALKER TANNERY STOCK.

WORCESTER, MASS.

J. H. WALKER.   G. M. WALKER.   S. D. DAVENPORT.

Notice that it says "Walker Tannery Stock." This is because J. H. was a partner in the Walker Oakley Co. of Chicago, which he formed with J. W. Oakley in 1867. They were burned out in the great Chicago fire and sustained losses of between $50,000 and $100,000. In spite of this, they went on to rank among the largest companies of their kind in the country. They had offices in Boston, which were under the direct control of J. H. Walker. They employed from 350 to 400 men in the two Chicago tanneries. An appreciation of the size of the operation can be gleaned from the following image of the Chicago plant.

CHICAGO : WALKER OAKLEY COMPANY.

The factories produced 400,000 wax calf-skins, 150,000 kips, and 50,000 satin calf-skins annually. They enjoyed continual growth due to their location near the supply of fine grades of leather. Chicago was, of course, the location of the stockyards. Offices were also opened in San Francisco. It became part of the American Hide and Leather Co. in August of 1899.[145]

In Worcester, a two-and-a-half story building known as the "Walker Storehouse" was built behind the new factory at 73 Winter Street, in 1879, for "aging" the boots. By 1880, more than 300 employees worked in the factory, producing heavy boots, which were widely sold in the American West. The J. H. & G. M. Walker Co. stayed in business until January, 1888, when the remaining members of the firm retired. Company assets were bought by F.W. Blacker, who continued making the "Walker Boot" in a different location.

---

[145] M. F. Sweetser, edited by Moses King, King's Handbook of the United States, (Buffalo, NY: Moses King Corporation, Publishers, 1891-1892), (including illustration of the Walker Oakley Company).

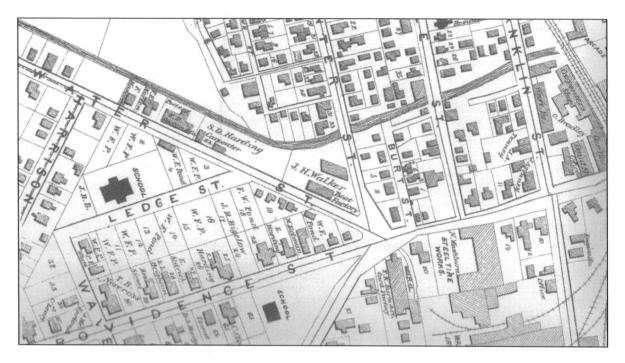

The 1870 factory on Water Street is shown in the center of this period map

Remarkably, the factory still exists, as seen in these two views. However, it is endangered since a modern use has not yet been found.

Boot and shoe factories were run by steam power generated on site. Distinct functions were conducted on each floor. Typically, in one room in the basement was the steam engine and in others were machines for cutting and rolling the leather, also shaping the soles. In the stories above, the upper leather was sewn together, generally by women, using steam-powered sewing machines. The upper leather was then secured to the last. The last was usually made of wood to the shape of a particular foot size. The outer soles were tacked on by hand in preparation for pegging. The pegging machine then took over. It was fed by a thin strip of wood, one hundred feet in length, and neatly coiled like a watch spring. The width of the coil matched the desired length of the peg. Pegs were cut and dropped into an individual cell, ready for insertion. The machines ran at a rate of fourteen pegs per second. Upon completion of this operation, the boots went up to the next floor for final finishing and packing in boxes for shipment.

Joseph Henry Walker married first, Sarah Ellen Harrington. They had two children, a boy, who died in infancy, and a girl named Ellen. After the death of his wife in 1859, he married Hannah Maria Clapp Kelly on the 3rd of April, 1862. They had three children, Joseph Henry Jr., George M., and Agnes M. Agnes was born in 1870. She married Adams Davenport Claflin.

J. H. Walker was considered the "father" of most of Worcester's twenty-three late-19th century boot and shoe manufacturers. Most had gotten their start in his shop. Like William Claflin, he went on to have success in politics, ultimately as a member of the United States House of Representatives from Massachusetts (1889-1899). He served as Chairman of the Committee on Banking and Currency. He was a member of the common council of Worcester (1852-1854) and president of the Worcester Board of Trade. He was a member of the American Academy of Political and Social Science from 1892 and the author of "Money, Trade, and Banking." He had a stock farm in New Hampton, NH. Joseph Henry Walker Sr. died in Worcester on the 3rd of April, 1907.

HON. JOSEPH H. WALKER.

Adams Davenport Claflin

He was born on the 7th of February, 1862, in Newtonville. Like his father, Governor William, Adams was also a very successful businessman. He was educated in private schools in Newton, Boston, and France. He received an A. B. from Harvard in 1886. Adams was with the Mather Electric Co. of Manchester, CT from 1887 to 1894. He built and managed the Commonwealth Ave. Street Railway in 1895. He was president and trustee of the Boston Suburban Electric Companies; director of the Middlesex & Boston Street Railway Co., the Westborough and Hopkinton Street Railway, the Washington Mills, and the Emery Manufacturing Co. The famous Norumbega Park (1897-1965) in Newton was built by his street railway company to encourage more riders.

On the 30th of October, 1888, Adams married Agnes Walker, daughter of Joseph Henry Walker of Worcester, thus uniting the two renowned boot manufacturing families of Massachusetts. Adams lived in Newton until his death in 1933.

Newton Center home of Adams Davenport and Agnes (Walker) Claflin

Adams Davenport Claflin (and child)

Agnes (Walker) Claflin with William and Mildred

On the steps of their home in Newton

Trolley Service

In 1901, the Westborough & Hopkinton Street Railway was incorporated. It connected Westborough and Hopkinton to the network running through Framingham to points east. Service from Hopkinton to Milford was also established. In 1908, the street railway was absorbed into the Middlesex & Boston Street Railway, which would eventually become the MBTA. From Ashland, the tracks followed the current Route 135 all the way to the center of Westborough, with an interesting exception shown here:

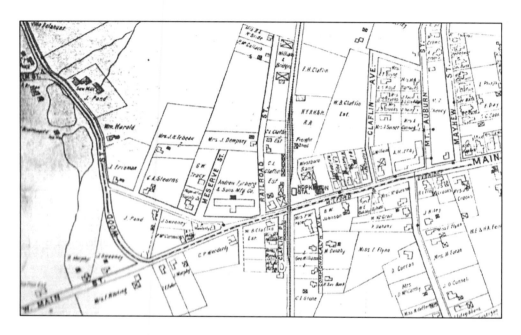

At the time this map was created about 1907, the street railway was known as the Milford & Uxbridge. Wood Street had been diverted down the hill to the west to accommodate the street railway, while not disturbing the houses at the old intersection. In 2013, Route 135 follows the original route of Wood Street and the intersection with Main is a point of traffic congestion, which now threatens these same houses.

With regard to this map, a few side points are worth mentioning. Andrew Fyrberg & Sons Mfg. Co. is shown to be occupying the abandoned factory at the intersection (see page 194). After this factory was torn down, it was the site of Patten's Plumbing for many years. Now, there is a day care facility on the site. Railroad Street has been renamed Meserve and the original Meserve Street is a driveway. Clement Meserve owned a house on this lot prior to the construction of the factory.

Notice too that the N.Y. N.H. & H. Railroad crossed Main Street with two tracks and they had a small freight yard behind the station and the "Westboro Bank." The bank was a former hotel for travelers. In Hopkinton, one had the choice of electric or steam travel.

At the Common, the street railway had a bypass track at the intersection with the line from Milford at Hayden Rowe. The tracks followed the east side of Hayden Rowe, passing the Common. Across the town line into Milford, the tracks did not follow Cedar Street. Rather, they paralleled the N.Y., N.H., & H. Railroad bed. If you take the Milford Upper Charles Trail, you will see the parallel rail bed just to the east. It was built later, but it has been out of operation longer, so it is sometimes harder to follow. It has melted into a swampy area in one section. More blasting was needed to build the street railway than the earlier, standard railroad. In a few areas, much rock had to be removed.

Here we have the 200th Anniversary celebration on the Common in 1915 and the welcome sign was out. With the advent of the electric street railway, lighting was starting to be converted to electricity in the houses surrounding the Common. In 1910, none of the schools at the Common had yet been supplied with electricity. They were still heated by iron stoves.

Here on Hayden Rowe, instead of a trolley, a car is coming from the direction of Milford. Industry was moving away, but the houses remained. The automobile would come to have a large impact on Hopkinton—one that continues to grow. Eventually, it meant one could live in Hopkinton and work far away. The need to travel quickly and in all kinds of weather, coupled with the need for reliable electricity, has resulted in few canopied streets like this. The loss of the great elm trees to disease didn't help either.

Increasing automobile traffic is putting pressure to redesign Main Street. Traffic lights continue to be added to the old "Central Turnpike." New housing developments have all but eliminated the farmland that survived into the 1970's. But much remains from the past to remind us of the uncommon people who lived here, the things they accomplished, and the changes they made to Meetinghouse Hill, with its enduring Common.

Subject Properties – Owners/Buildings

Common / Training Field
      Town of Hopkinton (c. 1725)

Cemetery
      Samuel Barrett I
      John Manning (1742)
      John Barrett I (1742)
      Samuel Barrett III
      John Barrett II & Nancy (Barrett) Freeland
      Town of Hopkinton (1807)

2 Main Street (Church building)
      Barrett Family (1725)
      Congregational/First Parish Church (church 1830-1883-1939)
      United Church of Christ (1961-1994)
      Korean Presbyterian Church (1997)

6 Main Street (Masonic building)
      Barrett Family (1725)
      Thomas & Nancy (Barrett) Freeland
      Nancy Freeland (1805)
      Samuel & Joseph Valentine (1806)
      Joseph & Fanny Valentine   First Parish Church (adjacent lot)
      Central Coffee House (Highland House) (1831-1882)
      Park House (c. 1883-1941) (Hopkinton National Bank, Post Office)
      John Warren Lodge (1951)

10 Main Street (Middlesex Savings Bank)
      Same as 6 Main through 1882
      A. A. Sweet (Dry goods store built on Coffee House lot)
      Highland Block (c. 1883-1900) (S. A. Knowles)
      Highland Block (S. A. Knowles) (rebuilt as one-story building)
      Drug Store
      Hopkinton Holliston Bank
      Middlesex Savings Bank (1992)

14 Main Street (Bill's Pizza & Restaurant)
     Same as 6 Main through 1840's)
     Claflin & Coburn Co.
     Braithwaite Block
     Brown & Smith
     Bill's Pizza & Restaurant

18 Main Street (Hopkinton Town Hall)
     Same as 6 Main through Valentine
     Claflin & Coburn Co. and E. Thompson Co. factories
     First Town Hall (c. 1850 to 1882)
     Second Town Hall (c. 1884 to 1900)
     Third Town Hall (1902 to the present)

20-24 Main Street (Commercial)
     Samuel B. Walcott (before 1831)
     Lucius H. Wakefield
     Post Office Block (with 28 Main)
     Bridges Block (after 1882 to 1900)
     E. L. Bridges (primarily vacant lot after 1900)
     Commercial building constructed c. 1920 (3 store fronts)

28 Main Street (Hopkinton Supply Co. building)
     Samuel B. Walcott (before 1831)
     Betsey Barber & Barber's store (by 1856)
     Mahon Bros. (until 1900) (Post Office Block)
     Hopkinton Supply Co. (1906) (building constructed)
     A&P and Edison
     Framingham Motor Parts

13 Main Street (Hopkinton Public Library)
     Joseph Valentine Estate
     Jefferson & Harriet (Valentine) Pratt (heirs) (dwelling constructed)
     (E. Thompson & Co. storehouse on site of future St. Paul's – 1888)
     Sarah (Pratt) Whitin (Mrs. John C.) (heir)
     Library and Episcopal Church lots (1895)
     (Library constructed 1895, St. Paul's Church constructed 1898)
     Library expanded to include former St. Paul's (1967)

15 Main Street (Commercial – Pan Thai Restaurant)
    Joseph Valentine Estate
    John L. & Miriam R. Valentine (heirs)
    Miriam R. Valentine
    Henry R. Valentine (heir) (house removed after 1899)
    Vacant lot 1904, 1910 (new bungalow constructed after 1910)

17 Main Street (E. A. Bates house – Commercial)
    Joseph Valentine Estate
    Dr. Jefferson & Harriet Pratt (heirs)
    Eliakim A. Bates (residence c. 1855)
    Arthur R. Crooks (by 1908)
    Annunziata Family

25 Main Street (Pratt-Crooks Mansion - Commercial)
    Joseph Valentine Estate
    Dr. Jefferson & Harriet Pratt (heirs) (residence constructed 1849)
    Abram & Ann Crooks
    Ann Crooks (1892)
    Archdiocese of Boston

35 Main Street (Erastus Thompson Mansion - Commercial)
    Joseph Valentine Estate
    Erastus Thompson (residence constructed c. 1860)
    Franklin & Mary (Crooks) Thompson

43 Main Street (E. Thompson house)
    Joseph Valentine Estate
    Erastus Thompson (residence constructed c. 1850)
    William B. Coburn

87 Main Street (S. D. Davenport Mansion)
    Thomas Walker
    Dr. Thomas & Sally (Claflin) Bucklin
    Samuel D. & Mary (Bucklin) Davenport (1822, residence also)
    Mary (Freeland) Davenport (1863)
    Daniel T. Bridges (1864)
    Charles & Priscilla Morse (1886)
    Horace & Helen Fenn (1906)
    Palmer Family

5 East Main Street (Stone Tavern)
> Samuel Barrett I
> John Manning (1742)
> John Barrett I (1742)
> Samuel Barrett III
> Isaac Claflin
> Samuel & Polly Valentine Jr. (1804)
> Polly Valentine (1823)
> Ann M. Claflin & Susan Tilton (1863)
> C. W. & Ann M. Claflin (residents)
> C. L. Claflin (after 1894)
> C. L. Claflin Estate (1905)
> Edward W. Pierce (heir)
> William & Martha Gleason
> Carrie Taylor (1907)
> Alice Tebeau & Mary Hines (1915)
> Stenzel (1942)

7 East Main Street (Wadsworth house)
> Barrett Family, same as for 5 East Main
> Willard Wadsworth
> C. W. & Ann M. Claflin
> Luther Taylor
> James F. & Carrie Taylor
> Alice Tebeau (1915)
> James McIlvenny (1918)
> Edward Ray (1924)
> Harold Gleason (1948)
> Chesmore Family

21 East Main Street (How house)
> John How
> Ephraim Read
> Emily Read (by 1831)
> Estate of Emily Read (Silas Mirick, executor)
> Lee Claflin (1854)
> Benjamin W. & Evelyn B. Johnson (1854)
> Phipps (1856)
> Michael Collary (1857)
> Collary (1906)

1 Ash Street (One Ash Street - Commercial)
    Town of Hopkinton (1715 – Land to support schools)
    Charles Morris (1735)
    Roger Price (1744-1752) (church & cemetery constructed c. 1748)
    William Price (1783)
    Madam Elizabeth Price (1802) (church destroyed 1815)
    Episcopal Church (1818) (church constructed 1818, burned 1865)
    Town of Hopkinton (Schools) (school constructed c. 1875)
    St. Paul's Episcopal parish house (1957)
    One Ash Street – remodel of 1875 building for commercial use
    (Episcopal Cemetery – East Main, became private Valentine/Claflin
    cemetery. Since 1956, Town of Hopkinton)

5 Ash Street (Madam Price Mansion or Price/Tucker/Kelly house)
    Same as 1 Ash to William Price (1783)
    Madam Elizabeth Price (1802) (residence constructed c. 1810-1820)
    Willard Aldrich (1820)
    Silas Moore (1832) (mortgaged 1833)
    William Godfrey (1836)
    Artimus Johnson (1840)
    Artimus Johnson & Sylvester Phipps (Greek-Revival remodel)
    Joshua Tucker (1842)
    Frances Tucker (heir)
    Martha Everett
    Sara Humphrey (1918)
    Honora Harrigan (1925)
    Kelly Family

11 Ash Street (Center School)
    Same as 5 Ash Street through Tucker
    Part occupied by house of Mrs. Timothy Lee
    Town of Hopkinton (Schools)
    Center School (1928, expanded 1950)

15 Ash Street (Morse house)
    Lands held in common
    Madam Elizabeth Price   Elijah Fitch (adjacent lots)
    Willard Aldrich
    Susanna Aldrich
    Willard Aldrich Morse (residence constructed about 1875)
    Susan E. Morse   Artimus Putnam (adjacent lot)
        George Ellard
        George Stedman
    John Woodbury (1877)   John Woodbury
    Amy Perkins
    C. L. Claflin
    C. L. Claflin Estate (1905)
    Edward W. Pierce (1920)
    William Stearns Morse

17 Ash Street (Gannon house)
    Lands held in common
    Elijah Fitch
    John Gannon

21 Ash Street (Woodbury house)
    Lands held in common
    Elijah Fitch
    John Woodbury

25 Ash Street (Hemenway house)
    Lands held in common
    Elijah Fitch
    Fisher Hemenway

2/4/6 Park Street (Allen house or Walker-Claflin Mansion)
    Town of Hopkinton (1715)
    Roger Price (1752)
    William Price (1783)
    Madam Elizabeth Price (1802)
    Trustees for the School Fund (1821)
    Moses Chamberlain (1821)
    John A. Fitch
    Timothy B. Allen (1832) (residence likely constructed 1833)
    Artimus C. Putnam & Jacob Fairbanks (1833)
    A. C. Putnam (1834)
    William Smith (1834) (residence mortgaged in November)
    Artimus C. Putnam (1835)
    Joseph Walker (1835)   A. C. Putnam (divided off part)
    Lee Claflin (1843)   A. C. Putnam
    Joseph Whitman (1853)
    Elenor Whitman (1854)
    Charles W. Claflin (1857)   John L. Pingry (1872)
    Charles L. Claflin (1884)   Pingry to Claflin (1900)
    C. L. Claflin Estate (1905)
    Edward Winslow Pierce & Winslow Claflin Pierce (heirs) (1919)
    Edward W. Pierce (1920)
    George & Carlotta Minard (1924)
    Framingham Co-op Bank (1930)
    William & Susan Arms (1932)   (not 4/6 Park)
    Framingham Co-op Bank (1935)
    Phil & Marjorie Clow (1943)
    Richard & Hazel Gallagher (May 1946)
    Clarence & Aline Farr (Dec 1946)
    Spiro & Sigrid Pantos (1950)
    Dockstader Family (1955)

4/6 Park (Claflin-Hayward house)
    Set off by C. W. Claflin (residence constructed)
    Lewis Hayward (1882)
    Martha (Claflin) Hayward (1897)
    C. L. Claflin (1897)
    C. L. Claflin Estate (1905)
    Edward Winslow Pierce & Winslow Claflin Pierce (heirs) (1919)
    Edward W. Pierce (1920)
    George & Carlotta Minard (1924)
    Framingham Co-op Bank (1930)

8 Park Street (Aldrich house)
      Town of Hopkinton (1715)
      Charles Morris (1735)
      Roger Price (1752)
      William Price (1783)
      Madam Elizabeth Price (1802)
      Trustees for the School Fund (1821)
      John Gibson Jr. (1821)
      Cornelius Gibson
      Willard Aldrich (1823) (residence constructed c. 1824)
      Susanna Aldrich (heir)
      Lucy Bixby (heir)
      William Mosher (1920) (property divided)
      Francis Kennedy (2 lots, 1927 and 1931)

2 Hayden Rowe Street (Valentine Mansion – site of Price Mansion House)
      Samuel Barrett II
      Charles Morris III
      Roger Price (1746)
      Sir Charles Henry Frankland, Bart. (c. 1751) (leased property)
      Admiral Henry Cromwell (lived there with his father)
      John Troutbeck (leased property)
      William Price (1783)
      Madam Elizabeth Price (1802)
      Lawson & Mary Ann (Price) Valentine & Olivia (Price) Hall (1820)
      Charles Valentine (1821) (leased property)
      Joseph Valentine (1825) (purchased from Lawson Valentine)
      Benjamin Herrick (leased property)
      Joseph Valentine (new residence built after Price Mansion burns)
      Joseph Valentine Estate (divided and house sold separately – 1845)
      William Claflin (1845)
      Nathan P. Coburn (c. 1855 to 1864)
      Hopkinton National Bank (became commercial/residential)

4 Hayden Rowe Street (Claflin-Page house)
      Joseph Valentine Estate (1845)
      Dr. Jefferson & Harriet (Valentine) Pratt (heir)
      Sarah (Pratt) Whitin (Mrs. John C. Whitin) (heir) (1883)
      C. L. Claflin & George McConnell (1892) Edwin Thompson land too.
      Charles L. Claflin (1892)
      Winslow Claflin Pierce (1892) (constructs new residence - 1892)
      Charles L. Claflin (1895)
      Webster W. Page (1898)

6 Hayden Rowe Street (Edwin Thompson house)
Joseph Valentine Estate (1845)
Erastus Thompson
Edwin D. Thompson (residence constructed before 1889)
Fred Wood (by 1898)
Butterfield Family

8 Hayden Rowe Street (Lee Claflin Mansion)
Joseph Valentine Estate (1845)
Lee Claflin (1845) (residence constructed c. 1853)
Polly Claflin (1871)
William Claflin (by 1889)
Dr. Edgar A. & Gertrude V. Briggs (by 1906)
Oakley Family
Wilson Family
Walker Family

10-12 Hayden Rowe Street (Part of 8 Hayden Rowe until at least 1875)
William Claflin (constructs new duplex residence before 1888)
Crowley Family

14 Hayden Rowe Street (Guy house)
Joseph Valentine Estate (1845)
Betsey Guy (1846) (residence constructed)
Betsey Guy Estate (1859)
Samuel Crooks (1859)
John, Samuel, and Abram Crooks
J. M. Stewart

16 Hayden Rowe Street (Crooks house)
Joseph Valentine Estate
Abram Crooks (residence constructed c. 1846)
John C. Adams

18 Hayden Rowe Street (Mosher house)
Joseph Valentine
Lee Claflin
Methodist Episcopal Church and parsonage (1858)
William Mosher (1922) (residence constructed 1922-1925)

20 Hayden Rowe Street (now Church Pl.)
    Joseph Valentine
    Lee Claflin
    Hopkinton Academy/High School
    Church Place (new street) (before 1910)

22-24 Hayden Rowe Street
    Joseph Valentine
    Lee Claflin
    Nathan P. Coburn (1843)
    Samuel Crooks Jr. (1855) (residence constructed by 1889)
    Mrs. A. McMullen (1907)

26 Hayden Rowe Street
    John C. Webster
    Nathan P. Coburn (1845)
    Samuel Crooks Jr. (1855) (residence constructed by 1889)
    Eames (1907)

28 Hayden Rowe Street (Samuel Crooks Mansion)
    Jefferson Pratt
    Samuel Crooks Jr. (residence constructed by 1856)
    Samuel Crooks Estate (1893)
    Thomas C. Dobson
    Robert & Mary Wilson (1924)
    Wright Family

30 Hayden Rowe Street (B. F. Coburn house demolished and now part of 34)
    Jefferson Pratt
    Samuel & Abraham Crooks (1867)
    Benjamin F. Coburn (by 1875)
    J. Cunningham (by 1907)

34 Hayden Rowe Street (Commercial – built for A. Coburn & Son)
    Francis Coburn
    Wilbur F. Claflin (Lee Claflin & Co.) (first factory constructed)
    Alonzo Coburn (A. Coburn & Son) (Wm. Claflin, Coburn & Co.)
    Coburn, Gauss & Co. (1891)
    Andrew Fyrberg & Sons (c. 1903)
    Hermina Silk Mill (c. 1905)
    Lawson Pink Food Products Co. (by 1912)
    Seamans & Cobb Thread Mills (1918 – at least 1946)
    General Packets (1958-1969) (factory remodeled)

44 Hayden Rowe Street (D. J. Coburn house)
>   J. Woodard (c. 1857)
>   Daniel J. Coburn (c. 1875)

50 Hayden Rowe Street (Schoolhouse – factory - now residence)
>   Moved from Common by Lee Claflin (after 1840)
>   Wilbur F. Claflin (one of several factory buildings)
>   A. Coburn & Son
>   Curtis Smith

52 Hayden Rowe Street (Alonzo Coburn Mansion)
>   Alonzo Coburn (residence constructed 1844-1848)

58-64 Hayden Rowe Street (formerly 78 – The F. B. Mansfield Mansion)
>   Ministerial Lot (possibly also part of Wilson lot)
>   Franklin Mansfield (1853) (residence constructed)
>   Edward Wiswall (1874)
>   Clarence A. Claflin (1877)
>   Hopkinton Savings Bank (c. 1886)
>   Adelbert E. Claflin
>   Celia A. & Daniel J. Coburn
>   Andrew Fyrberg (1903)
>   Paul A. & Nellie M. Hewitt (1911)
>   Levi & Annie L. Diamond (1914)
>   Arthur Bruerton (1919)
>   Allen/Boliver (1922)
>   Henry Wilson Co-op Bank
>   Samuel Berger (1927) (residence damaged in 1930)
>   Nathan Hyman (1931)
>   George Frye (1932)
>   Paul Keaney (1935) (residence burned or was demolished)

65 Hayden Rowe Street (W. F. Claflin Mansion – Spring Hill Farm)
>   James Wilson
>   Wilbur F. Claflin (residence constructed 1854)
>   William Bassett (by 1889)
>   Robert & Sarah Gillespie (c. 1905)
>   (Servant's wing removed in the 1950's) (Many transactions)

9 Church Street (S. A. Knowles house)
    Joseph Valentine Estate
    Jefferson Pratt
    Sarah Whitin
    Seymour A. Knowles (by 1889)
    James C. McColl

14 Church Street (A. A. Sweet house)
    Joseph Valentine Estate
    Dr. Jefferson Pratt
    Alvan A. Sweet (residence constructed c. 1863)
    Dr. William A. Phipps

73 Frankland Road – Ashland (original route of the Bay Path)
    James Gooch, Esq.
    Sir Charles Henry Frankland (1749) (residence constructed 1751)
    Jacques Joseph Villiers de Rouen (tenant c. 1765)
    Henry Cromwell, Esq. (1783)
    Dr. Timothy Shepherd (1793)
    Mrs. Mary (Stow) Shepherd (Widow)
        She married Brigadier General William Hildreth (1809)
    Becomes part of the new town of Ashland (1846)
    Mrs. Mary Hildreth to:
    Elias Nason (1857) (residence burned 1858, rebuilt 1861)
    Noyes (1876)
    W. Jennings
    (Residence burned c. 1904, rebuilt c. 1905)

133 West Union Street – Ashland
    Thomas Valentine (residence constructed)
    Samuel Valentine (1783) (residence burned and was rebuilt)
    Andrew Price Valentine (estate divided)
    William Price Valentine (residence remodeled 1870)
    Albert William Valentine, heir (died 1909)
    Miss Francis Valentine (by 1918 to at least 1952)
    Became part of the new town of Ashland (1846)
    (House and barn in jeopardy 2014)

Boot Manufacturers in Hopkinton
1850

This list is extracted (in order) from the Federal Census for 1850:

Name	Value of Real Estate Owned (in Hopkinton)
Fisher Hemmenway	2000
Gustavus Adams	------
Erastus Thompson (Merchant)	4000
Nathaniel Johnson (Merchant)	4300
William Claflin	9000
Charles N. Mellen (Merchant)	1500
Samuel D. Davenport	16000
Levi P. Coburn (Merchant)	3000
Jonas Woodard	2300
Willard Woodward	500
Samuel Crooks Jr.	700
Abraham Crooks	300
Wm. H. H. Loring	2500
John J. Loring	2500
Stephen Barnard	1500
Lowell Claflin	3500
Lee Claflin (Merchant)	11000
Abner Albee	2000
Enos King	4000
Lovett H. Bowker	5000
Benj. Phipps (Merchant)	3500
William A. Phipps	5000
Uriah Bowker	1800
James Bowker	2000
F. B. Mansfield	------
Joshua M. Weston	------
John Smith (Merchant)	800
Joseph L. Gamage	3500
Elbridge G. Rice	275

This is a list of "Bootmanufacturers" as opposed to "Bootmakers." Lee Claflin and others are listed as "Merchant" because of their focus on sales. On the other hand, E. A. Bates, with his store, is listed as a "Trader" instead of "Merchant." At least some of these Merchants were in the boot and shoe industry – certainly Erastus Thompson.

Acknowledgements

I would like to particularly acknowledge the assistance of the following:

The late *Rose Leveille,* Hopkinton Public Library Director from 1991 to 1994 and Library Trustee, acquired an extensive knowledge of Hopkinton's history. Her efforts greatly expanded upon the 1940's work of Beryl Osborn. She was always ready to share and she fostered my interest in the industrial development of the town.

Linda Connelly is a member of the Hopkinton Historical Society and Archivist Librarian for the Hopkinton Public Library. Her work in organizing the Treasure Room at the library has made research much easier.

Susan Marshall is the Adult Services Librarian for the Hopkinton Public Library. She scanned some of the photographs and provided editorial suggestions, encouragement, and frequent access to the Treasure Room. She also suffered through my use of the microfilm reader adjacent to her desk!

Russell Greve is the curator of the Hopkinton Historical Society. Russ helped me find numerous photographs and encouraged me to publish.

Sara Goldberg at Historic Newton provided help in finding images of the Coburn and Claflin families and properties.

Lyn Lovell at Memorial Hall, the Milford Historical Museum, provided assistance in researching the Milford home of Lee Claflin, and the Hopkinton Railroad.

A special thanks to *Mr. & Mrs. David Dockstader* for allowing me a close-up look at their home at 2 Park Street while it was undergoing an extensive and sensitive restoration. I know I am not alone in having wondered what the house must have been like a hundred years ago. It is what led me to begin this book.

Additional resources were made available by the following: Ashland Historical Society, Ashland Public Library, Boston University, Framingham Public Library, Harvard University, Hopkinton Town Hall, Hudson Public Library, Lancaster Public Library, Middlesex South Registry of Deeds, Milford Public Library, Newton Public Library, Worcester Historical Society, and the Worcester Public Library.

Bibliography

"A Brief History of Hopkinton," by Mrs. Frances A. Stafford, 1915.

"A Brief History of Leicester, Massachusetts," by Rev. Amos Hill Coolidge, 1890.

"A City So Grand, The Rise of an American Metropolis, Boston, 1850-1890," by Stephen Puleo, Beacon Press, Boston, 2010.

"A Report of the Record Commissioners of the City of Boston, Containing the Records of Boston Selectmen, 1736 to 1742," Rockwell & Churchill, City Printers, Boston, 1886.

"A Report of the Record Commissioners of the City of Boston, Containing the Boston Births from A. D. 1700 to A.D. 1800," Rockwell & Churchill, City Printers, Boston, 1895.

"A Report of the Record Commissioners of the City of Boston, Containing the Boston Marriages from 1700 to 1751," Municipal Printing Office, Boston, 1898.

"A Woman of the Century: Fourteen Hundred-Seventy Biographical Sketches Accompanied by Portraits of Leading American Women in All Walks of Life," edited by Francis E. Willard and Mary A. Livermore, published by Charles Wells Moulton, Buffalo, 1893.

"Annals of King's Chapel, From the Puritan Age of New England to the Present Day," by Henry Wilder Foote, 2 Volumes, Little, Brown, & Co., Boston, 1881/1882/1887/1900.

"Beacon Street: Its Buildings and Residents," by Robert E. Guarino, The History Press, Charleston, 2011.

"Biography of Henry Ward Beecher," by Wm. C. Beecher and Rev. Samuel Scoville, New York, 1888.

"Boyhood Days in Hopkinton, Massachusetts in the 1870's," by Edgar Homer Grout, Hopkinton, 1948 and 1950.

"Brampton Sketches," by Mary B. Claflin, copyright by Thomas Y. Crowell & Co., New York, published by C. J. Peters & Son, Typographers & Electrotypers, Boston, 1890.

"Commemorative Biographical Record of the Counties of Brown, Kewaunee and Door, Wisconsin," by J. H. Beers and Co., Chicago, 1895.

"Cyclopedia of Michigan, Historical and Biographical, Comprising a Synopsis of General History of the State, and Biographical Sketches of Men Who Have, in Their Various Spheres, Contributed Toward Its Development," published by Western Publishing & Engraving Co., New York and Detroit, 1900.

"Days and Ways in Old Boston," published by R. H. Stearns and Company, Boston, 1914.

"Dictionary of Canadian Biography," Volume IV (1771-1800), Morris, Charles (1711-1781), by Phyllis R. Blakeley, University of Toronto/Université Laval, University of Toronto Press, Toronto, 1979.

"Du Page County, Illinois," by Rufus Blanchard, O. L. Baskin & Co, Historical Publishers, Chicago, 1882.

"Eminent Nova Scotians of New England Birth," by Rev. Arthur Wentworth Hamilton Eaton, C. C. L., of Boston, the New England Historical and Genealogical Register, Volume LXII, 1913.

"Felling the Ancient Oaks, How England Lost Its Great Country Estates," by John Martin Robinson, Aurum Press Limited, London, 2011.

"Fighting for the King in America's First Civil War," by Thomas B. Allen, Harper Collins Publishers, 2010.

"Framingham – An American Town," by Stephen W. Herring, for the Framingham Historical Society, Framingham, 2000.

"Harvard Memorial Biographies," Volume I, by Thomas Wentworth Higginson, Cambridge, MA, Sever and Francis, 1866.

"Historic Homes and Places and Genealogical and Personal Memoirs Relating to the Families of Middlesex, Massachusetts, Volume I," by William Richard Cutter, Lewis Historical Publishing Company, New York, 1908.

"History and Directory of Hopkinton, Massachusetts," by Clement Meserve, A.E. Foss & Company, Needham, 1891.

"History, Gazetteer and Directory of Nottinghamshire," by William White, Sheffield, England, 1832.

"History of Framingham, Early Known as Danforth's Farms, 1640-1880," by Josiah Howard Temple, Framingham Historical Society, 1887.

"History of Hopkinton and Ashland," unpublished thesis by Byrle Osborn, c. 1940, reprinted by the Hopkinton School Committee, 1980.

"History of Littleton, New Hampshire," by George C. Furber, Edited by James R. Jackson. Volume III, Town of Littleton, University Press, Cambridge, 1905 – Information regarding the Barrett family.

"History of Middlesex County with Biographical Sketches of Many of Its Prominent Men," by Duane Hamilton Hurd, Volumes I-III, J. W. Lewis & Co., Philadelphia, 1890.

"History of the Town of Milford, Worcester County, Massachusetts, From Its First Settlement to 1881," by Adin Ballou, Franklin Press, Rand, Avery, & Co., Boston, 1882.

"History of Milton, Massachusetts, 1640-1877," by Albert Kendall Teele, Rockwell & Churchill, Boston, 1887.

"King's Handbook of the United States," text by M. F. Sweetser, edited by Moses King, Moses King Corporation, Publishers, Buffalo, 1891-1892.

"Loyalists of Massachusetts and the Other Side of the Revolution," by James Henry Stark, The Salem Press Co., Salem, Massachusetts, 1910.

"Marblehead's Pygmalion, Finding the Real Agnes Surriage,"by F. Marshall Bauer, The History Press, Charleston, 2010.

"Old Boston in Colonial Days or St. Botolph's Town," L. C. Page Co., Boston, 1908.

"Old Boston Taverns and Tavern Clubs," by Samuel Adams Drake, W. A. Butterfield, Boston, 1917.

"Our Little Old School Houses," by Harold S. Wood, for the Hopkinton Historical Society, 1960.

"Professional and Industrial History of Suffolk County, Massachusetts," Volumes I-III, by William T. Davis, The Boston History Company, Boston, 1894.

"Record of the Descendants of Timothy Rockwood," by E. L. Rockwood, 1856.

"Sir Charles Henry Frankland, Baronet: or Boston in the Colonial Times," by Elias Nason, M. A., J. Munsell, Albany, New York, 1865.

"Sketch of the Life of the Honorable John Read, of Boston, 1722-1749," by George Bowlend Reed, privately printed by Beacon Press, Thomas Todd, Boston, 1879.

"The Crooked and Narrow Streets of Boston, 1600-1822," by Annie Haven Thwing, Marshall Jones Co., Boston, 1920.

"The Fountain Inn, Agnes Surriage and Sir Harry Frankland" by Nathan Perkins Sanborn, Marblehead Historical Society, Marblehead, MA, 1904.

"The Framingham Evening News," 12 September, 1918, Framingham, MA.

"The Hopkinton Light," Vol. 1, No. 1, 15 October, 1894 and Vol. 2, No. 3, December, 1895, Hopkinton, MA.

"The Life of the Honorable Lee Claflin: A Christian Merchant and Eminent Philanthropist," by David Sherman, Boston, 1883 (Mugar Library, Boston University).

"The New England Historical and Genealogical Register," Volume LXLII, Boston, 1913 – Information regarding Charles Morris, also Volume XX, Boston, 1866 – Information on Madam Price and Willard Aldrich.

"The New England Palladium," published in Boston from 1803 to 1814 – regarding the death and reputation of Major William Price at the end of 1802.

"The Origin and Growth of the Boot and Shoe Industry in Holliston and Milford, Massachusetts, 1793-1850," by Ernest A. Bragg, Boston, 1850.

"The Royal Navy, A History from the Earliest Times to the Present," Volume 3, by Sir William Laird Clowes, Sampson Low, Marston and Company, Limited, London, 1898.

"The Shoemaker Who Looked Like a King," by Don Lochbiler, for the Detroit News, issue of June 11, 1998.

"The Site of St. Paul's Cathedral, Boston, and Its Neighborhood," by Robert Means Lawrence, M.D., published by Richard G. Badger, Boston, 1916.

"The Valentines in America, 1644-1874," by T. W. Valentine, Clark & Maynard, Publishers, New York, 1874.

"United States Investor," Vol. 15, Boston, New York, and Philadelphia, July 9, 1904.

"Wage Trends, 1800-1900," by Stanley Lebergott, in "Trends in the American Economy in the Nineteenth Century," published by The Conference on Research in Income and Wealth, UMI, 1960.

"What Style Is It? A Guide to American Architecture," by John C. Poppeliers and S. Allen Chambers Jr., Historic American Buildings Survey, John Wiley & Sons, Inc., Hoboken, New Jersey, 2003.

Image Credits

Cover –Hopkinton Historical Society (hereinafter HHS), Stereoscopic card: Photography by T. Lewis, Cambridgeport, MA (undated).

4 – Map: Town of Hopkinton, Assessors Office, www.hopkintonma.gov/home/government/boards/assessors.

5 – Map: United States Geological Survey, Milford, Massachusetts, Quadrangle, 7.5 Minute Series, 1946, surveyed 1942/1943 at: www.usgs.gov/pls/topomaps (MA_Milford_351896_1946_31680_geo.pdf).

6 – Photography by the author (hereinafter JFW).

10 – Hopkinton Public Library (hereinafter HPL).

11 – Map: Created by the author and based in part on a map by Beryl Osborne, Hopkinton, c. 1940.

12 – Map: Hopkinton & Upton deed books, Volume I, part II, p. 217, Hopkinton Town Hall.

13 – Map: "Plan of Portion of Charles L. Claflin Estate, Hopkinton, Mass.," E. C. & G. R. Hulme, Framingham, Mass., located at the Middlesex South Registry of Deeds, Cambridge, Plan book: 333, Plan: 49, December, 1923 (Author's Collection).

14 – HPL.

16 – JFW.

18 – "Days and Ways of Old Boston," Boston: R. H. Stearns and Company, 1914.

20 – Map: William Price, "A New Plan of ye Great Town of Boston in New England in America" Boston: 1769, Library of Congress, UNH Diamond Library, and multiple other sources.

24 – Mary Caroline Crawford, "St. Botolph's Town - An Account of Old Boston in Colonial Times," for L. C. Page & Company, Inc., Boston: The Colonial Press: C. H. Simonds & Co., 1908.

25 – usbornefamilytree.com/thirklebyhall.htm.

27 – HPL.

28 – James Henry Stark, "Loyalists of Massachusetts and the Other Side of the Revolution," Salem, MA: The Salem Press Co., 1910, pp. 416-417.

32 – HPL.

33 – JFW.

35 – Library of Congress Prints and Photographs Division. No known restrictions on publication.

36 – collections.rmg.co.uk/collections/objects/15076.html.

37 – the-athenaeum.org (public domain image of an oil-on-canvas painting).

38 – "Lost Heritage – Demolished Country Houses of England at: www.lostheritage.org.uk) and also available at: lh.matthewbeckett.com/houses/lh_sussex_munthamcourt_gallery.html.

41 – Peter Landry Collection, Dartmouth, NS, www.blupete.com.

44 – JFW.

45 – Henry Wilder Foote, "Annals of King's Chapel, From the Puritan Age of New England to the Present Day," 2 Volumes, Boston: Little, Brown, & Co., 1881/1887/1900.

50 – HPL.

51 – JFW.

53 – Map: "Plan of Hopkinton, Surveyed by Matthew Metcalf," Boston: Pendleton's Lithography (1825-1836), 1831 – Copy courtesy of the Hopkinton Public Library.

55 – Map: Detail of "Hopkinton Center" from: Henry Francis Walling, "Map of Middlesex County, Massachusetts," Boston: Smith & Bumstead, 1856 (Author's Collection).

56 – HHS.

57 – HPL.

58 – JFW.

60 – "American Women, Fifteen Hundred Biographies, With Over 1,400 Portraits, a Comprehensive Encyclopedia of the Lives and Achievements of American Women During the Nineteenth Century," Edited by Frances E. Willard and Mary A. Livermore, Volume I, Revised Edition, New York: Mast, Crowell & Kirkpatrick, 1897 – Page: 60.

61 – Map: Detail from F. W. Beers, "County Atlas of Middlesex, Massachusetts," New York: J. B. Beers & Co., 1875.

63 – JFW.

66 top – Ashland Historical Society.

66 bottom – JFW.

69 – HPL.

75 – Library of Congress, Prints and Photographs Division. No known restrictions on publication.

77 – HPL.

78 – HPL.

79 – HPL.

80 – HPL.

81 – HPL.

84 – HPL.

85 – JFW.

86 – HPL.

87 top – Original at the Whitinsville Community Center, Northbridge, Massachusetts.

87 bottom – HPL.

88 – HPL.

89 top – HPL.

89 bottom – Map: Detail from F. W. Beers, "County Atlas of Middlesex, Massachusetts," New York: J. B. Beers & Co., 1875.

90 – HPL, Photo from glass plate, original photography by T. Lewis, Cambridgeport, MA.

93 – JFW.

97 – JFW.

100 – Courtesy of the John L. Palmer Collection.

101 – Map: Detail of "Hopkinton Center" from: Henry Francis Walling, "Map of Middlesex County, Massachusetts," Boston: Smith & Bumstead, 1856 (Author's Collection).

102 – HHS.

103 – Map: "Hopkinton Center" from: Henry Francis Walling, "Map of Middlesex County, Massachusetts," Boston: Smith & Bumstead, 1856 (Author's Collection).

104 – R. S. Foster and Charles Tilton, "A History of the Milford Methodist Episcopal Church with Biographical Sketches and Portraits of Its Pastors," Cambridge, MA: Riverside Press, 1888.

106 – JFW.

107 top – "Cambridge Chronicle," Volume XXIII, Number 48, Cambridge, Massachusetts, Saturday, November 28, 1868.

107 bottom – "Cassier's Magazine, Engineering Illustrated," Volume XXXIV, New York: The Cassier Magazine Co., 1908.

108 – "Worcester Magazine," Volume 4, The Board of Trade, Worcester, Massachusetts, August, 1902.

109 – Author's collection, (public domain images).

110 – JFW.

111 – HHS.

112 – HPL.

113 – Framingham Public Library.

114 – Map: Sanborn Map Co., New York, (Framingham Public Library).

116 – Map: United States Geological Survey, Milford, Massachusetts, Quadrangle, 7.5 Minute Series, 1946, surveyed 1942/1943 at: www.usgs.gov/pls/topomaps (MA_Milford_351896_1946_31680_geo.pdf).

117 – "Village of Hopkinton, Town of Hopkinton," Geo. H. Walker & Co., Boston: 1889.

118 – HPL.

119 – Author's collection: from an early 1960's calendar photograph.

120 – JFW.

121 top – HPL.

121 bottom – JFW.

122 – JFW.

123 – JFW.

124 – HPL (photograph enhanced by the author).

125 – HPL.

126 – HPL.

127 – HPL.

128 – JFW.

129 – Map: Detail from F. W. Beers, "County Atlas of Middlesex, Massachusetts," New York: J. B. Beers & Co., 1875.

130 - "Cyclopedia of Michigan, Historical and Biographical, Comprising a Synopsis of General History of the State, and Biographical Sketches of Men Who Have, in Their Various Spheres, Contributed Toward Its Development," Detroit and New York: Western Publishing & Engraving Co., 1900.

131 – JFW.

132 top – Detail from photograph on page 124 (HPL, photograph enhanced by the author).

132 bottom left – HPL.

132 right - Ward, J. F., Computer-Aided-Design from original plans of Barker & Nourse.

133 – HPL.

134 – JFW.

135 – HPL.

136 - Ward, J. F., Computer-Aided-Design from original plans of Barker & Nourse.

137 – JFW.

138 left – Map: Sanborn Map Company, New York: March, 1904 (Hopkinton Public Library).

138 right – HHS.

139 – Map: Sanborn Map Company, New York: August, 1910 (Hopkinton Public Library).

140 – HHS.

141 – JFW.

142 – HPL.

143 – JFW.

144 – Map: "Plan of Portion of Charles L. Claflin Estate, Hopkinton, Mass.," E. C. & G. R. Hulme, Framingham, Mass., located at the Middlesex South Registry of Deeds, Cambridge, Plan book: 333, Plan: 49, December, 1923. (Author's Collection).

145 – Map: "Plan of Property Owned by Edward W. Pierce, Hopkinton, Mass., E. C. & G. R. Hulme, Framingham, Mass, located at the Middlesex South Registry of Deeds, Cambridge, Plan book: 339, Plan: 13, December, 1923. (Author's Collection).

146 – JFW.

148 – JFW.

149 – Photography by David Dockstader.

150 – JFW.

151 – Milford Historical Society.

153 – Map: Detail of "Hayden Row" from "Map of Middlesex County, Massachusetts," by Henry Francis Walling, Smith & Bumstead, Boston, 1856 – (Author's Collection).

154 – Map: Detail from: F. W. Beers, "County Atlas of Middlesex, Massachusetts," New York: J. B. Beers & Co., 1875.

155 – HPL.

156 – HHS.

157 – HHS.

158 – HHS.

159 – Map: Sanborn Map Company, New York: March, 1904 (Hopkinton Public Library).

160 – Map: Sanborn Map Company, New York: August, 1910 (Hopkinton Public Library).

161 – HHS.

162 top – HHS.

162 bottom – JFW.

163 – The State Library of Massachusetts, photograph c. 1868, archives.lib.state.ma.us
ocm33284813_1868HouseandSenateAlbumPage0016.jpg.

164 – JFW.

165 – HPL.

166 – HPL.

168 – Map: Detail of "Hopkinton Center" from: Henry Francis Walling, "Map of Middlesex County,
Massachusetts," Boston: Smith & Bumstead, 1856 (Author's Collection).

169 – HPL.

170 – HPL.

171 – Map: Detail from: F. W. Beers, "County Atlas of Middlesex, Massachusetts," New York:
J. B. Beers & Co., 1875.

173 – Library of Congress Prints and Photographs Division. No known restrictions on publication.

174 left – "The New England Historical and Genealogical Register," Volume LXI, Boston, 1907.

174 Right – Newton Historical Society.

175 – Newton Historical Society.

176 – Newton Historical Society.

177 top – Newton Historical Society.

177 bottom – JFW.

178 – Newton Historical Society.

179 – Map: Newton City Atlas, 1895, Plate 16, Historic Maps of Newton, Massachusetts.

181 – HHS.

182 top left – "The Colorado School Journal," Volume 10, Denver, April, 1894.

182 top right – M. F. Sweetser, "King's Handbook of Newton," Boston: Moses King Corporation,
1889.

182 bottom – Newton Historical Society.

183 – Map: Newton City Atlas, 1895, Plate 16, Historic Maps of Newton, Massachusetts.

184 – "The Colorado School Journal," Volume 10, Denver, April, 1894.

185 – JFW.

186 top – HPL.

186 bottom – JFW.

188 – JFW.

189 top – D. Hamilton Hurd, "History of Middlesex County, Massachusetts, with Biographical
Sketches of Many of Its Pioneers and Prominent Men," Volume III, Philadelphia:
J. W. Lewis & Co., 1890.

189 bottom – HPL.

190 top – D. Hamilton Hurd, "History of Middlesex County, Massachusetts, with Biographical
Sketches of Many of Its Pioneers and Prominent Men," Volume III, Philadelphia:
J. W. Lewis & Co., 1890.

190 bottom – JFW.

191 left – "King's Handbook of Boston, Fourth Edition," published by Moses King, Cambridge, 1881.

191 right – Boston Public Library and numerous online sources.

192 – HPL.

193 – Map: Sanborn Map Company, New York: March, 1904 (Hopkinton Public Library).

194 top – JFW.

194 bottom – HPL.

195 – HHS.

196 – HPL.

197 – HPL.

198 – JFW.

199 – HPL.

200 – HPL.

201 top – JFW.

201 bottom – Map: Sanborn Map Company, New York: March, 1904 (Hopkinton Public Library).

202 – Map: Detail from O. H. Bailey & Co., Lithographers and Publishers of Boston, 1898.

203 – Map: Sanborn Map Company, New York: 1903 (Framingham Public Library).

204 top – JFW.

204 bottom – Map: Detail from O. H. Bailey & Co., Lithographers and Publishers of Boston, 1898.

205 – "F. Brigham & Gregory Factory, Hudson, Mass.," by C. E. Sexton, post card
        (Author's Collection).

206 – "R. H. Long Shoe Factory, Framingham, Mass., post card (Framingham Public Library).

207 – JFW.

208 top – Framingham Public Library.

208 bottom – JFW.

209 – HPL.

210 – HHS.

211 – HHS.

212 – HHS.

213 – HHS.

214 – Map: Sanborn Map Company, New York: March, 1904 (Hopkinton Public Library).

215 – JFW.

216 – JFW.

217 – JFW.

218 – JFW.

220 – "Tricentennial Record of the Class of 1876 of the Sheffield Scientific School of Yale College," by
        Max Mailhouse, Class Secretary, New Haven, CT: The Tuttle, Morehouse & Taylor Company,
        1908, p.132.

221 – Map: Detail from "Hopkinton, Mass.," Boston: O. H. Bailey & J. C. Hazen, Publishers, 1880.

223 – Ibid.

225 – HPL.

226 – HPL.

227 – HPL.

229 – Map: Detail of "Hopkinton Center" from: Henry Francis Walling, "Map of Middlesex County,
        Massachusetts," Boston: Smith & Bumstead, 1856 (Author's Collection).

231 top – HPL.

231 bottom – JFW.

232 – HPL.

233 – HPL.

234 – HPL.

235 top – JFW.

235 bottom – HPL.

236 – HPL.

237 – HPL.

238 – HPL.

239 – HPL.

240 – HPL.

241 top – JFW.

241 bottom – HPL.

242 – JFW.

243 – Map: "Atlas of the City of Worcester," New York: F. W. Beers & Co., 1870.

244 – "The New England Magazine," New England Magazine Co., 1901, p. 561.

245 – M. F. Sweetser, "King's Handbook of the United States," edited by Moses King, Buffalo, NY: Moses King Corporation, Publishers, 1891-1892.

246 top – Map: "Atlas of the City of Worcester," New York: F. W. Beers & Co., 1870.

246 bottom – JFW.

248 – "Gunton's Magazine," Volume XIX, New York: Political Science Publishing Co., 1900.

249 – Author's collection.

250 – Newton Historical Society.

251 – Newton Historical Society.

Index

Polly (Sheffield), 98, 99.
Catherine (Poole), 105.
Puah (Herrick), 76, 99.
Sally Watkins (Adams), 99, 150, 151, 152.
Sally, (Bucklin), 98, 99, 100, 101.
Sally (Davenport), 54.
Sarah (Tilton), 76, 98, 99, 150.
Susannah (Holbrook), 105.
Susannah Willard (Wadsworth), 99, 105, 106, 107.
Tennessee, 49.
Thomas Jefferson, 105.
Victoria (Woodhull), 49.
Wilbur Fisk, 99, 151, 152, 153, 165, 166, 195, 219, 221, 224.
William Davenport, 172.
William (Governor), 49, 84, 95, 99, 149, 151, 152, 156, 164, 167, 168, 172, 173, 174, 175, 179, 191, 192, 193, 194, 200, 247, 249.
Winslow, 99.

Claflin-Allen Shoe Co., 167.

Claflin, Allen & Co., 167.

Claflin Coal Company, 107.

Claflin & Coburn (Claflin, Coburn, & Co., Wm. Claflin, Coburn, & Co.), 78, 114, 151, 168, 170, 180, 186, 190, 191, 192, 194, 195, 198, 199, 200, 207, 208, 220, 222.

Claflin-Sumner Coal Company, 109, 110.

Claflin University, 163.

Clark, Elizabeth (Hill), 69.
Frances (Fanny), 69, 70.
Isaac, 69.

Clarke, James Freeman, 172.
Mary (Barrett), 8.
Rhoda (Ware), 228.
Susanna (Copley), 8.
Hon. William, 28.

Clements, Hannah, 54.

Clifford, E. B., 236.

Clinton, General Sir Henry, 30.

Clow, Marjorie C., 147.
Phil H., 147.

Cobb, F. N., 81.

Coburn, Alonzo, 80, 180, 195, 196, 198, 209, 215, 221.
Benjamin Franklin (B. F.), 180, 196, 221.
Celia Augusta (Claflin), 99, 223.
Charles Henry, 195.
Daniel Jennings., 83, 99, 180, 222, 223.
Elenor (Wheeler Whitman), 180.
Emma Lucinda, 180.
Lucinda (Morey), 180.
Mary Elizabeth (Thayer), 215.
Miranda (Young), 129.
Nathan Parker (N. P.), 83, 84, 88, 103, 104, 157, 160, 168, 169, 180, 181, 182, 183, 184, 185, 187, 191, 195, 196, 200, 204, 205, 215, 223.
Sadie P., 147.
Sarah Elizabeth (Wentworth), 196.
Sarah Frances (Fanny) (Carpenter), 180.
William Burrage, 215.

Coburn & Claflin Boot Shop, 168.

Coburn, Gauss & Co., 205.

Coburnville (Framingham), 204.

Cody, Philip, 11.

Colella's (Supermarket), 169, 209.

Colorado College, 184, 185.

Colorado Springs, CO, 184.

Commonwealth Ave. Street Railway, 249.

Conant, Mary (Putnam), 96.

Congregational Church, 7, 16, 54, 78, 79, 81, 83, 90, 94, 147, 155, 171, 222, 226, 241, 242.

Cook, Robert, 167.

Copley, John Singleton, 8.
Susanna (Clarke), 8.
Corbett, Betsey (Elizabeth), 54.

Cordaville, 52.

Crompton & Knowles, 120.

Cromwell, Oliver, 23, 37, 196.
        Giles, 196.
        Henry (Admiral), 26, 30, 31, 34, 36, 37.
        Mary, 37.

Crooks, 169.
        Abraham (Abram), 88, 89, 96, 97, 135,
140, 154, 187, 188, 190, 192, 216, 231.
        Ann Maria (Guy), 88, 96, 187, 216.
        Arthur, 231.
        Emeline (Stearns), 187.
        Emily M. (Parker), 187.
        John, 97, 154, 187, 188.
        Mary A. (Thompson), 214, 216.
        Myra (Adams), 231.
        Sarah Bucklin (Guy), 96, 187.
        Sarah L. (Matthews), 187.
        Samuel, 96, 97, 154, 160, 187, 188, 189,
192, 221.

Crooks, Root & Co., 204, 205.

Cunningham, J., 196.

CSX Corporation, 207.

C. W. Claflin Co., 146.

C. W. Claflin & Co., 107, 108, 109, 112, 126,
146, 218, 222.

Daniels, Mary Harding (Davenport), 102.

Darby, Captain, 19.

Davenport Block, 101, 102, 192, 194.

Davenport & Gibbs, 9, 103, 192.

Davenport, 228.
        Betsey (Fuller), 102.
        Betsey (Godfrey), 100.
        Joseph Gibbs, 102.
        Mary Bucklin (Claflin), 47, 99.
        Mary Claflin (Bucklin), 99, 100.
        Mary Harding (Daniels), 102.
        Mary Sophia (Freeland), 54, 200.

Samuel Daniels (S. D.), 54, 93, 99, 100,
101, 152, 155, 167, 168, 200, 201, 230, 244.
        Seth, 100.
Day, Joanna (Rockwood), 228.

Delaware and Hudson Coal Co., 108.

Dennison, 206.

Diamond, Annie L., 224.
        Levi, 224.

Dockstader, David, 147, 264.

Draper, Daniel, 73.
        George, 120.

Drew, John, 30.
        Sophia (Goshia) (Thompson), 209.

Duke of Bedford, 40.

Duke of Buckingham, Henry Stafford, 23.

Duke of Newcastle, Thomas Pelham-Holles,
24.

Duke of Portland, 17, 22.

Dupee, John, 31, 44.
        Sally, 31, 44, 45.

Dupree (Leggett), Madelane, 41.

Dyre, 19.

E. A. Bates & Co., 225, 228.

Eames, D., 83.
        Izzanna (Jones), 152.
        Luther, 93.
        Phineas, 152.
        Polly Jones (Claflin), 152.
        Sally (Claflin), 99.

Earl of Litchfield, George Henry Lee, 23.

Edison Electric Company, 13, 110, 111.

Edward VII of England, 130.

Elizabeth I of England, 43.

Frye, George, 224.

Fuller, Arthur Buckminster, 102.
    Betsey (Davenport), 102.
    Joseph, 175.
    R. Buckminster, 102.

Fyrberg, Andrew, 223.

Gage, General Thomas, 22, 30.

Gannon, John, 60.

Gates, Rhoda (Putnam), 96.

Gauss, William T., 205.

General Packets Inc., 196.

George III of England, 30.

Georgian Colonial (style), 44.

Gerrish, Sarah (Barrett), 8.

Gibbs, Fanny (Pierce), 229, 230.
    Homer, 229, 230.
    Jacob, 9, 101.
    John, 101, 229.
    Lucy (Claflin), 98, 99.
    Martha (Howe), 101.
    Mary (Mellen), 98.
    Mehitable (Walker), 91, 98.
    Phineas, 98.

Gibson, Cornelius, 59, 64, 90, 94, 146.
    Edward, 17.
    Elizabeth (Barnes), 59.
    Maria (Stearns), 64.
    Patience (Aldrich), 59, 146.
    John, 59, 83, 90, 94.
    Martha (Wood), 71.

Glasier, Beamsley Perkins, 42.

Gleason, Martha M., 15.
    William H., 15.

Goddard, Keziah (Pond), 92.
    Samuel, 92.
    Samuel Brigham (S. B.), 54, 92.
    Susannah (Howe), 92.

Godfrey, Betsey (Davenport), 100.
    David S., 52.
    William, 52.

Godman, Elizabeth (Shirley), 24.

Goldsmith, John, 152.

Gooch, 21, 26.
    Elizabeth (Hobby), 68.
    Elizabeth (Valentine), 65, 67, 68.
    James, 29, 68.
    Joseph, 65.

Gooden, James, 12.

Gothic-Revival (style), 87, 240.

Gould, Jay, 72.

Goulding, John, 54.

Granary Burial Ground, 39.

Great Atlantic & Pacific Tea Co. (The) (A&P), 110, 111.

Great Gale, 48, 151, 242.

Greek-Revival (style), 50, 51, 55, 81, 86, 97, 100, 103, 123, 135, 149, 190, 210, 215, 216.

Greeley, Horace, 172.

Greenough, Thomas, 28.

Greenwood, Rosella (Isabella) (Wakefield), 230.

Gregory, William F., 200, 205.

Gregory & Co., 200.

Gregory, Shaw & Co., 204.

Grout, Edgar Homer, 168, 169.

Gunthwaite (Lisbon), NH, 180.

Guy, Ann Maria (Crooks), 88, 187.
    Charles Virgil, 96.

Robert, 74.

Holbrook, Anthony P., 105.
    Elsie (Aldrich), 105.
    Evelyn (Aldrich), 105.
    Mary Ann (Claflin), 105.

Holmes, Oliver Wendell, 23, 172.

Homer, Charles, 73, 74.
    Winslow, 74.

Hopkins, Edward, 2.

Hopkinton Branch Railroad Company, 115.

Hopkinton Gourmet, 215.

Hopkinton High School, 84, 98, 100, 154, 155, 157, 158, 187, 201.

Hopkinton, Milford, & Woonsocket, 115.

Hopkinton National Bank, 142, 154, 236.

Hopkinton (Public) Library, 2, 4, 9, 85, 87, 186.

Hopkinton Railroad Co., 13, 65, 114, 115, 116, 117, 118, 119, 120, 121, 122.

Hopkinton Savings Bank, 142, 163, 219, 222.

Hopkinton State Park, 21, 76.

Hopkinton Supply Co., 110, 226.

Hopkinton Town Hall, 2, 83, 170, 171, 199, 209, 225, 229, 236, 237, 238, 240, 241.

Houghton, Henry Oscar, 74.
    Lucy Heywood (Valentine), 74.

Houghton, Mifflin & Co., 74.

Howarth, Captain John, 36.

Howe (How), David, 14.
    John, 9, 10, 11, 14, 15, 54, 68, 92, 98, 101, 105, 167.
    Lucy Ann (Fitch), 94.
    Martha (Gibbs), 101.
    Martha (Walker), 105.

Nathaniel, (Rev.), 54, 94.
    Phineas, 92.
    Richard (Vice-Admiral), 36.
    Susannah (Goddard), 92.
    William, (General) 5th Viscount Howe, 30.

How & Claflin, 167.

How, Claflin & Cook, 167.

Howard, Bertha Ella (Knowles), 234.

Hull, Governor (General) William, 174.

Humphrey, Sara E., 56.

Hunting, Elizabeth (Betsey) (Morse), 62.

Hutchinson, (Royal) Governor Thomas, 28.

Hyde & Leather Bank, 163.

Hyman, Nathan, 224.

Imperial Shoe Factory, 194, 196.

Inman, Ralph, 30.

Italianate (style), 149, 174, 189, 218, 221.

Jefferson, Thomas (President), 37, 86.

John Warren Lodge, 242.

Johnson, Artimus Ward, 52.
    Elizabeth (Betsey) (Guy), 96, 103.
    Experience (Briggs), 52.

Jones, Anthony, 96.
    Elizabeth (Alden), 96.
    Elizabeth (Simpson), 71.
    Elizabeth (Valentine), 67, 68, 71, 76.
    Izzanna (Eames), 152.
    John, 68, 71.
    John (Colonel), 71.
    Lois (Claflin), 152.
    Mary (Mellen), 68, 71.
    Mary (Buckminster), 71.
    Nathaniel Alden, 152.

J. H. & G. M. Walker (Co.), 244, 245, 246.

Pepperrell, (Sir) William, 40.

Perkins, Amy W., 63, 135, 145.
    James, 83.
      Hannah (Clements), 54.
      Reuben, 54.

Phelps, Rev. Amos A., 54, 155.
    Jonas, 82.

Phipps, Doctor W. A., 233.
    Frank, 14.
    Horace A., 13.
    Laura A. (Briggs), 52.
    Sylvester, 52.

Phipps Livery Stable, 210.

Pickman, Martha (Walcott), 226.

Pierce, Edward Willard, 105, 108, 127.
    Edward Winslow, 64, 105, 108, 144, 145, 146.
      Emma (Moore), 105.
      Emma (Morse), 64, 105, 145.
      Emma Francis (Claflin), 105, 144.
      Fanny (Gibbs), 229.
      Mary, 31.
      Winslow Claflin, 105, 108, 110, 141, 142, 144.

Pine Grove Cemetery, 143, 164, 172, 217, 222.

Pingree & Smith Shoe Co., 130.

Pingree, Pingry (Pengry), 147.
    Adeline (Bryant), 129.
    Hazen Stuart, 129, 130.
    Mary Jane (Young), 129, 135.
    Jasper, 129.
    John L., 96, 124, 129, 135, 138, 139, 140.
    Moses, 129.
    Samuel Hoyt, 129, 167.
    William Morrill, 129.

Polley, Sadie B., 147.

Pond, Ebenezer, 92.
    Keziah (Goddard), 92.
    Sybelia (Brigham), 92.
    Zebiah (Fiske), 69.

Poole, Catherine (Claflin), 105.

Porter (Mr.), 147.

Portland Company, 119.

Post Office (building), 199, 229.

Pratt, Doctor Jefferson, 54, 78, 86, 87, 89, 97, 154, 169, 190, 229, 259.
    Harriet Jones (Valentine), 67, 86, 87, 190, 259.
      Sarah Elizabeth, 87, 141.

Preble, Jedediah, 40.

Prouty, Rebecca (Fiske), 232.

Prescott, Oliver, 45.

Preston, 26.

Price, 76, 98.
    Andrew, 17, 43, 46.
    Charles, Lord Mayor of London, 46.
    Elizabeth (or E.), 11, 17, 43, 45, 46, 47, 48, 51, 59, 62, 64, 72, 76, 126.
    Elizabeth (Bull), 17.
    Henry Yelverton, 17.
    James, 17.
    John, 17.
    Madam, 1, 43, 47, 48, 62, 64, 72, 76, 126.
    Mary, 17.
    Mary Ann (Valentine), 17, 22, 43, 47, 48, 67, 71, 76.
    Olivia (Hall), 43, 76.
    Roger, 12, 15, 16, 17, 19, 20, 22, 26, 39, 43, 46, 47, 49, 154.
    Thomas, 17.
    Major William (or W.), 11, 17, 43, 44, 45, 48, 71.

Price Mansion House, 11, 21, 22, 44, 45, 67, 71, 73, 76, 77.

Preble, Jedediah, 40.

Pulsifer, Nathan Trowbridge, 74.
    Lawson Valentine, 74.

South Station, 19.

Spillane Lodge, 201.

Spotsylvania Court House, Battle of, 130.

Spring, Eliza (Wadsworth), 105.

Spring Hill Farm, 165, 219, 221.

St. John's Catholic Church, 157, 160, 241.

St. Malachi's Catholic Church, 52, 103.

Stafford, Mrs. Francis A., 49.

Stark, James H., 28, 31.

Stearns, Alanson, 64.
    Hannah (Bridges), 199.
    Maria (Gibson), 64.
    Priscilla Almena (Morse), 64, 145, 201.

Stedman, George, 63.

Stick (style), 236 and 237.

Stimpson, George, 11.
    Mary (Claflin), 98, 99, 105.

Stone Tavern, 4, 13, 14, 15, 61, 67, 69, 70, 72, 90, 105, 106, 107, 126, 135, 145.

Stowe, Harriet (Beecher), 49, 172.

Streeter, Mary A. (Claflin), 99, 166.

Strong, Elizabeth (Betty), 9, 87.

Stuart, Gilbert, 37.

Sullivan, James S., 70.
    Jane (Valentine), 70.

Sumner Coal Co., 109.

Surriage, Agnes (Frankland), 23, 26, 27, 28, 30.
    Edward, 31.
    Isaac, 31, 54.
    Mary, 31.

Swain, Mary (McClester, Surriage), 31.

Sweet, Alvan Able (A. A.), 84, 154, 232, 233, 234, 236.
    Marion Eliza (Fiske), 232.

Sweet, Morse & Knowles, 234.

Taft, Peter Rawson, 102.
    William Howard (President), 102.

Talbot, George, 6th Earl of Shrewsbury, 43.

Talcott (Read), Ruth, 39.

Taylor, Carrie, 15.
    James F., 15.
    John, 10, 11, 54.
    Luther, 15, 106.

Tebeau, Alice D., 15.
    John H., 15.

Temple, Josiah, 9.

Terry Oil Co., 193.

Thayer, Arba, 83.
    Edwin, 163.
    Libby (Chapin), 91.
    Mary (Claflin), 99.
    Mary Elizabeth (Coburn), 215.

The Old Elms, 174, 175.

Thirkleby Hall, 25, 27.

Thompson, Adelia M. (Loring), 214.
    Arad, 209.
    Catherine Wheelock (Oakes), 214, 217.
    Charles E., 214, 218.
    Clarence A., 214, 219, 222.
    Doctor George, 84.
    Dorthea, 242.
    Edwin Davis (E. D.), 141, 142, 214, 218.
    Erastus, 115, 141, 209, 211, 213, 214, 215, 216, 217, 230, 233.
    Franklin O., 214.
    George, (MP), 155.
    Ira, 209.
    John, 223.

Mary (Fitch), 54, 61, 67, 68.
Mary Hoe (Harper), 74.
Mary (Lynde), 65.
Mary Wadsworth (Claflin), 70.
Miriam Rice (Haven), 89, 230, 231.
Mrs. (Polly Fiske), 55.
Patty (Burnap), 96.
Polly, (Mary Fiske), 54, 55, 67, 69, 105, 106.
Robert, 65.
Samuel, 9, 15, 48, 65, 67, 68, 69, 70, 71, 73, 76, 82, 83, 105, 106.
Samuel F., 70.
Susan Gilbert (Tilton), 70, 72.
Susan Isabella (Guy), 96.
Thomas, 29, 65, 67, 68.
William, 68, 96.
William Price, 65, 67, 72.

Valentine & Co., 73, 74.

Valentine & Bridges, 73.

Valentine Mansion, 77, 78, 80, 84, 85, 86, 88, 90, 103, 142, 167, 171, 219, 242.

Valspar, 73, 74.

Vanderbilt, Cornelius, 49.

Ventham (Cromwell), Mary, 34.

Victorian (period), 124, 142.

Villiers, Jacques Joseph, de Rouen, 30.

Wadsworth, Captain David, 105.
Eliza (Spring), 105.
Frances Ellen (Bridges), 106, 200.
Joseph, 106, 200.
Meriam (Woolson), 106, 200.
Susannah Willard (Claflin), 99, 105, 106, 107.
Virtue, (Willard), 105.
Willard, 106, 145, 200.

Wakefield, Lucius Henry (L. H.), 225, 230.
Rosella (Isabella) (Greenwood), 230.
Sarah Jane (Barber), 230.
Tubal Cain, 230.

Walcott (Wolcott), Martha (Pickman), 54, 226.

Mary (Baker), 226.
Jabez, 226.
Samuel Baker (S. B.), 52, 54, 82, 95, 155, 225, 226, 227, 230.
Walcott, William, 226.

Walcott Street, 15, 69, 111, 168, 171, 226, 229, 236.

Walker & Keith, 54.

Walker, 98.
Agnes M., 247, 249.
Andrew Chapin, 244.
Ann Maria (Claflin), 99.
Dexter, 93.
Elizabeth (Frail), 91.
George M., 247.
George Moore, 244.
Hannah Maria Clapp (Kelley), 247.
Hannah Thayer (Chapin), 91.
Henry, 91.
Jason, 11.
Joseph, 91, 92, 93, 95, 98, 104, 243.
Joseph Henry (J. H.), 91, 244, 247, 249.
Leonard, 91, 92, 93.
Lovett, 82, 91, 92, 93, 99.
Mehitable (Hitty) (Gibbs), 91, 98.
Mildred, 250.
Samuel, 104.
Sarah (Bullard), 91.
Sarah Ellen (Harrington), 247.
Solomon, 91.
Thomas, 11.
Widow, 54.
William, 250.

Walker Boot, 244, 245.

Walker-Claflin Mansion, 148.

Walker Mansion, 95.

Walker Oakley Co., 244, 245.

Walker Storehouse, 245.

Walker Tannery Stock, 244.

Ward, Margaret, 13.

Warren, (Mr.), 150.

Washington, George, 14.

Washington Mills, 249.

Watkins, Ede (Claflin), 55, 93, 99.

Wayside Inn, 14.

Webster, Daniel, 14, 191, 227.
    Fletcher, 227.
    Rev. John (Jessie) C. (J. C.), 155, 160.

Wellesley College, 172.

Wensley, Ann, 29.

Wentworth, (Royal) Governor Benning, 39.
    Sarah Elizabeth (Coburn), 196.

Wesleyan University, 164.

West, Benjamin, 37.

Westboro Bank, 253.

Westborough and Hopkinton Street Railway, 249, 250.

Wheeler, Elenor (Whitman, Coburn), 104, 180.
    J. W., 191.

Whitin, John Crane, 87.
    Sarah Elizabeth (Pratt), 87, 141.

Whitin Machine Works, 87, 120.

Whitman, Elenor (Wheeler) (Coburn), 104, 180.
    Joseph, 104, 180.

Whittier, John Greenleaf, 172.

William Claflin & Co., 167.

William Parker & Co., 72.

Wilson, 21.
    Doctor, 11.
    Henry, 172.
    James, 11, 12, 221.
    Widow, 12.

Wm. Claflin, Coburn, & Co., 114, 151, 180, 186, 191, 194, 195, 199, 220, 222.

Winthrop House (hotel), 180.

Wiswall, Edward, 222.
    Edward F., 222.
    Elisha, 222.
    George, 222.
    Lizzie M., 222.

Wiswall & Co., 222.

Wonderly, Charles P., 222.

Wood, Elizabeth (Buckminster), 71.
    Fred A., 219.
    G. P., 169.
    Hannah (Haven), 71.
    Harold S., 49.
    John, 71.
    Joseph, 71.
    Mable L., 219.
    Martha (Gibson), 71.

Woodard, Hannah, 169.
    Willard, 169.

Woodard Store, 169.

Woodbury, John A., 61, 63, 135.

Woodville (Hopkinton), 49, 53, 71, 187, 230.

Woodward, Mary, 19.

Woods, Gardner, 169.

Woolson, Eda (Adams), 151.
    James Adams, 88, 151, 152, 186, 191, 200.
    James Rix, 106, 151.
    Meriam (Wadsworth), 106, 200.
    Nathan, 186.

Worcester Board of Trade, 247.

Worcester Fuel Company, 110.

Worcester Historical Museum, 243.

Wright, Francis (Hewitt), 223.

Wyatt, James, 25.